Problematic and Risk Behav
in Psychosis

In spite of improved access to psychosocial interventions, many people with psychosis continue to experience persistent problems, which act as significant barriers to their recovery. This book investigates risk and problem behaviours in psychosis including staff and service factors that can impede the delivery of effective care.

Problematic and Risk Behaviours in Psychosis provides a new approach for assessment formulation and intervention within such problem behaviours in a team context. Of particular interest will be:

- the SAFE (Shared Assessment, Formulation and Education) approach
- an integrative model for understanding risk and problematic behaviour
- shared risk assessment and management processes
- approaches to reducing team and carer barriers to effective care
- the use of CBT in day-to-day interactions with clients
- a set of formulation-driven strategies for managing problematic behaviours
- case studies and vignettes providing guidance and highlighting the benefits of the approach.

This book will have particular appeal to professionals working in specialist community, hospital-based and residential services who often struggle to help those with the most complex mental health problems who are hardest to reach. It is also an excellent resource for those engaged in training in psychological therapies, risk assessment and management.

Alan Meaden is a Consultant Specialist Clinical Psychologist for Birmingham and Solihull Mental Health Foundation Trust who specialises in working with those most affected by psychosis. He is an active researcher, most notably in the area of cognitive therapy for command hallucinations, and has other research interests in engagement and staff factors.

David Hacker is a Principal Clinical Psychologist in Neuropsychology at University Hospital Birmingham Regional Neuroscience Centre. He is experienced in working clinically with psychosis, is an active researcher and a Cochrane reviewer. He has additional expertise in working with a range of forensic populations and has undertaken post-doctoral training in Neuropsychology, which is now his area of speciality.

Problematic and Risk Behaviours in Psychosis

A shared formulation approach

Alan Meaden and David Hacker

Routledge
Taylor & Francis Group

LONDON AND NEW YORK

First published 2011
by Routledge
27 Church Road, Hove, East Sussex BN3 2FA

Simultaneously published in the USA and Canada
by Routledge
270 Madison Avenue, New York, NY 10016

*Routledge is an imprint of the Taylor & Francis Group, an
Informa business*

© 2011 Alan Meaden and David Hacker

Typeset in Times by
RefineCatch Limited, Bungay, Suffolk
Printed and bound in Great Britain by
TJ International Ltd, Padstow, Cornwall
Paperback cover design by Andrew Ward

This publication has been produced with paper manufactured
to strict environmental standards and with pulp derived from
sustainable forests.

British Library Cataloguing in Publication Data
A catalogue record for this book is available
from the British Library

Library of Congress Cataloging in Publication Data
Meaden, Alan, 1961–
Problematic and risk behaviours in psychosis : a shared formulation
approach / Alan Meaden and David Hacker.
   p. ; cm.
   Includes bibliographical references and index.
1. Psychoses.   I. Hacker, David, 1973–   II. Title.
   [DNLM: 1. Psychotic Disorders—complications.   2. Behavior
Control—methods.   3. Cognitive Therapy—methods.
4. Psychotic Disorders—therapy.   5. Risk Assessment—methods.
6. Risk Reduction Behavior. WM 200 M481p 2010]
RC512.M37 2010
616.89—dc22   2010020905

ISBN: 978–0–415–49464–9 (hbk)
ISBN: 978–0–415–49465–6 (pbk)

Contents

Figures

Tables

Abbreviations

ABC	activating event, belief, consequence
AOT	Assertive Outreach Team
ARS	Attribution Rating Scale
ASPD	antisocial personality disorder
BFT	behavioural family therapy
CARM	Cognitive Approach to Risk Management
CBC-P	Challenging Behaviour Checklist for Psychosis
CBRS	Challenging Behaviour Record Sheet
CBT	cognitive-behavioural therapy
CFI	Camberwell Family Interview
CFT	Case Formulation Team
CPA	Care Programme Approach
CTO	Compulsory Treatment Order
CTT	Case Treatment Team
DRA	differential reinforcement of alternative behaviours
DRI	differential reinforcement of incompatible behaviours
DRL	differential reinforcement of low rate of responding
DRO	differential reinforcement of other behaviours
DSH	deliberate self-harm
EIS	Early Intervention Service
EWS-P	Early Warning Signs of Psychosis
EWS-R	Early Warning Signs of Risk
GAST	Goal Attainment Scaling Tool
GMT	goal management training
HDU	High Dependency Unit
IBMC-P	Idiosyncratic Behaviour Monitoring Checklist for Psychosis
ICIDH-2	*International classification of functioning and disability*, Beta-2 draft
LEE	Level of Expressed Emotion Scale
MDT	Multidisciplinary Team
OT	occupational therapist
PICU	Psychiatric Intensive Care Unit

PRN	*pro re nata* (as needed)
RTA	road traffic accident
SAFE	Shared Assessment, Formulation and Education
SMART	small, measurable, achievable, relevant and time-limited
TBCT	team-based cognitive therapy
TCO	threat control override
WHO	World Health Organization

Preface

Our approach detailed in this book is the product of nearly 15 years of work thinking about the needs of this client group and represents a long and at times difficult journey. One of my early experiences involved attempting to work with a young woman I shall call Lucy. I was asked to see her with a view to helping the staff manage her problematic behaviours better. She frequently attempted to harm herself by violently throwing herself against the wall and furniture in her room, she banged her head repeatedly, would masturbate in public areas of the unit and seemed cut off from others most of the time. I went to see her hoping to talk with her about her experiences, she was being restrained. The nursing staff explained that this was a common experience and they described feeling overwhelmed and stuck. I felt the same. My training in working with people with psychosis had not prepared me for this. I had spent much of my training learning about cognitive-behaviour therapy (CBT) with my supervisor (now Professor) Paul Chadwick. Cognitive therapy was just emerging then as an approach to working with people with distressing psychosis. Over the coming weeks I attempted to engage Lucy in discussions about her experiences, we made some progress in understanding her difficulties but her ability to internalise any new understanding appeared limited and she was often actively responding to voices in the sessions, was clearly distressed and at times sexually disinhibited and it was difficult to develop any sort of therapeutic relationship with her. In the coming weeks I attempted to draw on my work with learning disabled clients and implement a behavioural programme with the staff group. This met with little if any success. Lucy remained distressed, thought disordered and continued to harm herself on a regular basis. I did think that there must be a better way to work with Lucy and support the staff. Lucy had been a long-term inpatient although she was only in her early thirties. The team's concern about her risk was paralysing, thwarting any efforts to adopt a therapeutic risk-taking approach. It often seemed to me that staff factors were a key part of the work but I lacked a framework that brought all of the separate elements that seemed potentially helpful together into an integrated approach.

Later I attended a conference organised by the International Society for

Psychotherapy of Schizophrenia and related psychoses (ISPS) and had my first introduction to the need-adapted treatment approach (Alanen, 1997). The following year I heard Sarah Davenport speak at another ISPS event in Manchester and became interested in her adaptation of Professor Alanen's work using shared formulations. She was kind enough to share this with me on a subsequent visit to Manchester. This was the starting point of developing a much more integrated shared approach to working with people like Lucy.

Around seven years ago I began working with David Hacker. He brought with him both an interest and evolving expertise in forensic risk assessment and neuropsychology. Over the years that followed, we experimented with ways of integrating these different approaches and evolved what we have now termed SAFE and CARM.

When we first set out on the journey of writing this book together we had a clear idea of where we wanted to get to and the route we would take. However, along the way we became distracted by various places of interest and obscure landmarks. These detours have enriched the journey and have influenced our practice. Things we thought we understood or had evolved the right method for we questioned, tested them again in our clinical work with staff and clients and subsequently revised our approach. We also came to appreciate that in order to make this book of real clinical and practical value we would need to embed our ideas for working with problematic behaviours in people with psychosis within a broader set of rehabilitation and recovery principles. What has emerged therefore is in part a framework that can be adopted by services for rehabilitation and recovery work with such clients. It is much more than a set of techniques and a useful summary of the literature, it includes methods for organising the team's work and recording and planning care, supervising, supporting and training staff.

We hope that this book will provide a sense of optimism that even those who present with the most complex and challenging needs and do not engage in or appear to benefit from current psychological approaches can be enabled to lead fulfilling, meaningful lives.

Alan Meaden
September 2010

Acknowledgements

I dedicate this book to my wife Ann Meaden for her continuing support and inspiration along the journey of writing this book. I would also like to acknowledge Peter Hulme, Max Birchwood, Peter Trower and Paul Chadwick who have been some of my mentors along the way and from whom I have learnt and continue to learn so much.

Alan Meaden

I dedicate this book to my parents Elizabeth and Graham Hacker and my sister Julie for their support and encouragement through good and bad times. I would also like to thank Dan and Smita for their longstanding support and friendship over many years. Finally, thanks go to Dr Chris Jones, Mr Martin Preston and Professor Max Birchwood for sharing their time, knowledge and wisdom.

David Hacker

We would both like to further dedicate this book to the staff and clients who have survived alongside us in our ongoing efforts to develop effective solutions to their, at times, intractable problems. Without them we would never have written this book.

Finally, we would like to thank the brewers Daniel Batham and Son for being a continuing source of inspiration.

Introduction

The Shared Assessment, Formulation and Education (SAFE) approach described in this book offers an integrative approach to working in a multi-disciplinary context with people with psychosis who do not respond to the best-quality, evidence-based standard care currently available. Often these clients have so-called chronic residual symptoms but frequently the barrier to successful community living and integration is not these persistent symptoms but the problematic behaviours they present with (which may or may not be symptom related). It may be tempting to view this book as concerning risky individuals who are chiefly the province of forensic or specialist community services dealing with those perceived as presenting most risk. We have worked across many different service areas, however, and have found problematic behaviours in people with psychosis to be common. Frequently, these serve as barriers to obtaining effective care; generating hopelessness and pessimism in those involved. We hope that this book will offer new ideas and solutions to working with such individuals and those involved in their care.

We have illustrated the book throughout with case studies taken from our own practice, which we have anonymised as far as possible to maintain confidentiality whilst preserving the integrity of the clinical features of each case. John features as a major case study throughout the book in order to provide an illustration of the key aspects of the complete SAFE process. Of course, no one client, however complex, presents with the complete range of problematic behaviours described here and so we have drawn on additional case material to illustrate other key aspects of the approach.

This book can be read cover to cover and this is what we would recommend. Nonetheless, since different chapters may be more or less relevant to a given setting or clinical issue, the reader may wish to dip into the most relevant chapters based on the brief synopsis presented below.

OVERVIEW OF THE BOOK

Part 1: The SAFE approach; theory, models and processes

In **Chapter 1** we discuss why we consider problematic behaviours in psychosis to be an important but neglected area. We consider the definitions of problematic or challenging behaviours, their prevalence and impact. In **Chapter 2** we provide an overview of the SAFE approach, which sets the context for future chapters. Several different formulation methods are described, which can be used either together or in various combinations dependent on the goal to be achieved. These are discussed in later chapters in more detail. **Chapter 3** gives further consideration to common barriers to effective care for this group of clients. We discuss how problematic behaviours need to be understood in the context of a more holistic formulation of the client's goals and real-world limitations, and emphasise improving social participation over simple reduction of the problematic behaviour. Specifically, we discuss the use of the WHO ICIDH-2 model for a service level formulation, which can aid in goal setting and care planning. **Chapter 4** provides a review of the literature on psychological formulation, and offers a framework for a traditional cognitive-behaviour-therapy (CBT) based formulation of the client's difficulties and symptoms, showing how this might be achieved through a multidisciplinary Case Formulation Team. **Chapters 5** and **6** give consideration to the risk literature pertaining to psychosis and review the most pertinent factors for violence and suicide. The assessment of risk is discussed and a formulation framework for high-risk behaviours (the shared risk formulation) is provided. **Chapter 7** illustrates an integrative cognitive and behavioural model (the Cognitive Approach to Risk Management model: CARM) for conceptualising acute risk and problematic behaviours. We describe and provide a rationale for how this model successfully integrates the pertinent cognitive factors in psychosis, behavioural models of psychosis and current conceptualisations of risk into a functional analytic understanding that can be shared with Multidisciplinary Team members. This sets the scene for the intervention chapters in Part 3 of the book. **Chapter 8** reviews the literature on the importance of staff factors such as attributions and how they may impact on client care and should be considered a target for intervention themselves. We illustrate a process for this task, drawing on cognitive therapy principles to formulate staff beliefs that are subsequently addressed through our shared formulation methodology.

Part 2: Assessment

Part 2 is concerned with the process of assessment in the SAFE approach, which underpins the subsequent intervention chapters in Part 3. **Chapter 9** covers issues in the assessment of problematic behavioural excesses and provides methodologies and tools to achieve this. **Chapter 10** specifically describes how to construct idiosyncratic early warning signs of risk signature, which has relevance to both the CARM and shared risk formulations. It is particularly relevant to Chapter 13, which deals with interventions addressing high-risk behavioural excesses. **Chapter 11** deals specifically with the assessment of negative symptoms and behavioural deficits, forming the basis for Chapter 14, which deals with intervention for behavioural deficits.

Part 3: Interventions in SAFE

Part 3 deals with intervention approaches, building on the formulation and assessment chapters in Parts 1 and 2. **Chapter 12** deals with working with low-risk behavioural excesses and particularly emphasises the use of reinforcement-based interventions (based on the CARM model). **Chapter 13** specifically addresses working with high-risk behavioural excesses. This involves a unique use of staff-based CBT to reduce behavioural issues in conjunction with early warning signs monitoring. **Chapter 14** addresses the methods of intervention for behavioural deficits and negative symptoms and also discusses methods drawn from the neurorehabilitation field.

Part 4: Implementation issues: translating SAFE into routine clinical practice

Part 4 discusses the broader systemic issues of implementing SAFE in routine care settings. **Chapter 15** discusses and illustrates issues relating to effective care planning and ensuring implementation of SAFE-driven care programmes. **Chapter 16** draws together the information from earlier chapters to discuss the relevance of the different formulation and intervention approaches to different specialist settings in which people with psychosis are cared for. Finally, **Chapters 17** and **18** deal with issues relating to organisational change and implementation of the SAFE approach, as well as issues relating to the need for training and supervision.

Part 1

The SAFE approach
Theory, models and processes

Chapter I

Problematic behaviour in psychosis: a barrier to social inclusion and recovery

Definitions, prevalence and consequences

INTRODUCTION

Psychosocial interventions (e.g. behavioural family therapy, relapse prevention, psychoeducation and cognitive-behaviour therapy) for psychosis have received increasing attention and support for adoption into routine practice in recent years. Cognitive-behaviour therapy (CBT) for psychosis, for example, is now part of standard evidence-based practice, both in research and clinical arenas and latterly in government guidelines in the United Kingdom (National Institute for Clinical Excellence, 2002; National Institute for Health and Clinical Excellence, 2009). The focus of these interventions has often been on the reduction of symptoms and distress or the prevention of psychotic relapse. A large number of randomised controlled trials have, however, failed to show consistent evidence of sustained clinical outcomes (Jones *et al.*, 2002; Wykes *et al.*, 2007; Lynch *et al.*, 2010). The reality is that many people's psychotic symptoms and associated beliefs remain treatment resistant even to CBT and they continue to be cared for in long-term settings, by Multidisciplinary Teams (MDTs) where the emphasis is often on minimising risk. Perhaps surprisingly, much less attention has typically been paid to the multidisciplinary treatment and management of these clients who exhibit problematic or risk behaviours. This is in spite of the fact that behaviours such as aggression are a common issue in psychiatric inpatient treatment (Daffern *et al.*, 2004, 2007) and in the community (Swanson *et al.*, 1990; Monahan *et al.*, 2001). Individuals with psychotic disorders such as schizophrenia are also at greater risk of suicide (Pompili *et al.*, 2007) and self-neglect (ReThink, 2004). Furthermore, such behaviours may severely limit the individual's independence and freedom, significantly reducing their opportunities for community living and decreasing their quality of life. In this book we outline an innovative approach to the assessment and management of problematic and risk behaviours in psychosis. We term this the Shared Assessment, Formulation and Education (SAFE) approach. Our primary focus is on achieving integrated MDT working, aimed at eliciting changes in the client's problematic or risk behaviours, whilst concurrently promoting a reduction in distress. It is a collaborative process that values all perspectives and serves to normalise problematic behaviours, making them understandable through the use of shared formulation processes. SAFE aims to also increase staff[1] and carer empathy and promote shared effective care for managing such behaviours. Ultimately, our goal is to maximise the individual's independence by reducing barriers to living an ordinary life that problematic and risk behaviours can create and thereby enabling opportunities for recovery.

THE NATURE OF THE PROBLEM: DEFINITIONS AND CLASSIFICATION

A key source of empirical literature regarding what we have termed 'problematic behaviour' is to be found in the literature on challenging behaviour, based on research conducted in the field of intellectual or learning disability. Emerson's (1995, as cited in Emerson, 2001, p. 3) definition of challenging behaviour is now widely accepted in this field and is one we have adopted to guide our development of SAFE: 'culturally abnormal behaviour(s) of such an intensity, frequency or duration that the physical safety of the person or others is likely to be placed in serious jeopardy, or behaviour which is likely to seriously limit use of, or result in the person being denied access to, ordinary community facilities'. Challenging behaviour is therefore inherently defined by its impact. The definition encompasses both risk behaviours that are life threatening or likely to cause significant physical harm to self or others, and those that may cause distress or discomfort to self and others. The scope of this definition also extends to behaviours that result in the social exclusion of the individual concerned by either preventing the use of community facilities or alienating the person from potential social supports or relationships. Whilst the social, physical and psychological impact is a crucial and defining element, the appearance or type of the behaviour (the behavioural topography) may also be important. In our experience, MDT members may hold very different beliefs about behaviours based on their apparent characteristics rather than their function (we discuss this in more depth in Chapters 2 and 8). In one of the few texts to make reference to challenging behaviours in psychosis, Hogg and Hall (1992) identified those which they considered to be commonly reported in people with schizophrenia. These included:

- aggression (physical assaults on other people, damage to property, self-injury);

---

1 The terms 'staff' and 'team member' are used interchangeably throughout the text, reflecting their use in the literature being discussed.

- antisocial behaviour (shouting or screaming, swearing, spitting, recurrent and uncontrolled vomiting, smearing of faeces, stealing);
- sexually inappropriate behaviour (nakedness in public, exposure of genitals, masturbation in public, sexual harassment/assault);
- bizarre behaviour (stereotypic behaviour such as rocking or odd speech, using nonsense or jumbled-up words, unusual gait or hand movements, altered routine such as sleep reversal, unrestrained eating and drinking, including dangerous substances).

This list identifies many of the behaviours we encounter clinically and which prove problematic for the person or for others. It does not, however, encompass self-neglect or other behaviours that may make the person vulnerable in the community to either exploitation or abuse (e.g. wearing unusual clothes, talking back to voices out loud, walking alone at night in a dangerous area).

As a first step in beginning to understand and work with problematic behaviours, we offer a broad classification encompassing three dimensions:

- behavioural excesses versus behavioural deficits;
- high versus low risk;
- self versus other (the direction of the risk).

An individual with psychosis may display behaviours that are not typically exhibited within the cultural or social norm (depending on where they live) or age group to which they belongs (e.g. wearing excessive clothing in the summer, swearing loudly in public); we term these 'behavioural excesses'. Alternatively, the individual may fail to display culturally or age-appropriate behaviours that are the norm for their peers. They may, for example, fail to attend to hygiene or personal safety, fail to engage in conversation when addressed or fail to display a normal range of emotional expressions; these we term 'behavioural deficits'. Clearly, there is some overlap between these definitions and those symptoms used as criteria to define psychiatric disorders (such as those employed by the American Psychiatric Association, 2000). However, to some degree these symptoms relate to observable behaviours that are a result of more complex underlying processes. Behavioural deficits are a particular case in point. They may on the surface present as negative symptoms of schizophrenia (e.g. staying in bed all day). However, they may occur in response to positive symptoms (e.g. a voice telling the person that if they get up they will be punished). Our focus therefore is less on psychiatric diagnosis (although this is useful in defining some aspects of treatment and prognosis) and more on being clear about the behaviour exhibited, its function and its psychosocial impact.

A further dimension to defining problematic behaviour is whether the deficit or excess represents a high or low risk to self or others. Those with psychosis may exhibit behaviours that are clearly frustrating for those who care for them such as making excessive demands (e.g. asking for cigarettes or extra visits) or making inappropriate demands (e.g. banging on windows or making abusive phone calls). Such behaviours are clearly 'excesses' but do not necessarily pose a high risk. Other behaviours such as assaults on others or staff may pose a high risk of harm as well as being behavioural excesses. Similarly, behavioural deficits may present a relatively low risk (e.g. refusal to speak to certain team members or to tidy one's living space) whilst others (e.g. refusal to maintain an adequate diet, refusal to take prescription medication for physical health conditions) may pose a significant but perhaps slightly longer-term risk to the person or their dependants. Finally, the direction of the behaviour in question (self versus other) is also a defining feature. For example, aggressive behaviours directed at staff may elicit more anger and resentment in the team than aggression directed at self, which may evoke sympathy and a greater helping response (Dagnan and Cairns, 2005). The interaction of these dimensions may be important: staff may respond with sympathy to apparently high-risk attempts at suicide (e.g. hanging) whilst lower-risk self-directed behaviours (e.g. scratching or cutting superficially) may be viewed as attempts at manipulation and hence regarded with more anger or dismissiveness. Clearly, the type of behaviour may predispose staff to make particular attributions about its purpose and subsequently alter their inclination to offer help; we discuss the role of staff attributions and beliefs further in Chapter 8.

THE SCALE OF THE PROBLEM: FREQUENCY AND PREVALENCE

Violence and aggression in inpatient settings

Violence and threatening behaviour are relatively common problems in inpatient psychiatric settings and may be the initial precipitant for admission. Binder and McNeil (1988), for example, found that 26 per cent of acute inpatients had been assaultative in the previous six months and 36 per cent had caused fear in others. Monahan (1992) reviewed 11 studies and found a median rate of 15 per cent of patients[2] committing a violent assault prior to admission (range 10 to 40 per cent). Of course, these groups may not be representative of people with psychosis as a whole, since these studies tended to examine the history of violence in those already admitted to hospital, which may represent a particular high-risk group. It may also be the case that procedures that are involved in the lead-up to admission themselves

---

2 We adopt the term 'patient' in reviewing this and other subsequent areas in keeping with that predominantly used in the original research literature.

precipitate violent incidents (e.g. use of the police). During the stay itself, rates continue to be high. Daffern *et al.* (2007), for example, found that during one year, over 45 per cent of patients were aggressive on at least one occasion. Other similar studies indicate an overall rate of inpatient violence of between 10 and 40 per cent, with a median rate of 25 per cent (Monahan, 1992). It is notable that a small minority of patients tend to be responsible for a large proportion of incidents (Blumenthal and Lavender, 2000). In the United Kingdom, Commander and Rooprai (2008) studied problematic behaviour in a new long-stay population across 208 acute hospital beds, and found that 38 patients were identified who met the criteria (having a stay exceeding six months). Of these, 16 per cent had harmed another, whilst 34 per cent had been threatening or intimidating towards others. In longer-term rehabilitation settings, Cowan *et al.* (in preparation) found that 50 per cent of patients from their sample of 98 patients across ten units had a history of serious violence or dangerousness and that this was considered to be a serious barrier to moving on. Most (85 per cent) were currently in some form of low-secure rehabilitation.

Research attempting to identify the causes of violence and aggression in these settings suggests that aggression may be more commonly precipitated by external, interpersonal factors (Sheridan *et al.*, 1990; Shepherd and Lavender, 1999; Daffern *et al.*, 2007) but external, situational factors such as overcrowding, management practices and staff inexperience may also play a role (Davies, 1993; Whittington, 1994). Internal factors such as symptom severity, history of violence, illness, age and antisocial attitudes may also be important (Blumenthal and Lavender, 2000; Quinsey *et al.*, 2006; Nagi *et al.*, 2009).

The likely target of aggression (staff versus other patients) appears to vary depending on the function of the behaviour. Aggression directed towards staff is more commonly associated with avoiding demands made, forcing staff to acquiesce in the face of demands being denied, rules being enforced or in the context of belittling interactional styles (Daffern *et al.*, 2007).

Violence and aggression in community settings

In community settings, a number of methods of studying psychiatric patients have been used. Some studies have followed up patients discharged from hospital. Steadman *et al.* (1998) and Monahan *et al.* (2001) found that in a sample of over 1000 patients, 27.5 per cent had committed at least one violent act in the 12 months post discharge. This high rate was noted when information was gathered from self-report, agency records and collateral sources; this was in contrast to a rate of only 4.5 per cent when relying on agency sources alone. This pattern has also been noted in other studies (Mulvey *et al.*, 1994), underscoring the need to gather information from a variety of sources. Klassen and O'Connor (1988) found rates of violence of 25 to 30 per cent

within the first year following discharge (n = 304; all males) and Newhill *et al.*
(1995) rates of around 44 per cent for males and females followed up for six
months post discharge.

These studies have, however, largely focused on select samples (e.g. those
already hospitalised and then discharged) and this may influence estimated
violence rates. Other studies have attempted to use community-based samples
that are randomly selected and have matched community controls. Swanson
et al. (1990), in their Epidemiological Catchment Area (ECA) study of a
representative community sample of 10,000 adults, found an increased risk of
violence of four times in those presenting with a major mental disorder, with
rates for schizophrenia, bipolar disorder and major depression being comparable. Similarly, Link *et al.* (1992) found violence rates in their patient
sample to be two to three times that of controls. Other methodologies linking
cases across psychiatric and criminal records with matched population controls have broadly replicated the increased risk of violence in schizophrenia
(3.8 times for men, 5.3 times for women). Bonta *et al.* (1998), in their meta-
analysis of previous studies for offenders with mental illness (predominantly
schizophrenia; n = 11,156), found a rate of violent reoffending of 25 per cent
and 46 per cent for any offending.

Despite varying methodologies, there appears to be a consensus that violence amongst people with mental illness is a significant problem and that
people with mental illness, as a group, are at higher risk of violence and
aggression. The degree to which this can be applied to individual clients is a
topic which will be returned to in later chapters.

Risk of self-harm, attempted suicide and suicide

Risk of harm to self is of equal concern when working with psychotic individuals, especially since it increases the risk of suicide. Base rates for self-
harm vary significantly, from 21 per cent to as much as 61 per cent across
studies for clinical populations as a whole (Hawton *et al.*, 1997). Research
by Vanderhoff and Lynn (2001) suggests that self-harm is distinct from
suicide or attempted suicide in a number of ways. First, individuals describe
self-harm as a completed behaviour. Second, there is a reported fear that
self-harm may lead to death. Third, the behaviour itself often leads to
feelings of relief (from difficult emotional states) compared with suicidal
patients who report distress when an attempt has failed. Clients who self-
harm also tend to report no intent to die (Simeon and Favazza, 2001).
Parasuicidal behaviours tend to differ from self-harm in terms of method
(e.g. head banging as opposed to ingesting paracetamol) although they
may be the same (e.g. cutting). The functions of parasuicidal behaviours
compared with behaviours involving attempts to die are obviously different
(e.g. Brown *et al.*, 2002).

Actual suicide is a significant problem and is reflected in attempts to reduce it by as much as a third in mentally ill populations (DH, 2002). Contemporary reviews of the literature on suicide amongst inpatients and former inpatients with schizophrenia have found that the suicide rate in those who were followed-up for periods ranging from 1 to 26 years after their first hospitalisation was 6.8 per cent (Pompili *et al.*, 2007). It has been estimated that up to 10 to 13 per cent of individuals with schizophrenia die by suicide and that this is the main cause of death in this group (Caldwell and Gottesman, 1990). Other meta-analytic studies have, however, indicated lower rates of around 4 to 4.9 per cent and have noted that the risk of suicide in schizophrenic patients is around eight times that in the general population (Inskip *et al.*, 1998; Palmer *et al.*, 2005). Higher rates, of up to 50 per cent, are noted for attempted suicide (Meltzer *et al.*, 2003; Drake, 2007). These attempts also represent an increased risk for later death by suicide (Powell *et al.*, 2000), with an estimated 10 per cent actually committing suicide during their lifetime (Meltzer *et al.*, 2003).

Research efforts that have also focused on trying to identify the period of highest risk have found that the mortality rate is highest in first-episode patients or those in the early phases of their illness (Brown, 1997). However, one third of those with schizophrenia commit suicide over the age of 45 years (Hansen *et al.*, 2004). Increased risk of suicide is noted in patients shortly after admission to hospital or shortly following discharge (Roy, 1982) and the risk of suicide in the six months post discharge may be 34 times that of the general population (Pompili *et al.*, 2007). In Shah and Ganesvaran's (1999) review of 62 case studies of inpatients with schizophrenia, over 40 per cent of suicides occurred during a period of approved leave and a similar percentage occurred after absconding. Across a number of these studies (involving 813 patients), 147 committed suicide whilst in hospital, 395 shortly after discharge, 198 whilst still hospitalised but on regular leave and 73 whilst having absconded.

Risk factors for suicide which apply to the general population also apply in schizophrenia (see Chapter 5 for a fuller discussion), but there are risk factors that are more specific to the disorder (Siris, 2001). However, people with schizophrenia (and in particular males) who attempt suicide have a tendency to use more lethal means and consequently to have a higher likelihood of success with methods including jumping in front of traffic or trains, jumping off bridges, hanging or drowning (Farebrow *et al.*, 1961; Shah and Ganesvaran, 1999; Powell *et al.*, 2000).

Suicide continues to be a cause of concern amongst those with the most serious mental illness. Despite a greater focus on suicide reduction and greater access to psychological treatments, the number of suicides has remained unchanged (Meltzer *et al.*, 2003). Indeed, people diagnosed with schizophrenia now are 20 times more likely to die by suicide compared with those diagnosed 100 years ago (Healy *et al.*, 2006; Seeman, 2007). Powell *et al.* (2000) found that 26 per cent of suicides in a United Kingdom sample of inpatients were not on leave and were under observation by staff at the time of suicide. Some of the methodologies described in this book are designed to help address this problem, especially our early warning signs of risk tool (Chapters 10 and 13).

Other problematic behaviours

As already noted, the range of problematic behaviours exhibited by individuals with psychosis is far broader in scope than those that are of high risk to self and others. The prevalence of less high-risk behaviours such as self-neglect or bizarre behaviours is, however, less clearly documented. Morgan (1998) is one of the few authors to have considered the issue of self-neglect in risk terms. He noted that little attention had been paid to this area (which continues to be the case) but that such problems are widespread in people with severe mental illness. They extend beyond the scope of negative symptoms and tend to be judged (by others) as less serious. Clinicians may make different judgements regarding what constitutes self-neglect and its severity in the absence of clear guidelines. Our criteria concern whether self-neglect places the individual in a vulnerable position to others such that they may be exploited or abused (e.g. wearing inappropriate clothes, leaving their possessions in an unsafe place), places them at risk of physical health problems (e.g. malnutrition, risk of infection or disease) or serves to create a barrier to participation. Clients with psychiatric disorders have a higher risk of physical health problems (McCarrick et al., 1986) and early death (Martin et al., 1985). Across ten 24-hour nursed care residential rehabilitation services, Cowan et al. (in preparation) assessed the behaviour of 98 patients using the Challenging Behaviour Checklist for Psychosis (see Appendix 1). Seventeen per cent were rated as having compulsive behaviours and 29 per cent socially inappropriate behaviours potentially making them vulnerable to physical health problems, social exclusion or abuse or exploitation from others. One hundred per cent had behavioural deficits that could lead to social exclusion, result in abuse or exploitation from others as well as physical health problems. Indeed, 36 per cent were also rated (on the Resident Profile, originally developed by the Royal College of Psychiatrists Research Unit for the Mental Health Residential Care Study: Lelliott et al., 1996) as being at risk of developing a moderate-to-severe physical health problem. Hiday et al. (1999) found that their sample of people with severe mental illness had an increased risk of 2.5 times that of the normal population for violent victimisation. Brekke et al. (2001) found that those with mental illness were 14 times more likely to be victims of crime, with 91 per cent being victims of violence. Risk of victimisation was also heightened by additional factors such as poverty, homelessness and substance misuse. Being victimised has in turn been found to be linked to increased self-harm (Warm et al., 2003).

THE SAFE APPROACH

Clearly, despite the emergence of and steady translation into routine clinical practice of psychosocial interventions, developments in pharmacology and other areas of practice occurring alongside improved service delivery mechanisms (e.g. assertive outreach teams), problematic behaviours are an ongoing cause of concern. We believe that high-quality comprehensive multidisciplinary care is key to improving the management and treatment of these behaviours. We also argue that new approaches are needed that bring together developments in the fields of psychosis, forensic risk practice and developments in the fields of learning disability and neurobehavioural rehabilitation. We present these in this book in the form of the SAFE approach and our Cognitive Approach to Risk Management (CARM) model. These offer a uniquely integrated set of methods to facilitate improved shared working practices with those with treatment-resistant psychosis and problematic behaviours.

SUMMARY

Rates of suicide, violence and other less risky but equally problematic behaviours remain high in psychotic individuals. These behaviours are worthy of considerable focus in terms of both research and treatment resources. Such problems, even if not life threatening, may cause a significant drain on resources, be distressing to others and severely limit the individual's access to normal activities. Perhaps more importantly, these behaviours hinder people from achieving their valued life goals, and severely limit their quality of life. In the next chapter, we outline the current treatment approaches to such problems and their limitations, and provide an overview of the SAFE approach.

Chapter 2

The SAFE approach

An overview

In this chapter we provide an overview of the Shared Assessment, Formulation and Education (SAFE) approach to working with problematic behaviours in psychosis. We discuss the importance of adopting an integrative and formulation-based approach, which addresses a range of relevant intrapersonal, interpersonal and environmental factors. We begin by considering the useful aspects of existing approaches to the understanding, management and treatment of individuals with psychosis presenting with problematic behaviours along with their limitations. First, however, it is worth giving brief consideration to the term 'treatment resistance'. Traditionally, the term has been used to refer to people who do not respond to standard psychiatric care (e.g. medication and nursing). However, standard care now encompasses psychosocial interventions such as cognitive-behaviour therapy (CBT), behavioural family therapy (BFT) and psychoeducation. In this book we suggest that the term may more usefully be applied to those individuals who do not respond to routine best practice, such as that recommended in current guidelines (e.g. DH, 2001; National Institute for Health and Clinical Excellence, 2009).

CURRENT APPROACHES

Cognitive-behaviour therapy

Alongside medication, CBT is arguably the treatment of choice for individuals with positive symptoms of psychosis. Some have, however, questioned the efficacy of such approaches (Turkington and McKenna, 2003; Jones *et al.*, 2010; Lynch *et al.*, 2010). Certainly, the effective ingredients of CBT have yet to be clearly established and are often camouflaged in trials. It is not clear, for example, whether it is the educational aspects of the CBT intervention, the disputation techniques used, the devising and carrying out of behavioural experiments or the teaching of coping strategies that is the effective component or even whether all of these used in combination are necessary to effect meaningful change. A further difficulty, one that is common to all trials, is that those taking part in them are to some extent a select group who may not represent clients encountered in routine clinical practice. This is especially true for those who are hard to engage and often present with additional co-morbidities and other treatment-resistant factors. These clients are most frequently encountered on the caseloads of clinicians under the care of Assertive Outreach Teams, as new long-stay patients in acute hospitals or in longer-term inpatient settings and forensic services. Finally, many trials have focused on symptom reduction or reduced relapse as their primary outcome measures. This is in contrast to the traditional focus of CBT for neurosis, where reducing distress or problematic behaviours has been the primary motivation (Birchwood and Trower, 2006). Recent innovations in CBT for psychosis have refocused the goals of therapy on reducing distress (Chadwick, 2006). However, relatively less attention has been paid to understanding and reducing problematic behaviours in psychosis. This is surprising given the high rates of violence, suicide and other problem behaviours in this group, as evidenced in Chapter 1. Evidence also suggests that acting on psychotic beliefs (which may involve violence or self-harm) is common (Buchanan, 1993; Trower *et al.*, 2004). The relationship between psychotic symptoms and risk is considered more fully in Chapter 5, but it is notable that recent studies suggest that specific aspects of the phenomenology of positive symptoms appear to mediate risk behaviours (Buchanan *et al.*, 1993; Freeman *et al.*, 2001, 2007; Green *et al.*, 2006). A particular strength of cognitive-behavioural models of psychotic symptoms is an emphasis on the importance of understanding the phenomenological link between psychotic beliefs and behaviours or distress. Specifically, studies have found that acting on voices appears to be predicted by voice-related beliefs concerning power, omniscience and the need to comply (Trower *et al.*, 2004; Hacker *et al.*, 2008). Similarly, in paranoid individuals, acting in accordance with delusional beliefs can be conceptualised within a CBT framework as attempts to mitigate against perceived physical, psychological or social threats: as safety-seeking behaviours (Freeman *et al.*, 2001).

These studies highlight the importance of conceptualising the cognitive-behavioural phenomenology[1] of psychosis when working with individuals whose behaviour is problematic and may result in social exclusion and enforced treatments. One of the few CBT approaches to focus on problematic behaviour has been that of Byrne *et al.* (2006), who describe a type of cognitive therapy for reducing compliance with command hallucinations through the careful targeting of beliefs about control, power, omniscience and the

---

1 The cognitive phenomenology of psychosis refers to the way in which the individual experiences the world, constructs a psychotic understanding about it (e.g. beliefs) and subsequently interacts with it.

need to comply. However, whilst conceptually clear and, as preliminary results suggest (Trower *et al.*, 2004), a very effective approach, it is focused on a single psychotic symptom (which is rarely the case in clinical practice), it is based around one-to-one therapy and it crucially assumes that people's behaviour is almost fully mediated by their beliefs about their voices. In reality, there is often a complex interplay of multiple symptoms (Chadwick *et al.*, 1996). An individual may also act on their distress in some instances (e.g. cutting themselves to reduce distress associated with voices), rather than because of a specific compliance belief. Therefore, a more idiosyncratic, formulation-driven approach to treatment is implicated. This is in contrast to the large numbers of randomised controlled trials of CBT for psychosis, which are of necessity often protocol driven and therefore do not reflect general clinical practice in the use of idiosyncratic case conceptualisations and individually tailored treatments. Whilst the importance of such conceptual-isations continues to be endorsed by a number of authors (Persons, 1989; Morrison *et al.*, 2004; Kuyken *et al.*, 2009), mention of them is strangely absent from current clinical guidelines.

Behavioural (functional analytic) approaches

As noted in Chapter 1 and at odds with CBT models of psychosis, is the fact that clients' problematic behaviours are often driven not by internal factors but by environmental and interpersonal ones. The CBT literature has little to say about these factors. In contrast, however, a strong literature on chal-lenging behaviours in the field of learning disability (Emerson, 2001) has adopted a largely behavioural, functional analytic approach to the assess-ment and treatment of such behaviours. This emphasises the importance of observable triggers to, and reinforcers of, problematic behaviours. To date, little has been written of the direct application of behavioural, functional analytic models to understanding and intervening with risk or problematic behaviours in psychosis. Formulation is seen as important to this approach but has a different focus from that usually employed in CBT: 'the process of operationalising target behaviours (determining their form) and evaluating relationships amongst target behaviours and potential controlling factors (determining function) for an individual client' (O'Brien *et al.*, 2003, p. 164).

A formulation should clearly specify the relevant maintenance factors and targets or points of intervention for a specific problematic behaviour. Emerson's (2001) model offers a formulation which highlights a range of factors that both trigger and maintain problem behaviour (e.g. staff reac-tions, environmental events), and distinguishes between those factors which establish motivation for the behaviour (establishing operations or setting events) and those which trigger its occurrence (discriminative stimuli). Once the behaviour has occurred it is said to be maintained or extinguished by the consequences that follow (operant reinforcement). Beer (2006) is one of the few authors to draw on these behavioural principles in recent times. Employing Emerson's (2001) model as a basis for assessment and formulation, he suggests the benefits of the RAID approach (Davies, 1993). The acronym RAID is derived from the approach it recommends – Reinforce Appropriate (behaviour), Ignore Difficult or disruptive (behaviour) – and is a commonly taught method. It is based broadly on an operant conditioning model: problematic behaviours are addressed using a differential reinforcement paradigm, ignoring undesirable behaviours and reinforcing more appropriate ones.

In our experience, a number of difficulties arise when purely applying a functional analytic model in this way to a psychotic population. First, because it is based originally around a learning disability population, it does not clearly provide a method for integrating the relevant phenomenological and cognitive factors that are so pertinent in psychosis. Second, the emphasis on triggering factors and reinforcers alone is problematic. In the former case, triggers are often not obvious as they may be internal (as in the case of voice commands). In the latter case, differential reinforcement methods necessitate altering the consequences that follow the behaviour in order to attempt to reduce its future occurrence. However, it is difficult to address high-risk behavioural excesses in this way since, on the grounds of safety and professional ethics, efforts must necessarily focus on safety. An additional issue is that a purely reinforcement-based approach fails to account for the potential strength of internal reinforcement for such behaviours in psychosis. It may be that few if any reinforcement programmes will override an immediate but delusional threat to one's own life or the lives of one's loved ones. Finally, functional analytic models concerned with setting events and triggering events give an emphasis to the acute management of risk and less consideration to the longstanding psychological dispositions of the individual, which are often implicated in driving risk in the longer term. These psychological dispositions or 'dynamic stable' risk factors (Douglas and Skeem, 2005) are considered in contemporary models of risk (DH, 2007). They are distinct from 'acute' factors, which indicate an imminent likelihood of the risk behaviour occurring. This distinction is particularly useful in conceptualising changes in mental state associated with increased risk, in people who are treatment resistant, have persistent residual symptoms or experience frequent relapses. Because persistent delusions, voices or other symptoms are frequently present in this group, they do not provide a good means of predicting when risk is likely to occur. It is here that the distinctions drawn within the risk assessment literature are particularly informative and useful.

Approaches to risk prediction and prevention

The forensic literature has traditionally emphasised risk prediction over risk prevention (Blumenthal and Lavender, 2000). This is reflected in current assessment methodologies that emphasise historical or demographic risk markers, which are mainly informative in assessing the client's risk 'status', that is, their likelihood of displaying the risk behaviour compared with other people. These methods have given less emphasis to the person's 'risk state' (Douglas and Skeem, 2005), that is, how likely the person is to display the risk behaviour at a given point in time. Making such a judgement depends on understanding the circumstances under which the risk behaviour is likely to occur and subsequently determining how this risk might best be managed given this knowledge. The literature delineates 'static' or 'historical' factors, such as gender or number of offences, from more 'dynamic risk factors' (Beech and Ward, 2004; DH, 2007). Dynamic stable factors (e.g. antisocial attitudes, delusions, trait anger) may be amenable to change but tend to be enduring characteristics of the individual. These can usefully be viewed as the traditional target of CBT. Dynamic acute factors are more rapidly changing factors, such as mood state, increased preoccupation with delusions or intoxication, which indicate the presence of a high-risk state and a high and imminent likelihood of the risk behaviour occurring. Recent Department of Health guidelines (DH, 2007) strongly emphasise the need for structured assessment of risk behaviours, the use of risk formulation and the monitoring of early warning signs of risk.

Emerson's (2001) model of challenging behaviour can be viewed as mapping onto the acute risk factors of contemporary forensic models. A synthesis of the two approaches provides a useful framework for formulating risk or problematic behaviours. Further integrating these two approaches with contemporary models of CBT for psychosis (Chadwick et al., 1996; Meaden et al., 2010) offers a more comprehensive framework for conceptualising, managing and treating problematic behaviours in treatment-resistant psychosis. However, it is equally important to note that these individuals often have multiple needs and are cared for in a complex care system with its own set of factors, which can help to facilitate or impede therapeutic efforts and change for the individual. Understanding the Multidisciplinary Team (MDT) and service context and culture are therefore equally important.

STAFF AND SYSTEM FACTORS: BARRIERS TO EFFECTIVE CARE

Staff factors

When working with complex care systems caring for complex individuals with psychosis, it is important to consider the broad range of factors that might impact on management and treatment. In MDTs, risk and behaviour management requires that the staff have a good (ideally psychologically informed) understanding of their client and be fully engaged in a consistent treatment approach. Additionally, they should attempt to minimise aspects of interactions that might reinforce dysfunctional beliefs and behaviours in the client. It is well documented in the learning disability literature, for instance, that staff attributions about clients and their behaviour are important determinants of care (Leggett and Silvester, 2003; Dagnan and Weston, 2006); these findings have been replicated in forensic populations (Sharrock *et al.*, 1990). Staff's attributions are often embedded within broader staff beliefs about the care process itself and about the causes and treatment of mental health problems. They have been shown to mediate staff emotional reactions and subsequent care responses (Sharrock *et al.*, 1990; Dagnan and Cairns, 2005). Factors identified that impact on treatment efficacy include: a lack of staff compliance with interventions; poor understanding of the rationale for the intervention; and negative feelings engendered by the client's challenging behaviours (Hastings and Remington, 1994). There is, additionally, a tendency for staff to consider the topography of the behaviour rather than its function, and to have an emphasis on crisis management rather than on promoting longer-term change (Hastings *et al.*, 1995; Hastings and Brown, 2002). Addressing these staff factors may be necessary in order to facilitate consistency in risk and behavioural management as well as reduce staff burnout, unhelpful team splitting and other dysfunctional team dynamics (Davenport, 2006).

Our process for constructing and sharing formulations is designed to increase staff understanding of the client's problems and background history (the shared person level formulation) as well as their more specific beliefs about the client and their difficulties (the staff ABC formulation). Of course, individual members of teams themselves are embedded within a care system that can vary in the degree to which it emphasises the needs of the individual over those of the organisation (e.g. to meet certain targets) and where clarity of goals and care planning can often be lost. It is crucial therefore that in dealing with problem behaviours the team has an overarching framework of values and goals for the service that can drive and support care planning for the individual in question. Our shared service level formulation has been developed to address this.

Care system factors

The SAFE approach encourages a systematic formulation of the client's problems, leading to an in-depth formulation of particular problematic behaviours (our Cognitive Approach to Risk Management [CARM] formulation). These behaviours, amidst a range of other factors, can result in the client with psychosis experiencing significant social exclusion and having their movements restricted (e.g. detention under the Mental Health Act, Compulsory Treatment Orders, restrictions on places to live). In turn, this impedes their ability to achieve their life goals and begin a recovery journey. 'Positive risk taking' is now an important part of Department of Health guidance (DH, 2007) but requires a framework to achieve it, safely balancing risk management with the rights and wishes of the client. Whilst treatment and management of problematic or risk behaviours is, by necessity, often a service priority for the purpose of protection of the client and the public, reduction of this should not be seen as solely an end in itself. Enabling recovery and reducing barriers to participation in ordinary community living should also be the goals of services. However, this focus is often hard to maintain in the face of persistent problems with engagement, poor motivation to change, complex risk issues and often substantial co-morbidities such as substance misuse or personality difficulties. The client's goals are all too often lost in the need for risk management and staff can often be unclear about what is expected from the client. Clients may unsurprisingly fail to perceive any relationship between the demands made of them by services and their own wishes or aspirations. This may lead to frustration with and disengagement from services.

In the United Kingdom, the Care Programme Approach (CPA) (DH, 1990) has been adopted as the method for developing care plans and their review. However, problems have consistently been encountered when implementing this process (Holloway, 2006). Assessment findings and formulations are all too often not reflected in the client's care plans. Rather, care plans are often centred on broad goals, such as 'improving personal hygiene' or 'reducing risk'. These care plan goals are so broad and non-specific as to be meaningless and it is unlikely that they will lead to any meaningful change in the delivery of the client's day-to-day care. Staff and carers are more likely to employ over-generalised approaches to management and intervention. This ambiguity and lack of specificity often result in different team members arriving at their own subjective interpretation of which approach to take, leading to contradictory or overlapping approaches being employed across the team. We argue that an overarching framework that incorporates the person's own unique personal goals, hopes and values as well as environmental, social and person-based barriers to participation in ordinary community living is required. The 1999 *International classification of functioning and disability*, Beta-2 draft (ICIDH-2), World Health Organization (WHO) model (WHO, 1999; Wade and de Jong, 2000) is arguably a useful framework for underpinning care planning in clients with treatment-resistant psychosis. It provides a framework for service level formulation and care planning into which clear interventions for addressing problematic behaviours is usefully integrated. The use of the ICIDH-2 model for idiosyncratic care planning in SAFE is discussed more fully in Chapter 3.

The WHO ICIDH-2 framework contains four key levels. Level 1 is concerned with the disease process (*pathology*) or diagnosis from which the person is suffering (e.g. schizophrenia). Level 2, *impairment*, is concerned with signs or symptoms and might include psychiatric symptoms and mood, cognitive deficits and somatic sensations. Level 3, *activity limitations*, is concerned with changes in the quality or quantity of the individual's behaviour as a result of levels 1 and 2; it includes both subjective and objective views on the person's abilities regarding interactions with their environment. We might consider this to include behavioural deficits, behavioural excesses and appropriate functional skills. Level 4, *social participation*, is concerned with changes, limitations or abnormalities in the position or role of the person in their social context. For example, an individual with schizophrenia (level 1) may have voices (level 2) and cognitive problems resulting in difficulties in motivation and in self-regulation (level 2), which result in problem behaviours such as violence (level 3) and poor maintenance of personal hygiene (level 3). These problems may result in the individual being excluded from local community facilities such as the library or local pub (level 4). The WHO ICIDH-2 model is therefore a useful framework for integrating the client's life goals and service goals (level 4) with an understanding of exactly which components of the client's symptoms (level 2) are preventing participation (level 3). The emphasis is therefore on life goals and reduction of barriers to participation and not simply on symptom reduction (many individuals who hear voices do live in the community without exhibiting violence or needing to be detained).

One of the advantages of the WHO ICIDH-2 model is its emphasis on understanding the impact of impairments and symptoms on the person's behaviour in their interaction with their social environment. In turn, limitations or alterations in the person's behaviour are considered relevant only in so far as they limit the person's ability to successfully participate in normal community and social activities that are appropriate for their culture and age-matched peers. Therefore, whilst contemporary behavioural models confer the advantage of understanding the function of the individual's behaviours, the WHO model provides a broader understanding of their impact on the client's level of participation and their ability to achieve their goals.

Adopting the WHO perspective is in keeping with behavioural principles. Barriers to participation or activity limitations are often behavioural in nature, not emotional or symptom based (although these may be important contributors to the person's behaviour). This initial focus on behaviour may seem reductionist. However, we find that it is almost without exception that these are the things that teams most struggle with and have the biggest impact on the individual. It is actually the behaviour resulting from other factors that most often leads to social exclusion and restrictions being placed on them. Discussion with staff and clients often does not begin in this way, but with further examination this is usually what we agree is the focus for developing our understanding and further work.

Case example: Linda

Consider Linda, who remains troubled and distressed by voices. She lives alone and in impoverished circumstances, refusing all but the most meagre possessions and comforts. She explains this as a need to suffer imposed by powerful voices. The team are frustrated that they cannot engage her in any meaningful activities and that she will not allow them to furnish her flat or help with her shopping and diet. Where does the problem lie? Arguably with the voices, however, we may further ask what is it that they prevent Linda from doing? Could it be then that it is her compliance behaviour that is the problem? This then becomes the task of assessment and understanding, although the approach ultimately adopted may not be a behavioural one.

Both the WHO ICIDH-2 framework and the behavioural aspects of our SAFE approach have in common a focus on arriving at clear definitions and goals. The WHO model is therefore useful in providing a basis for one particular aspect of the SAFE approach, the Service Level Formulation. This is the structure used to provide teams with an overarching framework for care planning and service values and which provides the focus for arriving at more detailed behaviour-focused interventions.

THE SAFE APPROACH

So far in this chapter we have outlined the range of existing approaches to addressing problematic behaviour in different populations. All have merits but used as standalone interventions are often inadequate to address the complex range of factors that drive and maintain problematic behaviours in treatment-resistant populations. MDT care planning aims to bridge this gap. As Harrison (2006) has noted, the majority of longer-term care requires the manifold skills of a MDT since a number of processes have to progress in order to achieve success. However, these are often carried out inconsistently or lack a clear service focus. We have developed what we now term SAFE over a number of years of clinical practice working with those who experience such difficulties. By integrating the models and approaches set out above, adopting a formulation-led process and importantly placing this in a service context, we offer a practical but theory-driven solution. An overarching theme across the different aspects of the approach, and indeed the chapters of this book, is the collaborative nature of MDT assessment and formulation we adopt. Good-quality comprehensive care is a key aim. Working alone and offering individualised treatments is unlikely to be effective with such individuals.

Key aspects: the four principles of SAFE

The ultimate aim of the SAFE approach is to promote social participation and inclusion (the *social participation principle*), not just reduce
behaviours. Of course, not everyone will want to live or socialise with others,
the point is that we should work towards reducing the barriers that prevent this so that the person concerned has a choice about whether to
participate more fully. In the SAFE approach, barriers to participation
are clearly identified as targets for intervention and such barriers are clear
problematic behavioural excesses or deficits; the SAFE approach is therefore clearly behaviour and goal focused. This understanding itself, however, is guided by the empirical literature and existing evidence base about
what factors may be important to consider in understanding problematic
behaviours in this client group (the *evidence-based principle*). The other key
aspect of the evidence-based principle is that the target of intervention, triggers and maintaining factors as well as methods of intervention should be
clearly and behaviourally defined. In addition, assessment, formulation and
intervention should be based on that which can be measured and assessed
and for which there is convergent evidence across a number of sources. A
client may report that their violent acts are linked to their voices but other
evidence may point to a refusal of their demands as the key trigger. A key
aspect to consider is the function of the client's behaviour and to develop a
shared understanding of the client's internal world along with the phenomenology and unique features of their psychosis (the *shared understanding of
phenomenology principle*). This is an area often lacking in teams who can lose
sight of the knowledge of the person's history and life experiences, and who
may not fully grasp or understand the client's internal world or reason
for their behaviours. In this sense, the inclusion of consideration of staff
beliefs and attributions is an important aspect of the shared understanding
of phenomenology principle.

By drawing on and integrating CBT models with contemporary approaches
to risk and challenging behaviour, SAFE offers an opportunity to apply CBT
in a novel, multidisciplinary fashion. This is the focus of our CARM model.
CARM incorporates aspects of the CBT literature but maintains a strong
behavioural focus, providing a clear rationale and focus for subsequent interventions. Finally, the process of formulation is seen as equally, if not more
important, than the end product itself. It provides a collaborative problem-
solving framework for staff and clients that is tailored to the unique changing
needs of the client and the setting. We have termed this the *need-adapted
principle*. In this we have been much influenced by the need-adapted treatment approach (Alanen, 1997), which highlights the need to consider the
case-specific and changing needs of individuals with psychosis. It emphasises
continuous hypothesising as well as developing a shared understanding with
the person and all of those involved in their care. An important principle of

need-adapted treatment is that different therapeutic activities should support and not counteract each other.

Further aims of the SAFE approach

SAFE values the perspectives of the person and potentially all of those involved in supporting them and providing their care, including their family and carers. It serves to normalise problematic behaviours and to increase understanding throughout the network of supports available, facilitating compassion and effective intervention. The primary focus is on achieving integrated MDT working, reducing overlapping or competing approaches. The specific aims in implementing SAFE are:

1   to promote team engagement with the client and adherence to treatment plans (by impacting on staff beliefs and attributions about the client and their behaviours);
2   to identify and prioritise specific treatment goals and targets, with a clear rationale for their choice that is transparent to staff (formulation-based treatment planning);
3   to engage staff in using a psychologically informed cognitive-behavioural approach in their day-to-day interactions with and management of problematic behaviours;
4   to more accurately and appropriately target behavioural interventions;
5   to reduce distress and problematic behaviour and thereby barriers to living an ordinary life and so enable recovery (in our terms 'social participation').

These aims are underpinned by the four principles of SAFE as described above.

SAFE formulation frameworks

SAFE formulations provide the frameworks for effective MDT working. First, they help to challenge unhelpful staff attributions, emotions and behaviours and provide a clear focus for clients, staff and the service. Second, they help the team to better understand the range of contributory factors. Third, they provide valued roles for all in contributing to the assessment process. SAFE care plans (Chapter 15) are a further mechanism for enhancing team working; they specify who should do what and when. Finally, the integration of models in SAFE is encapsulated in our formulation frameworks. These provide for a broad range of intervention strategies that can be delivered in an integrated MDT care package. These strategies are designed to address specific measurable goals in a multidisciplinary manner: co-opting MDT staff into working as behavioural and CBT therapists, providing daily CBT and promoting shared risk management.

A number of interlocking methods of formulation are presented in this book, which can be utilised at different times depending on the focus of the intervention or assessment and the setting in which it is being conducted. These formulation frameworks are built on best practice principles of formulation. Formulation has been most succinctly described by Bieling and Kuyken (2003, p. 53) as: 'a map of a person's presenting problems that describes the territory of the problems and explains the processes that caused and maintain the problems'. In SAFE, this broad perspective is best represented by our shared person level formulation which allows treatments to be tailored in a way that most closely matches the unique characteristics of the client (Haynes and Williams, 2003). This is a further important need-adapted treatment principle, reflecting the case-specific and changing needs of the individual.

Adopting best practice in SAFE formulations

Case conceptualisation, at least in CBT terms, cannot be said to be truly evidence-based practice (Bieling and Kuyken, 2003). Nevertheless, there is agreement that a formulation should both describe and explain presenting problems in clear and operationally defined terms (e.g. affect, cognition, behaviour), have validity and reliability, provide guidelines for intervention, and be responsive to new data. Johnstone and Dallos (2006) suggest five key areas in formulation: presenting problems, precipitating factors (distal and proximal), predisposing factors, perpetuating factors and protective factors. The social context of the clinical problem (e.g. social support) is also important in understanding both risk behaviour and recovery from psychosis (see Chapters 3 and 5). A crucial issue is whether or not clinicians can agree with proposed formulation elements. Persons et al. (1995) found that clinicians can agree on the client's overt problems and underlying cognitive mechanisms. Persons and Bertagnolli (1999) subsequently reported similar findings; with trained therapists being more accurate in identifying patients' problems. Mumma and Smith (2001) have also demonstrated that clinicians can achieve good reliability and convergent validity in their formulations for independently generated, cognitive-behavioural or cognitive-interpersonal scenarios. Similar findings have been reported in the psychosis literature (Kuyken et al., 2005). However, reliability tends to be less evident when clinicians are required to hypothesise regarding core beliefs. The use of more systematic methods or frameworks tends to minimise this as well as training and the experience of the therapist and their ability to make theory–practice links (Kuyken et al., 2009). The Plan Formulation Method (Curtis and Silberschatz, 1997), based on cognitive psychoanalytic theory, offers a systematic method of case formulation and defines the key elements of formulation based on theory (e.g. goals, obstructions, traumas). It utilises a structured process that enables a panel to achieve consensus on a formulation and its included elements. This method involves judges rating transcripts of therapy, obtaining consensus ratings of the relevance of different aspects of the client's presentation to their problems (assessed for reliability across judges) and the use of a standardised formulation format. This method has been well researched but for clinical purposes it may be less practical for use on an MDT basis since it is very time consuming. The core principles of this method are, however, useful in developing consensus, reliability and validity.

The question remains as to whether formulation actually improves outcomes. The evidence on this, however, is somewhat disappointing (Kuyken *et al.*, 2009). In some cases, clients report increased levels of distress and may actually disengage from therapy as a result (Chadwick *et al.*, 2003). This highlights the importance of adopting a collaborative approach where the clients, or as in the case of SAFE the team, are involved with the process from the beginning rather than the completed formulation being shared at an advanced stage.

Less attention has been paid to formulations with teams. Davenport (2002) is one of the few researchers to have reported utilising shared formulation frameworks in multidisciplinary settings; in this case on an acute setting with some success. Berry *et al.* (2009) conducted a pilot intervention with psychiatric staff helping them to develop psychological formulations for individual service users. Staff perceptions of service users' mental health problems were measured before and after the intervention using Likert scales. Staff perceptions of clients' control over their problems increased as a result along with reduced feelings of blame and increased optimism about treatment. Staff also reported an increase in their understanding of clients' problems.

Being mindful of these findings, SAFE formulations are based around clearly defined problem areas; which are the focus of our CARM, risk and shared service level formulations. Training is provided (see Chapter 18) to improve the team's knowledge and skill and formulations are always expertly facilitated. Formulations are constructed collaboratively with members of the care team and, if possible, the client. Several interlocking templates are adopted, which provide a systematic method for implementing shared formulations (see Figure 2.1). We believe that the use of these templates allows the above criteria to be more easily satisfied. Drawing on the empirical literature, SAFE incorporates:

- a collaborative approach (involving MDT members, the client and others involved in their care and support);
- structured and consistent templates with pre-defined elements (allowing staff to become familiar with the structure over time and through training and incorporating the evidence-based principle);
- team members and relevant others being involved from the first step (increasing ownership of the process, providing a framework for collaborative problem solving and underscoring Westermeyer's, 2003, view that formulation is as much process as end product).

- collaborative construction of the formulation (reducing the tendency to miss out crucial information);
- multiple methods of assessment (including interview, notes, behavioural observations and relevant psychometrics) and findings that are triangulated across multiples sources (including staff, family, the client themselves);
- triangulation of evidence across three main sources: (a) background and clinical history, (b) clinical presentation of the client during assessment and (c) psychometric assessment. In theory, evidence should converge to the same conclusions across these three different sources. For example, a client scoring high on antisocial personality traits on a self-report measure but with no concurrent history or clinical presentation may lead to some doubt about the validity of their self-report on the questionnaire rather than a diagnosis of antisocial personality disorder being assumed from test results;
- assessment methods that are embedded within a systematic process for sharing emerging elements and agreeing their relevance and importance;
- the evidence-based principle, which is applied to deductions and formulations (by reference to multiple and reliable sources of information, sound assessment procedures, collateral sources, reviews of relevant documentation and structured staff observations).

SAFE formulations are constructed in such a way that they can be used with clients who do not engage in one-to-one assessment or therapy (although this is always desirable). By involving the MDT as a whole, SAFE is also of use in helping to generalise skills and belief change outside of the therapy room. It is advantageous, and of course ethical, that where possible clients should be directly involved in the SAFE process. It should be noted, however, that sharing formulations with clients, at least as a *fait accompli*, may not necessarily improve outcome and may in some cases increase distress and hopelessness (Chadwick *et al.*, 2003). It may be, therefore, that formulations are helpful to clients directly only if they themselves are involved in the process and perhaps if the process is future oriented and relevant to the client's own goals. Our shared person level formulation involves a sharing of ideas and knowledge, resolving disagreements and facilitating a more complex, psychological understanding of the individual with psychosis. It is, however, ultimately embedded in the very goal-focused service level formulation emphasising the promotion of social participation.

The components of the SAFE approach

The SAFE approach has four key components, which are essentially levels of formulation, using structured and pre-defined methods where the content may vary but the structure remains the same. These are illustrated in Figure 2.1 and all are underpinned by the four principles of SAFE. The shared service level formulation provides the overarching framework and value of the SAFE approach. It allows a clear identification of treatment targets based on the client's life and recovery goals and increasing the degree of social participation whilst minimising risk (this formulation is discussed at greater length in Chapter 3). The shared person level formulation provides a useful summary of the client's life history, experiences, symptoms and presenting problems. It aims to educate all staff about the client as an individual and to provide an initial challenge to any unhelpful staff beliefs. The shared risk formulation and CARM provide a narrowing of focus on barriers to participation (activity limitations) indentified in the service level formulation, where these are problem behaviours. The shared risk formulation deals specifically with high-risk behavioural excesses. The CARM formulation, by contrast, provides a broader approach to the treatment and management of behavioural excesses and deficits be they high or low risk. The staff or team activating event, belief and consequences (ABC) (emotional and behavioural) formulation is of use in addressing unhelpful staff attributions

PROMOTE SOCIAL PARTICIPATION			
	Formulation level	Key elements	Intervention focus
SHARED UNDERSTANDING OF PHENOMENOLOGY	The person level formulation	Emphasises person's life history and overall understanding of the person's symptoms, beliefs and difficulties	Defines broad potential problem areas; increases staff knowledge of, and empathy for, client
	The service level (WHO) formulation	Incorporates client goals and service concerns; highlights how symptoms and other impairments become barriers to achievement of goals and social inclusion	Allows clear identification of specific treatment targets in context of client goals and risk management
	The shared risk formulation	Emphasises high risk behaviours to self and others	Allows grading of risk level, identification of risk treatment goals and risk management plan
	The CARM formulation	Specifies vulnerability factors, triggers and maintenance factors for both high and low risk behavioural deficits and excesses	Clearly specifies potential points of intervention for problem behaviours
	The cognitive ABC formulation (client)	Specific inferential beliefs (e.g. delusional/beliefs about voices) mediating emotional distress	Reduction of distress at early stages to prevent subsequent behavioural disturbance
	The cognitive ABC formulation (staff)	Formulation of unhelpful staff attributions	Reduction of negative staff feelings and increase in helping intention/response
EVIDENCE BASED			

(right vertical header: NEEDS-ADAPTED REFORMULATION OVER TIME)

Figure 2.1 An overview of the key components of SAFE.

and beliefs that have not been adequately addressed using the person level formulation or which are interfering with care. The client ABC formulation, by contrast, is useful both in the assessment of triggers to problem behaviours and in helping staff to act as cognitive therapists in their day-to-day interactions with clients, thus preventing the occurrence of problem behaviours.

The SAFE process

The SAFE templates can be used individually as required. However, they are intended to build on each other in order to provide an integrated approach. The idealised SAFE approach typically starts with the person level formulation to identify broad problem areas and to place the person's problems in the context of their life history and current circumstances. There may be times when this is not feasible due to time restrictions or it may not be necessary as the whole team has a good understanding of the client; under such circumstances the service level formulation may prove a useful starting point. The completed person level or service level formulation is subsequently used as a basis for team discussion to identify the relevant barriers to participation (see Chapter 15 for useful care planning questions) that are preventing the individual from achieving his or her goals or the relevant service goals (if the individual lacks capacity or will not engage in making such decisions for themselves). These can then form the basis of goal setting for care plans and if necessary this can be broken down into smaller short-term goals as we discuss in Chapter 15. Subsequently, the shared risk formulation or CARM formulation can be used to inform in more detail how and when interventions designed to manage problem behaviours should be carried out. This final stage is the detailed care planning used to inform CPA.

Initially, the process of implementing SAFE is carried out by what we have termed the Case Formulation Team (CFT): those most involved in working with the client. Later, this is extended to the whole MDT and relatives and carers where appropriate. This process serves to gently and systematically challenge any unhelpful attributions held about the client and their behaviour, helping those involved in their routine care to better understand situational problematic behaviours from the client's perspective. This conceptualisation also facilitates the application of traditional CBT principles, in a novel way, bringing them into day-to-day staff interactions with the client; targeted at reducing emotional distress and problematic behaviours.

The idealised stages of the SAFE approach can be summarised as follows:

1   *Identification of long-term goals and broad treatment targets (the service level formulation)*

This stage includes an assessment of the client's individual life and recovery goals (using the Recovery Goal Planning Interview, see Appendix 2) and where appropriate the service goals for the client. The identification of activity limitations and barriers to social participation/ achievement of goals is carried out at this point. These form the broad long-term treatment targets for the team and should match to service outcomes.

2 *Construction of a person level formulation*
This is based on a thorough assessment and review of background information. It serves to ensure that everyone in the MDT is aware of the individual's unique history, problems and strengths.

3 *Problem-focused formulations (CARM and shared risk formulations)*
Next, the CARM or shared risk formulation is constructed to guide intervention in more detail. If relevant, the client ABC formulation may be used in conjunction with CARM, as described in Chapter 7, to help to reduce high-risk behaviours.

4 *Tackling staff attributions*
If necessary at this stage, dysfunctional team attributions about the client or their difficulties can be more specifically addressed using the ABC formulation of staff beliefs (see Chapter 8). This is useful where the team is inherently stuck or polarised or where education and formulation at stages 2 and 3 have not been sufficient to result in a beneficial shift in staff attitudes.

5 *Detailed idiosyncratic care planning*
Finally, detailed care plans are constructed that are clearly operationally defined. These are devised using our adaptation of SMART (small, measurable, achievable, relevant and time-limited) goals for the client and the impact of interventions measured using the Goal Attainment Scaling Tool as described in Chapter 15.

In subsequent chapters we describe each of the components of SAFE in more detail and illustrate the process of formulation more fully.

SUMMARY

People with psychosis may present an increased risk to themselves or others that often creates a barrier to leading an ordinary meaningful life and may severely limit their recovery. Understanding the factors that lead to such behaviours and developing effective multidisciplinary treatment approaches is one of the key aims of this book. In this chapter we have shown how adopting a single model or theory approach is inadequate. We offered (and subsequently elaborate on) an integrative model (CARM), which we implement within a shared formulation methodology (SAFE). In the following chapters we provide an in-depth manual, illustrating the process of shared formulation, treatment planning and behaviour management through discussion and illustrative case examples. We also, where appropriate, include a number of formulation templates and innovative assessment tools for use by multidisciplinary staff.

Chapter 3

Improving care planning

The WHO ICIDH-2 model and service level formulation

INTRODUCTION

A great deal of time and resources is often devoted to ensuring that the complex needs of individuals with treatment-resistant psychosis and problematic behaviours are met. In order to make the most effective use of these resources, we argue that there is a need for a framework to act as a service level formulation, in order to ensure that the result of these efforts (often involving lengthy assessments and sometimes case formulations) are explicitly incorporated and translated into care plans with clearly defined goals. In this chapter we focus on the context of care planning. We show how, using the *International classification of functioning and disability*, Beta-2 draft (ICIDH-2), World Health Organization model (WHO) model outlined in Chapter 2 (WHO, 1999), as a collaboratively constructed shared service level formulation, provides a clear focus for care planning. The ultimate goal of this process is to engage the client and help them to achieve their goals and improve their quality of life, social participation (as long as this is wanted) and ordinary community living despite persistent symptoms and impairments.

CARE PLANNING BARRIERS

Clinicians are increasingly faced with a range of clinical guidelines regarding the treatment and management of a range of mental health problems and disorders (e.g. DH, 2007; National Institute for Health and Clinical Excellence, 2009). These guidelines have been deemed necessary in order to improve access to treatment, promote consistency, ensure the competent delivery of interventions and improve clinical outcomes. Similarly, attention has been given to standardising the types of services available (e.g. DH, 1999), making best-practice interventions (e.g. cognitive-behaviour therapy [CBT] and behavioural family therapy) and recovery-based care (Care Services Improvement Partnership *et al.*, 2007) routinely available for all. However, this increasing emphasis on standardisation of healthcare runs the risk of promoting a cookbook approach to treatment using protocol-based therapies. These are likely to be especially unhelpful when clients present with chronic, multiple problems and symptoms or when clients fail to engage in treatment (Kukyen *et al.*, 2009). Furthermore, the practising clinician continues to be faced with the problem of translating these general guidelines into individual treatment plans and integrating different aspects of care into a shared and coherently integrated multidisciplinary approach. Such treatment guidelines are often based on randomised controlled trials with a select group of patients being provided with a manualised treatment under conditions which do not typically reflect those found in general clinical practice. Guidelines, however well intentioned, are also likely to fail to fully address some of the important issues that create barriers to providing these interventions effectively in routine clinical settings and in the context of multidisciplinary care.

Case managers typically take responsibility for the process of translating assessment findings and guideline recommendations into care plans and may act as a broker for or provider of subsequent care. Case management systems are widespread in the United States (e.g. in Assertive Outreach Teams). Sherrer and O'Hare (2008) describe how these systems of providing care evolved in the 1970s following guidance from the National Institute of Mental Health in the United States and subsequently through the community support programme in 1977. Case management was identified as critical to community care clients who were being discharged from institutions and hospitals. The initial focus was on brokering and coordinating services with little emphasis given to directly providing clinical interventions. In the past two decades, however, the scope has been broadened to include the coordination of complex interventions and improving access to social, material and environmental resources. Continuity of care is a guiding principle of this approach, intended to avoid fragmentation and any undermining of interventions. In the United States, various forms of case management have been implemented in a range of community treatment programmes, most commonly assertive community treatment programmes. Case management is emphasised as needing to occur within a multidisciplinary context and one that operates 24 hours a day and has long-term open-ended contact with patients in their natural environment. Case management caseloads may vary between 10 and 25; although this is often exceeded in the United Kingdom.

This model of working in the United Kingdom is underpinned by the Care Programme Approach (CPA) (DH, 1990). This was one element from a range of reforms to health and social care (Thornicroft, 1994) that has endured to the present day. In its current form (Care Programme Approach Association, 2008), CPA has a renewed focus on the role of the care coordinator and continues to be the cornerstone of mental health assessment in England. The four main elements focus on appointing a care coordinator, assessing health and social needs, the development of care plans and their review. All of these serve to ensure high-quality, robust and flexible care. CPA also emphasises person-centred care and the adoption of recovery principles, including relapse plans and risk assessment, positive risk management and the use of outcome measures. Our Shared, Assessment, Formulation and Education (SAFE) approach supports all of these process, but more importantly also provides guidance and clear mechanisms for achieving them. It also ensures that the process is multidisciplinary, avoiding the tendency for some care coordinators to work in isolation from the team and construct separate care plans. Historically, standard CPA in England was applied to those people whose problems were less severe or chronic and who were more able to engage in one-to-one treatment and present fewer risk issues. For those who presented a higher risk and who may have been less able, or willing, to engage in either collaborative one-to-one therapy or care planning, enhanced CPA was provided as a structure and process for ensuring the delivery of good-quality, skilled, comprehensive mental healthcare and risk management. In Scotland, the use of CPA has been prioritised for this group. The current system adopted for use in England is to assign people to CPA or not, removing the standard/enhanced distinction.

Effectiveness of case management and the Care Programme Approach

Surprisingly little evidence has emerged to support the routine use of case management in the United States (Sherrer and O'Hare, 2008). One problem is that it is often difficult to distinguish case management from wider team processes (e.g. those in assertive community treatment). Furthermore, activities are not consistently described in the literature and little is known about how best to train and support workers in adopting case management practices. Case management has been found to be superior to brokerage models (Morse et al., 1997) but possibly this is a reflection of the lower caseloads in teams where case management operates. In line with this suggestion, most benefits are to be found in assertive community treatment programmes. These offer a comprehensive range of interventions and have much greater resources available to them. Consequently, improvements may be the result of many factors, not just case management.

CPA in the United Kingdom has not been subject to the same level of research and evaluation (other than as a feature of assertive outreach teams). Whilst CPA provides the frameworks and paperwork for recording information, it offers little actual guidance on the process of how assessment and information gathering should be translated into clinical goals or how these should be prioritised. Marshall et al. (2004), in their study, found that routine assessment of need for the purposes of care planning often failed to address high levels of unmet need in people with mental illness.

Approaches to implementing CPA vary greatly. At its worst, in the context of target-based care, CPA can become a tick-box exercise where completion of paperwork can actually take the emphasis away from client care. Care plans can also become so vague that they fail to ensure that robust, timely interventions are delivered that can meet the changing needs of the individual. Care plans that simply record phrases such as 'improve independence', 'monitor early signs' or 'improve mental state' lack specificity for ensuring high-quality care and yet are not uncommon. Electronic systems designed to monitor and ensure that CPA is regularly and consistently carried out may fail if they only capture cursory changes aimed at meeting performance targets. Frequently, care plans reflect current healthcare policy targets (e.g. CBT for all people with schizophrenia) or professionally defined goals such as prevention of risk. In sum, they lack a truly idiosyncratic process of assessment or goal setting. This may mean a clash between current guidelines and what is realistic for that client in achieving their life goals. In this way the care plan becomes increasingly one-step removed from the day-to-day care of the client and their interactions with team members and carers. Additionally, service goals such as reducing the number of untoward incidents and reaching targets (key performance indicators) may serve to reduce the focus on therapeutic risk taking and the life goals of the service user.

Current failures in care planning for those presenting with problematic or risk behaviours are evident in regularly occurring high-profile incidents involving violent offences committed by mental health patients (usually reported as having paranoid schizophrenia) with often tragic consequences. Cases such as Christopher Clunis and the recent Glaister Earl Butler inquiry are testament to this fact. These cases highlight the need for a clear process that:

- prioritises robust risk assessment and management;
- promotes shared goals to achieve *realistic* changes;
- matches service aims and goals to care plans;
- matches care plans to clinical and personal recovery goals.

The SAFE approach can help to increase the meaningfulness and relevance of care planning in general, and CPA specifically, for both the Multidisciplinary Team (MDT) and for the client.

TEAM BARRIERS

A crucial factor underpinning failures in care and care planning is that of unhelpful team dynamics. We discuss this issue and a broader range of solutions in Chapters 8 and 18. Here, it is important to note that team dynamics play an important role in achieving and maintaining consensus on realistic recovery-based care plan goals. Davenport (2006) notes that psychotic clients and those with abuse histories will often display difficult-to-manage inter-personal behaviours and dynamics, which are likely to negatively influence engagement. Staff may inadvertently re-enact early patterns of abuse and become enmeshed in unhealthy, destructive interactions. Davenport notes that processes such as 'splitting' (where teams develop polarised ways of viewing and interacting with clients) and 'projective identification' may be common when working with such complex cases. Projective identification, for example, may involve parts of the client's intrapsychic world, such as aggres-sive feelings, being projected onto others. The client may then react to these others as if they are the victim of hostile intent. Alternatively, staff may project their own dependency needs onto clients and behave towards them in an overly protective way, thereby limiting their independence. Such pat-terns of interaction can also be explained using cognitive-behavioural or attributional theories (discussed in detail in Chapter 8), whereby staff develop unhelpful attributions about the client or their problems, which reduce team members' sympathy, increase angry feelings and/or reduce the inclination to help. Such attributions may be driven by the team member's own life experi-ences and beliefs and their beliefs about care and mental health, for instance. Lack of adequate knowledge regarding the causes and treatment of mental health problems may also be a factor. Since individual team members views will likely vary, this creates the potential for team conflict about the best way forward. These processes can ultimately result in emotional distance and hostility in staff–patient relationships (so-called malignant alienation syn-drome), which can significantly increase the risk of behaviours such as suicide (Watts and Morgan, 1994).

SHARED FORMULATIONS

At least part of the solution to these care planning problems is to adopt a shared formulation process (Meaden and Van Marle 2008). This can be even more effective if this formulation reinforces a service philosophy, its aims and values. The most frequently cited limitation of formulations in a recent study by Summers (2006) was their lack of impact on patient care. A broad service level formulation process can enable clinicians, the individual with psychosis, carers and relatives to have a shared view of the way forward. It should both address the barriers to effective care and recovery whilst setting clear goals in the context of the case-specific and changing needs of the individual. We use the service level formulation to ensure that assessment results and other SAFE formulation templates are incorporated into the person's care plan since this overall framework is likely to have most direct relevance to MDT staff. For people with psychosis who present with problematic behaviours this is especially important. It can serve to reduce risk and improve communica-tion between team members and carers and facilitate multi-agency working.

Problematic behaviours limit access to ordinary community living and often camouflage the individual from staff so that they see only the behaviour and not the person behind it. Various approaches to shared formulation have been proposed. Some are essentially generic cognitive-behavioural formulations based around specific problems such as substance abuse and anger (Haddock and Shaw, 2008). These formulations usually represent an essentially psychological formulation of the individual. They are potentially useful in informing individual therapy but are not readily translated into MDT care plan goals, especially by non-psychologists who make up the bulk of care coordinators. The WHO model offers a service level formulation with direct relevance to care planning and goal setting that can be utilised by the broader team. It is also a person-centred methodology and if used appropriately is highly recovery focused.

SERVICE LEVEL FORMULATION USING THE WHO ICIDH-2 MODEL

Adapted from early work by Wing (1963), the WHO model is based on the notion of disability and handicap. It has been described by Craig (2006) as a means of conceptualising the impact of serious mental illness. It has received wide acceptance in neurorehabilitation services but has also been adopted in mental health in parts of Australia as a component of their approach to rehabilitation services and care planning (NSW Health Department, 2002). The model contains four main levels. Level 1 is the disease process itself (*pathology*) with which the individual is diagnosed (e.g. schizophrenia). Level 2 is that of *impairment*, which is concerned with symptoms or signs and might include psychiatric symptoms such as mood, cognitive deficits and somatic sensations. These two levels are clearly somewhat medicalised in their description of the individual but this is a useful feature in that the medical model remains the predominant model in healthcare settings and so the framework is readily familiar and acceptable to the broader MDT. However, the model goes further than being purely a focus on symptoms with its third and fourth levels. Level 3 – *activity limitations* – is concerned with changes in the quality and quantity of the individual's behaviour as a result of levels 1 and 2. This level includes both subjective and objective views on the person's abilities in terms of their interactions with their environment (we might consider this to include behavioural deficits, behavioural excesses and appropriate functional skills). The fourth level is *social participation*, which is concerned with changes, limitations or abnormalities in the position or role of the person in their social context. The model thus emphasises the impact of the individual's symptoms on their everyday functioning and implicitly incorporates life goals since the person's social participation level is inherently linked to their desired life goals and valued roles. The social environment, including

access to support, social relationships, work and safe housing, is an important determinant of mental health and wellbeing. Findings from the AESOP
(Aetiology and Ethnicity of Schizophrenia and Other Psychoses) study
(Morgan and Fearon, 2007; Reininghaus *et al.*, 2008) show that social adver-
sity factors across the lifespan (e.g. living alone, social isolation, unemployment, failure to achieve expectations and neighbourhood characteristics) are
related to the onset of psychosis. Overcoming barriers to achieving social
inclusion, accessing appropriate accommodation and achieving one's life
goals are likely to be significant factors in recovery also.

We have adopted the WHO model and framework as a shared service level
formulation to provide socially relevant points of intervention and care goals
that do not rely solely on symptom reduction or elimination. It places participation centre stage, sitting much more comfortably alongside the related
concepts of recovery and social inclusion.

THE SERVICE LEVEL FORMULATION FRAMEWORK

In our service level formulation framework we have found it useful to divide
level 3 of the WHO model into two aspects: (a) activity limitations or internal
barriers to participation and (c) external barriers to participation. The term
'barriers to participation' adds emphasis to the notion that level 3 problems
concern what is actually blocking the individual from leading an ordinary or
fulfilling life. The further distinction between internal and external barriers to
participation is particularly helpful for care planning purposes and serves to
better target interventions, making clearer the contribution of those factors
emanating from the individual and those in the broader social and sometimes
physical or care environment. The service level formulation framework is
illustrated below:

Level 1: Pathology/diagnosis

- What diagnoses does the person have (DSM-IV Axes I–III)?
- Consider the symptom cluster/syndrome and course.

Level 2: Impairment/symptoms

- What symptoms does the person have?
- What impairments does the person have?
    - Cognitive problems (e.g. poor concentration, poor initiation, poor memory)
    - Skills deficits (e.g. lack of social skills, ability to reflect on one's own thoughts or behaviour objectively)

Level 3i: Activity limitations/internal barriers to participation

- What specifically can the person not do (e.g. follow conversations, attend to personal hygiene)?
- What specifically is it about the person's psychosis that prevents participation (e.g. bizarre speech or behaviour)?

Level 3ii: External barriers to participation

- Restrictions or impositions imposed by others.
- Lack of required support or level of support.
- Lack of required amenities.

Level 4: Social participation

- Changes or restrictions in the interaction between the person and their environment.
- What roles, aspects of normal life or desired goals is the person prevented from accessing fully?

In individuals with psychosis, barriers to participation in ordinary community living may be said, in this model, to occur both internally and externally. Both positive and negative symptoms can be conceptualised as creating these barriers (see Table 3.1).

External barriers may be clearly imposed as in the case of the Mental Health Act or Ministry of Justice sections. External barriers can also be more subtle and may comprise any of the following:

- The person may lack a social network (family and friends may have disengaged or moved away).

Table 3.1 Positive and negative symptom barriers

Barriers created by positive symptoms	Barriers created by negative symptoms and cognitive impairments
Bizarre, socially stigmatising behaviours	Problems initiating actions without
Risk behaviours	prompting
Distractibility	Problems with goal planning
Avoidance of others	Lack of communication
Lack of appropriate investment in realistic	Lack of self-care
life goals (e.g. 'I own ASDA therefore I don't	Others attributing their behaviour to
need to receive any benefits or have to work')	laziness (decreased helping intention)
	Problems recalling important information
	Problems sustaining concentration

- The person may lack the understanding of others (family and team members may see only the behaviour/s).
- Low staffing levels restrict the opportunity for leave (as in inpatient settings) or reduce the opportunity for community interaction in those too afraid or underconfident to leave their house, use public transport etc.
- Unclear goals and expectations may mean that the person is unclear about what is expected of them in certain situations. Negative symptoms, paranoia or a lack of social skills may create significant barriers for people here.
- Sanctions may be imposed directly: restricted leave or orders to live in a certain place away from previous social networks.

In the following section we illustrate the application of the service level formulation framework through two case studies.

Case study 1: John

John's case (used throughout the book) illustrates how the WHO ICIDH-2 model can be applied successfully to someone presenting with positive symptoms and problematic behaviour in an inpatient High Dependency Unit (HDU). John has a long psychiatric history, beginning with a first episode of psychosis at the age of 19. This was followed by a series of compulsory inpatient admissions with increasing disengagement from services, poor adherence to treatment and a pattern of assaultative behaviour (currently manifested by hitting other residents and inpatient staff). John's difficulties can be formulated using the WHO model as a service level formulation:

Level 1: Pathology/diagnosis

- Paranoid schizophrenia.

Level 2: Impairment/symptoms

- A paranoid belief that other residents are trying to kill his mother, coupled with ideas of reference and the belief that other residents can hear his thoughts via sounds (thought broadcast).
- A grandiose belief that he can play the guitar just like Jimmy Page.
- Inflexibility and perseveration in his thinking: getting stuck on particular topics.
- Lack of insight into his mental illness.
- Highly distractible, with poor concentration and attention.

Level 3i: Activity limitations/internal barriers to participation

- Inability to pay attention to the context of information without prompting.
- Seemingly bizarre speech and behaviours (e.g. believes that hand driers transmit his guitar music so that he spends time loitering in the toilets).
- Assaults on other patients (punching them in the face).

Level 3ii: External barriers to participation

- Family and staff lack a detailed understanding of John's delusions and dismiss his seemingly bizarre communications.
- Limited amount of support to leave the unit (e.g. to go to the local shops or visit his mother).

Level 4: Social participation

- Unable to go to the local shops or pub alone.
- Lost contact with friends (lack of social network).
- Other residents avoid him.
- Unable to move home from hospital to live with his mother.

Case study 2: Maria

Maria also has a long psychiatric history characterised by poor engagement with services and interventions and gradually worsening social functioning. She lives with her partner Tony who is also a user of mental health services and is her main carer. Their relationship is described as chaotic and neglecting with Tony spending the majority of his time out with friends drinking and using cannabis. Maria is under the care of an Assertive Outreach Team who find her quite frustrating to work with. The team are divided about the best way forward.

Level 1: Pathology/diagnosis

- Schizophrenia.

Level 2: Impairment/symptoms

- Cognitive difficulties with planning and sequencing activities.
- Poor concentration and working memory.
- Low motivation and loss of pleasure in previously enjoyed activities.

Level 3i: Activity limitations/internal barriers to participation

- Unable to follow conversations.
- Unable to set goals and work towards them without repeated prompting.
- Difficulty with complex instructions or several step actions (e.g. tidying the house).
- Gives up easily on tasks.
- Personal hygiene and grooming is poor.
- Spends most of the day in bed and complains of constant tiredness, lack of energy and fatigue.

Level 3ii: External barriers to participation

- Belief of some team members and her partner that Maria is simply lazy.
- Lack of knowledge by her partner about how to best to help with negative symptoms and behavioural deficits.

Level 4: Social participation

- Spends long periods smoking/staring at the television.
- Personal hygiene limits friends and access to local shops, which she used to enjoy.

Adopting the WHO model and setting it within a service level formulation in this way poses a different set of care planning questions. The focus is now on participation, an important step in the recovery journey. Working to reduce problematic behaviours is not an end in itself, rather these are now conceptualised as barriers to participation, both internally (e.g. voice-driven violence) and externally (e.g. increased restrictions, attributions by key others of laziness).

THE PROCESS OF COMPLETING THE SERVICE LEVEL FORMULATION

Our two worked examples above illustrate how different clinical presentations can be viewed when placed within a service level formulation informed by the WHO model. These are completed as part of the broader SAFE process, utilising information obtained from our other formulation templates and process, set out in detail in subsequent chapters. However, should a team feel that they know the person well then an initial formulation of this type may be constructed. However, we would still recommend completing at least the shared person level formulation.

Typically in creating a service level formulation, the process is not sequential from levels 1 to 4. It is often best to begin with levels 1 and 4, requiring clarification of diagnosis and the client's goals. This can then be progressed by clarifying the nature of the symptoms in phenomenological terms at level 2 (e.g. what is the nature of this individual's voices and delusional beliefs?). Finally, those aspects of symptoms or impairments that create barriers to participation should be considered. These will form the focus of team care plans and subsequent intervention targets.

SUMMARY

In this chapter we have described problems with both the care planning and care delivery processes (CPA and team-based barriers). We addressed these problems by offering a shared service level formulation based on the WHO ICIDH-2 model. We show how these can be used for care planning purposes in Chapter 15. Further assessment and formulation processes are, however, usually required before completing the service level formulation. We turn in the next chapter to the first of these, the shared person level formulation.

Chapter 4

Formulating the person
Arriving at a shared view

INTRODUCTION

In line with the current evidence base and much of the current best practice literature on formulation (e.g. Kuyken *et al.*, 2009), we have adopted a largely cognitive therapy-based model for constructing our shared person level formulation template. We have been most influenced in this regard by the work of Chadwick *et al.* (1996), who have developed a clear cognitive model for explaining and treating belief-related distress in psychosis. We utilise their ABC format, adapted from rational emotive behaviour therapy, where the 'A' is seen as the activating event, 'B' represents the beliefs about 'A' and 'C' the emotional and behavioural consequences (Ce and Cb) of the beliefs, given the activating event. Structuring the model in this way clarifies how distress and problematic behaviour is a consequence at C, and as such becomes the 'problem', the relief of which becomes the goal of treatment. It also identifies the beliefs (B) as mainly responsible for the consequent distress and behaviour at C. This simple but elegant and powerful explanatory framework is used in later chapters for formulating both the client's beliefs and staff beliefs. It further provides a framework for the staff's day-to-day interactions for managing distress and problematic behaviours in their clients.

A good formulation should maintain strong links to the evidence base and good practice literature to help inform its key elements (our evidence-based principle). The proposed interrelationships between causal, moderating and problem variables also need to be linked to sound theory. Certain elements, however, may be more important in some cases than in others. Cognitive elements have now been well researched and there is good evidence for the role of beliefs in mediating distress and behaviour in psychosis (e.g. Mawson *et al.*, 2010; Hacker *et al.*, 2008; Birchwood *et al.*, 2010). Evidence for higher-level components (e.g. early experiences, including trauma, parental separation and other early adversities) are increasingly recognised as being important in the development of psychosis (Read *et al.*, 2005; Larkin and Morrison, 2006; Morgan and Fearon, 2007) and should be considered as an important element in any formulation of the person. Family dynamics (e.g.

expressed emotion) are also well-recognised factors involved in the course of psychosis (Kuipers *et al.*, 2002) and can both pre-date and be a sequel of the person's psychosis and their problematic behaviours. In relation to schizophrenia specifically, organic and developmental factors are now considered important in assessment and understanding the person and planning their treatment (Ferrel and McAllister, 2008) as are cognitive deficits (Harvey and Sharma, 2002). Other co-morbidities should also be routinely considered such as personality disorder (Meaden and Farmer, 2007) and substance misuse (Graham *et al.*, 2004). The stress vulnerability model (Zubin and Spring 1977) and the need to consider triggering events are now widely accepted processes in understanding schizophrenia, its onset and course. McKenna (2007) has recently cast doubt on their utility in general. We, however, by adopting the ABC model, take a more idiosyncratic approach, carefully attempting to understand the events and unique stressors that individuals may encounter and how these impact (if at all) on the person and their beliefs and subsequent emotional and behavioural reactions (our need-adapted treatment principle). Finally, the role of reinforcement (interpersonal reactions) is well established both in the family therapy literature, already alluded to, and in learning theory (e.g. Emerson, 2001; Beer, 2006) and we would argue are key components in understanding the maintenance of problematic behaviours.

Our shared person level formulation is usually the starting point of the Shared Assessment, Formulation and Education (SAFE) process as it provides an overall map of the person's problems. It includes the important key properties and elements as outlined above. These are embedded within the ABC model. Staff can often relate most readily to this, and there is good evidence to support it. Importantly, it sets the scene for subsequent formulations of staff and client beliefs, which are key ingredients of the SAFE approach and the Cognitive Approach to Risk Management (CARM) model.

KEY COMPONENTS OF THE PERSON LEVEL FORMULATION TEMPLATE

Our person level formulation has 11 key components:

1 Developmental history
   (This includes important predisposing factors.)

   • Co-morbidities such as developmental or personality disorders and their impacts (e.g. rigidity in thinking, poor memory).
   • Family history and relationships.
   • Childhood abuse (sexual, physical and emotional).
   • Trait mood and temperament.

2 Relevant life events
   (Of relevance here are further predisposing factors occurring through-
   out the lifespan, some of which may act as significant maintaining
   factors.)

   • Family expressed emotion (e.g. criticalness, overprotectiveness etc.),
     both pre-morbidly and later illness-related family patterns.
   • Family illness, loss and bereavements.
   • Educational attainment and employment history.
   • Social history (including problems in peer relationships).
   • Psychosexual development (intimate, romantic relationships and
     sexual life and interests).
   • Any historical traumatic events such as acquired brain injury and its
     impact (e.g. disinhibition, poor attention), being a witness or victim
     of violence or sexual assault, compulsory hospital admission.

3 Triggers to illness onset or previous relapses
   (These highlight plausible reactions to key life events as well as other
   lifestyle and coping patterns.)

   • Substance misuse.
   • Stressors (academic, interpersonal or work related, life transition).
   • Trauma (as above).

4 Core beliefs (self, others and the world) and interpersonal schemas
   (In our cognitive therapy model these are the core psychopathology, shaped
   by past and present events, and are often evident in the person's psychotic
   thinking.)

   • I am/others are, others see me as: bad, weak, a failure, worthless,
     unlovable, inadequate, incompetent.
   • The world is a dangerous place, others are not to be trusted.
   • I must be respected.
   • I am vulnerable.

5 Rules for living
   (In our cognitive therapy model these are broad beliefs reflecting strategies
   that the person uses across a range of situations in order to adapt and
   survive often in difficult circumstances. They usually function to maintain
   core beliefs and may be psychotic or non-psychotic in nature.)

   • If I make mistakes, bad things will happen.
   • I must do things perfectly in order to be loved/be worthwhile.
   • I must be vigilant to avoid exploitation and harm.
   • Without someone to guide me I will not survive.

6 Protective factors
   (This element focuses on the person's strengths and assets and other factors

which support recovery and reduce the risk of relapse, including psychotic and risk factors.)

- Ability to form a therapeutic alliance and trusting relationships.
- Presence and involvement from supportive others (care staff, family and friends) who hold hope.
- Connected to others and socially included.
- Prosocial attitudes.
- Absence of negative symptoms and cognitive deficits.
- Absence of substance misuse.
- Good intellect/problem-solving skills.
- Safe housing and environment.
- Secure finances.
- Good employment history.
- Valued and meaningful roles.

7   Current stressors
(These represent important maintenance factors and may function as immediate triggers for distress and problematic behaviour. They may relate to previous life events or be novel.)

- Substance misuse.
- Stress (academic, interpersonal or work related, life transition).
- Trauma (as above).
- Family expressed emotion (as above).
- Family illness, loss and bereavements.
- Financial problems.
- Accommodation problems.

8   Psychotic experiences, pan-situational and in-situation beliefs
(Pan-situational beliefs are those beliefs which are ever present across a range of situations; they can give rise to specific interpretations in situations that then mediate distress and behaviour.)

- Pan-situational psychotic beliefs (e.g. hearing a voice and believing that it is the voice of the devil and very powerful).
- In-situation psychotic beliefs (current voice commands, delusional preoccupation and high conviction in current threat).
- General psychotic and collateral symptoms (e.g. thought broadcast, thought insertion, threat control over-ride symptoms, visual and somatic hallucinations, passivity experiences).

9   Emotional consequences (Ces)
(These attempt to encapsulate at a broad level the person's distress and emotional functioning as well as more specific belief-related distress.)

- Anxiety, depression, anger, guilt, jealousy, shame, humiliation.

- Delusional and voice-related distress.
- Feelings of entrapment and hopelessness.

10 Behavioural consequences (Cbs)
(These attempt to encapsulate at a broad level the person's problematic behaviour as well as more specific belief-related problem behaviours.)

- Historical behaviours (e.g. past suicide attempts, assaults on others etc.)
- Current behaviours (e.g. assaults, verbal aggression, damage to property etc.).

11 Interpersonal reactions
(This element captures the reactions engendered in others by the person's expressed concerns, their distress and behaviour and helps to formulate [at an early stage] potential reinforcing mechanisms.)

- Staff avoidance or use of restraint procedures.
- Family/carer avoidance.
- Restricted leave/social exclusion.
- Giving of extra medication.

CONSTRUCTING A SHARED PERSON LEVEL FORMULATION IN SAFE

Person-based formulations place the person's beliefs, distress and problematic behaviour in the context of the broad phenomenology of their psychosis and their life history and experiences. The formulation process is staggered, with increasing levels of dissemination across the care team. We begin with what we have called the Case Formulation Team (CFT). This consists of those who have the most responsibility or involvement on a day-to-day basis with the client and their care. It may be extended to involve other team members who have frequent contact with the person and may include carers or family.

Stage 1: The initial formulation meeting

At the first meeting, the knowledge and attributions of key members of the CFT with regards to the client, their current difficulties and problematic behaviours are assessed. Members are asked to identify a list of emotions, which they believe to be problematic for the client as well as a list of problematic behaviours (these may be problematic for the client and/or for others). Simple questions with encouragement to elaborate are a helpful starting point here:

- What do you know about this person?

- ○ What have been their life experiences?
- ○ What do they want out of life?
- ○ What symptoms do they have or beliefs do they hold?
- ○ What are their likes and dislikes?
- ○ What do they think is the problem?
- ○ What are their strengths and positive attributes?

- • How do you feel generally about working with this person?

- ○ How would you like to be able to work with them?
- ○ What are your aims in working with them?

- • What would need to change for this person to be participating more fully in the community? What barriers exist for them here?
- • What would need to change for this person to be of less concern to others?
- • Do you feel hopeful or pessimistic about this person's future? What factors influence your view?
- • What are the key behaviours that cause problems for the person or those around them?
- • What appears to distress them and in what way do they show this?

This stage serves to clarify the presenting problems along with identifying general maintenance factors and possible triggers. Hypotheses can be made at this point, which can be subsequently ruled out or confirmed (with triangulation of evidence) as the formulation is developed. As noted earlier, if at this stage, staff are resistant to considering the client's problems, are pessimistic regarding their expectations of change, there is team splitting or other unhelpful dynamics engendered by the client or their behaviour, then it may prove useful to examine staff beliefs and their emotional reactions and current care approaches to working with them in more detail. This may serve also to promote engagement at this early stage (see Chapter 8 for more detailed guidance). Ideally, however, following this initial discussion, tasks are assigned and a series of further meetings arranged. This also helps to embed a culture of assessment in the team and provides multidisciplinary roles in the assessment process. Key tasks and roles are detailed below and may be carried out in parallel to each other by different members of the Multidisciplinary Team (MDT).

Stage 2: Assessment and information gathering in SAFE

1 Reviewing the clinical case notes

Case notes are an important source of factual information and will often have detailed descriptions of critical incidents such as relapses, problematic behaviours and interventions. They may be less useful, however, in providing a picture of change over time and may be incomplete, representing periods of disengagement with services or transient lifestyles, where the person has moved in and out of area. Notes may also point to periods of wellbeing or improved functioning, which are helpful when considering recovery factors. The involvement of many professionals and professions may have led to a variety of attitudes and approaches, to the detriment of a clear and objective history, and to disagreement about the nature of the person's difficulties and their treatment. These disagreements and conflicting approaches may subsequently be used to elicit staff beliefs and attitudes about the client and their behaviour.

Often, team members are less familiar with background history and the value of reviewing this quickly becomes evident. This is especially true where problematic behaviours have occurred but not for some time. Completing the Challenging Behaviour Checklist for Psychosis (CBC-P) (see Appendix 1) requires looking back over the client's history in order to check whether any of the behaviours listed have ever occurred, thus guiding the risk assessment process described in Chapter 5. Providing a useful summary of past behaviours, and psychotic relapses, can be especially useful if these are plotted against possible triggering or stressful life events.

Case example: Keith

In Keith's case, despite initially engaging in assessment regarding his risk of violence towards his partner, he subsequently withdrew from this process. A systematic review of his notes, however (together with discussions with the care team, an examination of criminal records and interviews with family members), made it possible to complete a checklist of early warning signs of psychotic relapse (adapted from the Early Warning Sign Monitoring Form developed by Birchwood et al., 1989). This revealed a pattern of depressive symptoms, increased feelings of hopelessness, anger, an increased tendency towards social isolation, drinking alcohol and becoming preoccupied with certain ideas. It was subsequently possible to complete a timeline matching risk incidents and known psychotic relapses. This was used to help determine whether risk episodes occurred around the time of psychotic relapses and hence support working hypotheses concerning the role of psychosis in his risk behaviour.

2 Assessing and interviewing the client

A range of assessments are used in the development of person level formulations when interviewing the client if they can be meaningfully engaged in this process. A standardised semi-structured interview guide (see Appendix 3) is also used to collate information regarding personal, social, developmental and psychiatric history. This also helps in reviewing clinical notes by guiding the clinician regarding key information (rather than simply summarising what is in the notes).

Assessment tools

The Beliefs About Voices Questionnaire–Revised (Chadwick et al., 2000), Cognitive Assessment of Voices (Chadwick and Birchwood, 1995) and the Beliefs and Convictions Scale (Brett-Jones et al., 1987) may be used to help elicit pan-situational and in-situation psychotic beliefs. The Psychotic Symptom Rating Scales (PSYRATS) (Haddock et al., 1999) are also useful for providing a measure of belief-related distress, its frequency and severity. The Safety Behaviour Scale (Freeman et al., 2001; Hacker et al., 2008) is a useful semi-structured interview for assessing the ways in which people may act on their delusional beliefs or voices as well as the type of threat they perceive (social or physical threat). The Antecedent and Coping Interview (Tarrier, 1992) is a useful schedule for identifying antecedents and modifiers for psychotic symptoms and the efficacy of any coping strategies.

Ideally, core beliefs and interpersonal schemas should be accessed through cognitive interviewing adopting the ABC framework of Chadwick et al. (1996). This contextualises clients' beliefs in terms of their developmental history and current circumstances compared with relying on questionnaire-based measures. We have also found the Young's Schema Questionnaire (Young and Brown, 1990), and its companion assessments, the Young Parenting Inventory (Young, 1994), the Young–Rygh Avoidance Inventory (Young and Rygh, 1994) and the Young Compensation Inventory (Young, 1995), particularly helpful when developing shared formulations. The Evaluative Beliefs Scale (Chadwick et al., 1999) may also provide access to evaluative beliefs and their direction as well as indicating more personality-based traits and characteristics.

A wide variety of mood assessments are available but we have found a select few to be of most use. The Calgary Depression Scale (Addington et al., 1993) provides a useful measure of depression relatively independent of negative symptoms. The Beck Anxiety Inventory (Beck et al., 1988) and the Spielberger State-Trait Anxiety Inventory (Spielberger et al., 1983) provide useful measures of anxiety. Meanwhile, the State-Trait Anger Expression Inventory-2 (STAXI-2: Spielberger, 1996) is useful for examining different aspects of anger such as the degree to which the individual's anger is part of their temperament or is situationally determined, their degree of control and the likelihood of expressing anger as outward aggression. Finally, the Novaco Anger Scale and Provocation Inventory (NAS-PI: Novaco, 2003) provides a useful assessment of likely triggers to anger as well as the cognitive, emotional and behavioural aspects of the individual's anger.

Few structured assessments for assessing the client's point of view regarding their own problematic behaviour exist. It is often useful, however, to interview the client about recent risk incidents or about their view of these behaviours. This can usefully be done using the CARM framework illustrated in Chapter 7. The client's awareness of their own distant and immediate triggers can be assessed as can their own subjective reasons for their behaviour. This can often prove useful in clarifying the link between psychotic symptoms and behaviour.

The Millon Clinical Multiaxial Inventory III (Millon, 1994) is a 175-item self-report inventory that assesses clinical personality patterns, severe personality pathology and clinical syndromes. It is designed only for people presenting with clinical symptoms and maps onto DSM-IV-TR (American Psychiatric Association, 2000) diagnosis but requires clinical validation. This can be a useful tool for defining personality traits not just for diagnosis but also for clinical formulation.

A useful approach to assessing insight has been developed by Amador et al. (1993), in the Schedule for Assessing Insight. This is a structured interview process that evaluates three dimensions: awareness of illness, capacity to re-label psychotic experiences as abnormal, and treatment compliance. The Personal Beliefs About Illness Questionnaire (Birchwood et al., 1993) offers a broader picture of the person's views about their diagnosis when the label of schizophrenia has been applied, including perceptions of stigma and feelings of hopelessness and entrapment.

In assessing cognitive problems in people with psychosis, a vast number of tools are available. The Wechsler Adult Intelligence Scale (4th edition) (WAIS-IV) provides a useful measure of current intellectual functioning and problem solving; the Wechsler Memory Scale (4th edition) (WMS-IV) provides a useful measure of memory function. One of the key areas to assess in schizophrenia is executive functioning. Executive functioning is an umbrella term encompassing a range of higher-level cognitive tasks, including planning, multi-tasking, self-monitoring, divided attention and selective attention. Useful tools in this regard are the Delis Kaplan Executive Functions System (DKEFS: Delis et al., 2001), the Hayling and Brixton (Burgess and Shallice, 1997) and the Behavioural Assessment of Dysexecutive Syndrome (BADS: Wilson et al., 1996). In addition, it is often important to assess whether the person has declined from their pre-illness abilities and the Wechsler Test of Adult Reading (WTAR) can be useful in this regard. Finally, it is essential that clinicians consider the validity of the test results obtained in these and other instruments by considering the degree to which the individual has applied themselves to the test situation (Bush et al., 2005). A number of tools exist but the Test of Memory Malingering (TOMM: Tombaugh, 1996) has been shown to be relatively insensitive to the symptoms of schizophrenia and so is valid for use in this population as a symptom validity test (Duncan, 2005).

3 Team-based observations

Teams-based assessments help to supplement the process of individual assessments and are a valuable tool where, as is all too often the case with less well-engaged and treatment-resistant clients, client assessments cannot be used. Informal observation may reveal whether the person is hearing voices (talks to themselves, shouts when no one is around, uses naturalistic coping strategies: wears earphones all the time), or whether they are experiencing any cognitive problems (e.g. problems in planning when out shopping, difficulties in concentration when watching television).

The CBC-P and Challenging Behaviour Record Sheet (CBRS: see Appendix 4) may be used at this stage to clarify which behaviours are problematic (for staff and for the client), and under what conditions or circumstances they are likely to occur. The client's perspective is also included in the CBRS to, where possible, clarify the reasons for their behaviour as close in time to the incident as possible. A more detailed description of how to use this tool is given in Chapter 9. Actuarial risk tools may also be completed at this stage (e.g. STATIC–99 for sexual offending: Hanson and Thornton, 1999; the HCR–20 for risk of violence: Douglas *et al.*, 2008) if high-risk behaviours are present.

We find the Early Signs Scale (Birchwood *et al.*, 1989) useful for initiating relapse plans and monitoring for early signs of psychotic relapse and, as noted above, to identify whether these have been apparent at all and thus match them against a timeline of life events and possible triggers. These may then be linked (or not) to any risk or problematic behaviours (although a much more detailed functional analysis will subsequently need to be undertaken to establish any actual functional links).

4 Assessing family needs and perspectives

Engaging the family or other carers in the assessment process is also important. They may know the person best and will often need to be engaged if subsequent intervention is to be appropriately supported. The Camberwell Family Interview (CFI), although mostly used for research purposes, is useful for identifying patterns of expressed emotion (Leff and Vaughan, 1985). However, it is unlikely that services will train up a staff member in using the CFI for this purpose and briefer measures may need to be adopted. Magaña *et al.* (1986) offer a brief semi-structured interview method for assessing expressed emotion derived from the CFI. It uses a variation of the five-minute speech sample to examine responses made by a patient's key relative when prompted to give their thoughts and feelings about them for a five-minute period. A coding system scores behaviours analogous to those rated on the CFI, such as criticism and emotional over-involvement. The relationship between ratings made adopting this method correspond closely with those obtained from using the CFI. Cole and Kazarian (1988) developed the Level of Expressed Emotion Scale (LEE) on the basis of a conceptual framework derived from the expressed emotion literature. The 60-item scale provides an overall score and assesses four characteristic attitudes or response styles of significant others: intrusiveness, emotional response, attitude towards illness and tolerance/expectations. The LEE has sound psychometric properties of internal consistency, reliability and construct validity.

It is also often helpful where possible to clarify patterns of expressed emotion that may have been in operation pre-morbidly as opposed to those that may have arisen following the client's subsequent psychosis. Information from carers' assessments carried out as part of the Care Programme Approach (CPA) can also serve to highlight key problems, particularly the frequency and severity of any problematic behaviour for those in community settings. Information on developmental history, important life events, possible past and current triggers and maintenance factors can also be obtained and cross-verified. Our standardised semi-structured interview guide can again be used here to collate information regarding personal, social, developmental and psychiatric history from the carer's perspective. The relative's or carer's knowledge about the person's diagnosis, difficulties and treatment and, importantly, how these result in the person's behaviour, are also important in understanding the relative's and carer's attributions in the same way as those of team members.

5 Assessing the client's goals

A key feature of the SAFE approach is that interventions and care plans should be directly related to the client's own goals as much as is practical. CPA does not in itself generally provide a clear means of client-centred goal planning, which is often the norm both in learning disabilities services and in neurohabilitation. Our Recovery Goal Planning Interview (see Appendix 2) is used at this stage in order to help identify the client's life and recovery goals. It addresses a number of goal-related domains in a semi-structured interview format, which is useful for developing an explicit focus on goals in areas such as social functioning, education, employment and family life. This can easily be carried out with the client by any member of the team. This tool also serves to identify barriers to achieving these goals and meeting broad needs. The interview is also designed to help the team arrive at a set of collaborative goals with the client that will subsequently feed into the service level formulation and the care planning process.

Stage 3: Completing the person formulation template

Having completed where possible the assessments described so far, the CFT reconvene to discuss and construct the initial person formulation template (see Figure 4.1). Key agenda items concern:

- resolving disagreements regarding the relevancy of formulation items;
- rating the relevancy of these items (with the highest-rated items retained) if needed in order to resolve any differences of opinion;
- triangulating evidence to support the inclusion of formulation items (members being encouraged to cite evidence for and against their inclusion). This helps to further socialise the team into the cognitive model and adopt the evidence-based principle. We also encourage CFT members to treat any items not clearly supported through triangulation of evidence as hypotheses that require further testing, either during the shared formulation process or over the course of the intervention, when reformulation may be required (a need-adapted principle);
- identifying other information required;
- deciding who will make any agreed changes to the initial template.

Stage 4: Dissemination and re-validation

Once agreed changes to the initial template have been completed a broader MDT meeting is arranged where the formulation is presented to the wider team. Agenda items at this stage concern eliciting team reactions to the template and further rating the relevancy of items where there are disagreements. The CFT subsequently reconvenes to examine the formulation in light of this review, make any amendments to the template and seek further information if necessary. Some elements may require longer-term validation and in these cases they are retained but clearly marked as hypotheses. After agreeing to make any final-stage changes, the completed template is acknowledged as the final working person level formulation. Over time, and as needs change or more confirmatory or disconfirmatory evidence becomes available, the template may be revised and used to inform new care plans (the need-adapted principle). The CFT continues to be involved with the person and may subsequently form the core treatment team, carrying out further assessment and reformulation as required. Ensuring that initial benefits derived from this process are translated into practice often requires reformulating. It should be noted that any formulation only offers working hypotheses, which should be tested and modified over time (Kinderman and Lobban, 2000).

Undergoing this process helps to resolve team disagreements and serve as an educational process for the team, carer and client. The client and the carer should ideally be involved in the process of disseminating and agreeing the relevancy of items. The team must consider here if this will be beneficial and engaging or likely to promote disengagement and increase distress. It is often useful to examine past experiences of psychoeducation with carers and clients and what they themselves might find helpful. We view the carer's assessment and life and recovery goals assessment as key aspects of SAFE. These contribute to the construction of collaborative goals and shared understandings of what is important to them. However, SAFE is also designed to help address the needs of often disengaged treatment-resistant clients and the person level formulation process is therefore designed to be used predominantly with the care team where necessary.

Case Study 1: John – Developing a shared conceptualisation

John is a 40-year-old male with a history of treatment-resistant paranoid schizophrenia. At the time of beginning the SAFE process, John had been in hospital on a High Dependency Unit (HDU) for over eight years. Attempts to work with him individually using cognitive-behavioural therapy (CBT) had met with very limited, if any, success. John had developed a highly elaborate and systemised belief system and had some cognitive impairment following his involvement in a road traffic accident in which he had been knocked down by a car and suffered a fractured skull and a severe traumatic brain injury. John has subsequently suffered from epilepsy (now well controlled by medication).

John's CFT consisted of his clinical psychologist (the second author), his inpatient named nurse and his community team care coordinator, as well as an unqualified member of the inpatient nursing team who knew John well. The CFT initially generated a list of difficult problematic emotions and behaviours (client Cs or staff As), which included:

- verbal threats of violence to other patients;
- hitting doors and on one occasion putting his fist through a plaster wall;
- breaking a bench outside in the ward courtyard by hitting and kicking it;
- physical assaults on other male patients, involving John punching them repeatedly in the face;
- suicide attempts (over 10 years ago);
- engaging in repeated delusional speech with others (which made him look odd to others and in the past had resulted in threats from members of the public).

Violence directed towards other patients was chosen as the formulation focus based on the CFT's discussion and on a CBC-P completed by staff prior to the meeting. Other behaviours such as violence to objects occurred at a similar frequency and were kept in mind as potential precursors to John's assaultative behaviour.

At the first meeting, non-psychology members of the CFT were familiar with John's paranoid ideas but were unclear (given that these were always present: they were pan-situational) why they only sometimes resulted in violence. There was a general consensus that change did not seem likely. As a result, staff beliefs about John were formulated in order to better engage the team. They were encouraged to voice their own frustrations and engage in an open discussion about differences in opinion. This ABC formulation of staff beliefs about John's behaviour is illustrated in more detail in Chapter 7. For the moment, it is relevant to note the themes present within staff beliefs. John's behaviour was attributed to personal characteristics or uncontrollable illness with little opportunity for intervention or change. Emotional reactions emerged as quite mixed and care responses focused on avoidance and increasing restrictions. Staff members tended to perceive any attempt to change John or his behaviour as futile given the longstanding nature of his difficulties. An initial suggestion was made at this point that symptom reduction itself may not be necessary and better management might be possible as increased understanding emerged during the formulation process. This was intended to engender some optimism for change and encourage staff to temporarily suspend their beliefs. At the end of this meeting, further tasks were assigned to individual CFT members:

- review clinical notes (named nurse);
- interview John about recent incidents of violence (psychology);
- assess his delusional beliefs and symptoms (psychology);
- conduct a neuropsychological assessment (psychology);
- complete Young's Schema Questionnaire and companion assessments (Young and Brown, 1990; Young, 1994; Young and Rygh, 1994; Young, 1995);
- assess daily living skills (named assistant);
- meet and interview John's mother to obtain a personal history (community care coordinator);
- involve the broader MDT by using the CBRS to record incidents and apparent triggers (team manager and nursing assistant);
- complete the Recovery Goal Planning Interview with John (nursing assistant).

Assessment findings

Psychometric testing revealed that John had some impairment of mental processing speed and executive functioning (cognitive perseveration). Case notes and interviews with John and his family revealed that he was a victim of bullying and frequently truanted from school, leaving with no qualifications (in contrast to his siblings). He was circumcised at age 10, which was very traumatic for him and gave him concerns that his penis would not work properly. John had long-standing difficulties relating to women and had not had any significant romantic relationships. Prior to his psychosis he suffered panic attacks associated with a fear of going mad and losing control.

John's father suffered from bipolar disorder and he used alcohol problematically; he died in 2004 from physical health complaints. Despite numerous admissions to hospital and frequent verbal hostility, John has always held his father in high esteem and relied heavily on him for advice and guidance. John's mother suffers from longstanding osteoarthritis and has a history of depression; she lives at home with support from carers and John's siblings.

John's risk history is extensive. He was assaulting other patients on a regular basis, which was distressing for other residents and staff alike and resulted in frequent limits being placed on his leave. Previous attempts to manage John's behaviour had involved restraint, time out and sanctions on his community leave. All had been unsuccessful. In the distant past, John had made a number of serious attempts at suicide, including an attempt at hanging himself and ingesting bleach.

Cognitive therapy assessment revealed that John held paranoid beliefs about a female (the 'Killer Queen') who he believed wanted to hurt him (by crucifying him, removing his eyes, cutting off his genitals) or to hurt his mother and steal her soul. He sometimes believed that others, under the influence of the Killer Queen, intended to harm his mother. John had, at times, believed that the Killer Queen had killed his father; at other times he put this down to real medical reasons or blamed himself. John often misperceived information from conversations or from the television as referring to him in a threatening way. In addition, he described that he could alter sounds, by which he meant that others could hear his own private thoughts in the presence of sounds (thought broadcast). Consequently, he felt quite vulnerable and threatened, becoming exceptionally anxious in the presence of noises such as aeroplanes, electric fans and vacuum cleaners. John also exhibited grandiose delusions, believing that he had special powers linked to extra electricity in his head. These special powers were linked to his watch he believed, which gave him the ability, but also the responsibility, to heal others (he found this very stressful but also a source of self-esteem). John frequently became concerned that he had not managed to save others or that he may have accidentally harmed them by trying to help (e.g. his father). John also heard the voice of his deceased father and felt comforted by this, believing that it indicated that his father was in heaven and safe.

The CFT reconvened to discuss and construct the person level formulation based on this information. (John's person level formulation is presented in Figure 4.1).

Addressing staff beleifs

The CFT, facilitated by the second author, were asked to consider how the template completed so far might affect their own original attributions (staff Bs), their feelings and helping response (staff Cs) as well as their understanding of the function of John's behaviour. Staff appeared to have developed a clearer understanding of the phenomenology of John's psychotic symptoms and their relevance to the problem behaviour (e.g. the staff A appeared to have moved from focusing solely on the client's behaviour to understanding the causes for it (the actual 'A' for the client). Staff appeared to now view John's violence as understandable given the degree of his delusional threat and this diffused some of the difficult feelings as well as eliciting some degree of sympathy. A general consensus emerged for the first time that John's behaviours might be both understandable and predictable now that their function could be understood.

The completed template was then shared with the broader MDT and few disagreements were noted. However, the broader MDT raised the issue of needing clearer guidelines on how to manage John's violence on the unit and so it was agreed that the CFT would work with them to complete a CARM formulation template and management plan. This is discussed in Chapter 7. In this sense the CFT now became John's treatment team, guiding the development of his care plan and both implementing the care plan themselves and supporting others to do so.

Developing a collaborative care plan

John identified a number of longer-term life and recovery goals:

- to move home to live with his mother;
- to be able to have guitar lessons in the community;
- to have greater access to shops;
- to be able to go to the local pub and meet old friends;
- to stop staff threatening and persecuting him (delusional);
- to have a girlfriend (who was one of the members of staff);
- to be able to cook meals for his mother and himself at home and use the appliances.

These goals were discussed with John using the Recovery Goal Planning

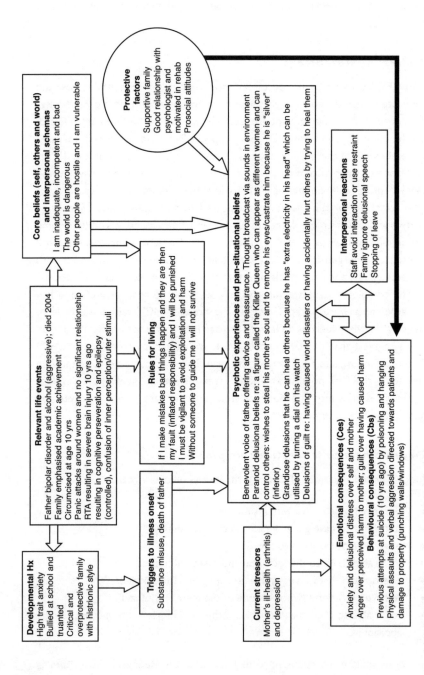

Figure 4.1 John's shared person level formulation template.

Interview (see Appendix 2) to establish the barriers to achieving these goals and to establish which ones were most realistic for him. It was noted that it was not possible or realistic for John to have a relationship with a staff member and the reasons for this were discussed with him. The process of developing relationships, however, was seen as a relevant life goal and it was agreed that a first step would be increasing John's social opportunities outside of the unit. It was also noted that the MDT were not entirely in agreement with his view that staff were persecuting him but understood that this was how he viewed their relationship at times and that it caused him considerable distress. Staff agreed to keep an open mind and discuss distressing incidents with John and attempt to resolve them (using cognitive therapy techniques). Another goal, moving home, was agreed as a long-term goal to work towards, with clear shorter-term goals devised to work towards it: extending periods of leave, if successful introducing overnight leave at home. The following goals were identified as those that could most usefully form the basis of an initial care plan:

- to move home to live with his mother;
- to have greater access to shops;
- to be able to go to the local pub and meet old friends;
- to stop staff threatening and persecuting him (delusional).

It was agreed as part of this process that a key barrier to achieving these goals was (although understandable within the terms of John's belief system) his ongoing assaultative behaviour.

At the same time, the CFT worked with the MDT to complete a service level formulation. This was used to develop the following service goals matched to John's identified barriers to achieving his own goals:

1   Barriers to participation (treatment targets, activity limitations)

- Violence to others as a result of his belief that they are going to hurt him or his mother (including the domestic employed by his mother).
- Bizarre speech content when out, rendering him vulnerable to assaults from others.
- Lack of cooking skills and skills in using appliances at home.
- Problems coping with noises (and thought broadcast) at the day centre.
- Staff shortages restricting the opportunities for leave.
- Not knowing where guitar lessons were or how to get there.
- Mistrust of staff in discussing incidents.

2   Collaborative goals (social participation)

- Increase leave home.
- Be able to cook meals for his mother and self at home.
- Increase social opportunities in the community by attending the local day centre.
- Going to a local pub (accompanied).
- Review incidents of threatening behaviour (of violence) with staff and elicit John's perspective (staff to use CBT techniques to address John's in-situational beliefs).
- Start guitar lessons in the community.

The following broad treatment plan was subsequently agreed and formed the basis of John's CPA care plan:

- Team to look out for signs that John is distressed and encourage him to seek support from trusted members of staff (initially the psychologist and named nurse).
- These staff to attempt to resolve issues before John feels he has to resort to violence; to be gradually broadened to include other staff as John feels comfortable.
- John to have increased leave home but to have psychology and occupational therapy sessions at home, in order to (a) dispute beliefs about the domestic and (b) increase domestic skills.
- John to have escorted leave with prompts regarding speech and behaviour when in the community; to be reduced over time.
- John to develop coping strategies with psychology for thought broadcast and to be aided by a nursing assistant at the day centre initially in generalising these strategies.
- Resources to be provided by the community team to address resource issues regarding leave.

The resulting care plan for John is illustrated in Chapter 15 along with the process for translating these broader goals into achievable short-term specific intervention targets. John's case demonstrates how findings from the person level formulation are used to both inform the service level formulation and crucially develop the basis for a MDT (psychological, nursing and occupational) care plan incorporating specific goals with specific strategies to achieve them: a true multidisciplinary recovery oriented care plan. More detailed issues regarding how behaviours are managed are dealt with in later chapters and we will return to John again at that point. In the next chapters we will turn to

the subsequent stages of the SAFE approach, which allow more detailed intervention planning.

OTHER METHODS OF IMPLEMENTING SAFE

The full SAFE approach is clearly time consuming and intensive and perhaps
most easily implemented within a healthy team and care system (Margison,
2005). However, many clients with the types of treatment-resistant psychosis
and problematic behaviours as described here often remain in long-term care
settings or remain on specialist team caseloads (e.g. Assertive Outreach
Teams) for many years. The full SAFE approach is perhaps most appropriate
in settings where there is a small caseload, managed by a consistent team, and
where there is a sufficient length of service involvement to enable comprehensive assessment and intervention to take place. Where this is not the case, a
more parsimonious approach may be warranted, whereby a skilled clinician
takes the lead in developing the initial person level formulation and then
shares it with the MDT. The service level formulation can also be used in this
way as a standalone tool or in conjunction with the CARM or risk formulations described in following chapters. Similarly, our CARM model (Chapter
7) may usefully be carried out during extended 'case-busting' sessions,
particularly in inpatient settings. This can be helpful in addressing team disagreements regarding the management of the person's problematic behaviour
in the short term but is no substitute for carrying out the full process when
addressing staff attributions and selecting treatment targets. Case-busting
sessions can also be a useful means of introducing the templates and the
concept of formulation in the first place. Templates can be completed in case-
busting sessions and then amended in a subsequent session if necessary. We
have, for example, successfully used the risk formulation alone in assertive
outreach settings.

Implementation of the complete SAFE process usually necessitates some
team training in the models and methods outlined. It also offers a gradual
framework for changing staff understandings; in cognitive therapy terms,
people rarely change their beliefs in one session and it is perhaps unreasonable to expect staff belief change processes to be any different.

SUMMARY

Shared person level formulations provide an historical and developmental
interpersonal context for understanding the person's symptoms, difficulties
and interactions (day to day) and allow tailoring of the overall MDT
approach and intervention style. Information presented in the person level
formulation highlights broad treatment targets for CPA purposes and can be

used to minimise more general exacerbations or relapses in the person's psychosis and be used to select interventions to address broad maintenance factors. It does not, however, allow explicit, specific hypotheses (functional analysis) to be made regarding behaviours, distress or symptoms. More detailed care plans are best derived from subsequent CARM or shared risk formulations, which are the focus of the next three chapters.

Chapter 5

Shared risk assessment in psychosis

INTRODUCTION

In this chapter we address an issue of increasing importance to clinicians, the assessment and management of risk. Risk assessment and management is a core task for mental health professionals, particularly those working in forensic settings (Blumenthal and Lavender, 2000; DH, 2007). This is even more the case with the move in the United Kingdom towards mental health professionals other than psychiatrists working as Responsible Clinicians with a much broader range of staff now being appointed as Approved Mental Health Professionals (Mental Health Act, 2007). Risk assessment outcomes inform decisions about whether someone is ready for discharge from hospital, their level of community leave, the need for initial detainment as an inpatient under the Mental Health Act (2007), the need for Compulsory Treatment Orders (CTOs) and more broadly the level of supervision and allocation of resources required for the individual concerned. As noted in Chapter 1, individuals with psychosis are at a higher risk than the general population of committing violence to others and suicide (Swanson et al., 1990; Powell et al., 2000; Monahan et al., 2001; Daffern et al., 2007; Pompili et al., 2007). People with psychosis may, however, be at risk in a number of other ways, which have been less rigorously studied: risk of deliberate self-harm; risk of damage to property or arson; vulnerability to self-neglect or to exploitation by others; neglect of dependants; risk of being the victim of violence due to bizarre or unusual behaviours; and risk of accidental injury due to poor attention/concentration or distraction by psychotic phenomena.

In this chapter we view risk assessment as forming part of the Shared Assessment, Formulation and Education (SAFE) process in that we conceptualise risk in terms of a shared assessment and formulation process, which serves to educate clinicians and others regarding relevant risk factors and thereby promote therapeutic risk taking (the social participation principle). We explore a framework for risk assessment paralleling that suggested by a number of authors (Douglas and Skeem, 2005; Beech and Ward,

2004). This framework provides a means of organising the vast amount of information obtained during a risk assessment into a coherent risk formulation that can be shared and co-constructed with Multidisciplinary Teams (MDTs). This further serves to reduce problems of miscommunication and information sharing, making decision processes more transparent and guiding judgements regarding the level of risk posed, the risk management plan required and the targets of treatment to mitigate risk in the longer term. We illustrate this framework through a number of case examples. We then summarise some of the main research findings regarding the relevant risk factors for violence and for suicide to aid the clinician in conducting a sound and defensible risk assessment within this framework (the evidence-based principle). Sexual offending is not addressed as a risk issue here since psychosis has not been identified as a risk factor for sexual offending (Hanson and Bussière, 1996); the reader is referred to authoritative texts on this issue (e.g. Craig, Browne and Beech, 2008).

DEFINING RISK ASSESSMENT

Risk assessment can be seen as a means of achieving a balance between the protection of the client concerned and the protection of the public, with the need for positive risk taking (DH, 2007) and promoting the rights and freedoms of the individual. The forensic literature has traditionally emphasised risk prediction over risk prevention (Blumenthal and Lavender 2000). Reflecting this there exists a range of tools providing methods that attempt to predict the level of risk posed or the likelihood of recidivism over a particular time period. Clinicians are, however, usually interested not only in a prediction of risk but in answering a number of risk-related questions to guide their management and treatment of the client:

1   What exactly is the nature of the risk posed?
    A number of useful subsidiary questions are:

    • What precisely has the person done before (therefore what are they likely to do again)?
    • What is the likely impact or severity of harm?
    • Who is the likely target (self versus others, children versus adults, strangers versus family, males versus females)?

2   How likely is the individual to display or repeat this risk behaviour in the longer term?
    A number of useful subsidiary questions are:

    • Compared with other clients in general?
    • Compared with other clients on my caseload?

3   Why does this risk occur in this individual?
     A number of useful subsidiary questions are:

•   What factors drive it?
•   How do the factors relate to each other?
•   What are the most sensible treatment targets to reduce the likelihood of risk?
•   Can these factors be changed (treatability)?

4   When is the risk more likely to occur/how imminent is the risk right now?
     A number of useful subsidiary questions are:

•   What are the likely triggers or early warning signs?
•   Are these circumstances currently present (imminence of risk)?
•   How is the risk best managed?

Several methods of conducting a risk assessment have emerged from the general risk literature (Doren, 2002), each of which has their useful aspects along with limitations. The *unstructured clinical judgement approach* is simply based on one's own general clinical experience and specific experience of the client. Information is not gathered systematically or necessarily based on research data. Therefore, the process is prone to missing important but less intuitive risk factors and is prone to influence by one's own feelings towards the client and to normal reasoning biases (Kahneman and Tversky, 1979). For example, someone working in a GP surgery assessing violence risk is likely to have a very different view of what constitutes 'high risk' to someone who has worked in forensic services (the first may overestimate risk, the second may underestimate it). Furthermore, recent experience of the client's violence may artificially inflate one's judgment of longer-term risk, the so-called 'availability heuristic' (Tversky and Kahneman, 1974).

By contrast, the *actuarial approach* to risk assessment focuses on factors that have been shown to be statistically associated with increased risk in large samples of people. These factors are scored by means of a set of algorithms and the client's total score is compared with cut-offs, which provide a percentage estimate of the probability of the risk occurring over a particular timescale (usually years). Whilst these methods are undoubtedly an accurate method of predicting risk in large samples, there are a number of problems associated with applying this approach to individuals. First, the actuarial tools themselves, such as the Violence Risk Appraisal Guide (VRAG: Quinsey *et al.*, 1998), are heavily reliant on so-called 'static factors' (e.g. gender, number of previous offences), which do not allow for changes in risk over time and have few implications for the treatment or management of risk (Otto, 2000). Second, much of the data is based on samples from the United States and Canada and generalisability to other populations, or individuals who are not similar to the normative sample of the scale, cannot be assumed.

Finally, it is a common mistake to assume that the group data applies directly to a given individual. Just because a person has characteristics in common with a group with a 45 per cent chance of recidivism in the next five years, it does not mean that this particular individual is 45 per cent likely to commit a particular crime in the next five years. In sum, actuarial tools should be used only as part of an overall risk assessment process and only if the client concerned bears a close resemblance to the group on whom the scale has been validated.

The *anamnestic risk assessment approach* involves examining the person's life history in relation to dispositional and contextual factors that are associated with risk for that individual. Current circumstances are then examined for the presence of the identified risk factors. This method has the advantage of being focused on the idiosyncratic history and circumstances of the client under assessment but is not necessarily based on risk factors with empirical support. Furthermore, there is an assumption that future incidents of risk will be driven by the same factors as previous incidents.

The *structured clinical judgement approach* combines three elements of information together: (a) research-based factors known to be associated with the risk in question, (b) the clinician's knowledge of the client and their risk behaviours and (c) the client's own view of their experience (DH, 2007). Adopting this method allows the combining of information from various sources (including those from the anamnestic approach) and allows the inclusion of more dynamic variables (e.g. psychotic symptoms), which may change over time either spontaneously or through treatment. This approach reflects the recent conceptual shift towards a risk management oriented process that emphasises the repeated reassessment of dynamic variables (Belfrage and Douglas, 2002). It is also probably the most commonly adopted methodology and one recommended by the Department of Health (DH, 2007). In order to be successful, however, it relies on the clinician having a working knowledge of the literature on the risk factors for the risk in question for the population under consideration. It is essential that risk behaviours be tightly defined and based on a full personal history, with corroborative evidence sought from clinical notes and, if relevant, from police and judicial records. Risk factors for sexual offending, for example, differ from those of non-sexual violence or arson and each behaviour may have its own risk trajectory. Furthermore, it requires the clinician to have some structured framework for formulating the information they obtain into a coherent summary, which can then be used for care planning and risk management purposes. This follows Andrews *et al.*'s (1990) principles of risk, need and responsivity: greater resources should be allocated to high-risk individuals, treatment should target risk-specific factors and it should be tailored to the abilities and learning styles of the individual. We aim to provide such a framework for risk formulation in this chapter alongside a methodology for developing a shared multidisciplinary risk assessment.

Whichever method of risk assessment is used, the estimation of risk will always be probabilistic and contain a great degree of uncertainty. If the bar is set high to determine who constitutes a high risk then few will reach the criteria and a large number of risky individuals will be missed. Conversely, if the bar is set too low then all risky individuals will be detected but so will many individuals who do not pose a high risk. Furthermore, even if methods with nearly perfect sensitivity (the ability to accurately detect high-risk individuals) and perfect specificity (the ability to accurately detect low-risk individuals) could be developed, the prediction of risk is fraught with inaccuracies since the clinician is attempting to detect behaviours that occur very rarely. For example, if only 4 per cent of individuals were to commit suicide in a particular population, then all else being equal and with no other information available, an individual has a pre-assessment chance of not committing suicide of 96 per cent. With such low rates, the clinician will always be more accurate overall by stating that individuals do not pose a risk. In reality, the consequences of missing a risky individual are great and clinicians will err on the side of caution but will tend to be wrong more times than they are right when they classify someone as being at high risk. Risk prediction is therefore a somewhat inaccurate business by nature. The emphasis must therefore be on making risk decisions that are transparent and defensible but not always correct. Risk assessments that state the likely risk and the conditions under which it will occur are always more useful than a simple statement of whether the individual is 'high' or 'low' risk. The shared risk formulation process described in the rest of this chapter delineates different types of risk factors to provide a holistic multidisciplinary risk assessment.

A FRAMEWORK FOR SHARED RISK ASSESSMENT AND FORMULATION

The forensic literature delineates three types of risk factors (Douglas and Skeem, 2005; Beech and Ward, 2004): static/historical factors, dynamic stable factors and dynamic acute factors. Each of these is useful in answering some but not all of the risk questions posited earlier (what, how likely, why and when?).

Static/historical factors

These are those factors, typically identified through research findings, which predict future occurrence of the risk behaviour in question. They are static in that they are by nature unchangeable by treatment (e.g. gender, age, number of convictions, age at first offence, number of previous suicide attempts etc.) or over time (with the exception of age). They are loosely based on the notion that past behaviour is the best predictor of future behaviour. Such factors are useful in considering the overall level of risk and answer the question: 'How likely is this individual compared with other individuals to display the risk behaviour in question in the future (normally the longer term)?'.

They are comparable with the types of factors commonly used to assess all risk such as those in the insurance industry (e.g. marital status, nature of employment, number of previous claims, gender, age, postcode). This places less emphasis on the individual and is more concerned with accurate prediction based on information of the broader population. These group-based factors, however, do not tell us what the person is likely to do, neither do they tell us about the likely features of the act (e.g. use of weapons, likely victim etc.). These must be obtained from a detailed clinical history, a review of clinical notes and other collateral information.

Dynamic stable factors

These are enduring factors linked to the likelihood of offending but are factors that may change over time or through treatment, although they are likely to do so only gradually. These may range from active symptoms of major mental illness (e.g. command hallucinations commanding violence) to longer-term dispositional characteristics (e.g. trait anger, antisocial attitudes). Beech and Ward (2004) describe these factors as psychological dispositions (they are often, although not necessarily, attitudes, values or beliefs), which predispose the person towards the risk behaviour. Beech and Ward (2004) see the historical risk factors as markers of these dispositions in action in the person's past. Assessment involves understanding the factors that originally contributed to previous risk behaviours: whether the behaviour was driven by mental illness or not. It is at this level that a formulation of the offence will be most useful and may involve understanding not only which dynamic stable factors are relevant but also how they interact with each other (the person may have impulsive personality traits, for example, exacerbated by problematic alcohol use). Assessing and formulating dynamic stable factors is closely related to identifying which aspects of the person's presentation are potential, usually longer-term targets, for treatment by medication or psychosocial intervention.

Case example: Michael

Michael hears voices and is distressed by them. He is brought into hospital having set fire to his flat and assaulting two police officers when being arrested. It is important to understand the interaction between his psychotic symptoms and his fire-setting. Within our framework for risk assessment we need to consider the following:

- Did Michael set the fire in response to voice commands?
- Did Michael set the fire not because of commands but because he was distressed by persistent and derogatory voices?
- Did Michael set the fire not because of voices but because of harassment from neighbours, a limited social support network and poor problem-solving skills?

If the answer to the first question is yes then we would need to carry out a further assessment of voice-related beliefs, distress and behaviour. We may then, depending on Michael's ability to engage in individual therapy, consider cognitive therapy for command hallucinations to reduce his compliance behaviour (Byrne *et al.*, 2006), alongside encouraging medication compliance. In response to the second question, we may consider an approach based on enhancing Michael's coping strategies. Again this would lead to further assessment. However, if the third instance is correct then interventions directed at voices will not be effective in reducing fire-setting risk. Since dynamic stable factors are likely to change slowly, if at all, they may form the targets of treatment over months or even years and involve broader social and team-based interventions aimed at addressing housing needs, teaching problem-solving skills and developing a support network. Changes in dynamic stable factors do not negate the static or historical factors. If Michael had set five fires previously then he will remain at high risk (compared to the general population) of setting further fires: static and historical factors lend more weight to long-term risk prediction.

Dynamic acute factors

Dynamic acute factors constitute more rapidly changing factors (e.g. substance abuse, isolation, distress, increased preoccupation with delusions) that signify an elevated likelihood of the risk behaviour occurring. They represent a 'red flag', indicating the need for urgent action to prevent risk. Dynamic acute factors can be seen as the pushing of stable traits (dynamic stable factors) into a high-risk state (Douglas and Skeem, 2005). They relate most closely to the short-term management and prevention of risk behaviours and the titration of the level of supervision required.

Case example: Kevin

Kevin typically interprets any misfortune (e.g. experiencing problems with his benefits) as being caused by his MDT. He believes that they have done so intentionally, out of a lack of respect and disregard for him. Kevin believes that he must always be treated with respect (a trait anger belief) and that violence is an acceptable way of solving problems (antisocial attitudes developed in the context of a violent upbringing). Kevin does not always act aggressively in response to such situations and triggers. However, when additionally under the influence of alcohol, Kevin may become sufficiently disinhibited to act aggressively: his traits are pushed over into a high-risk state.

The application of the dynamic stable/acute distinction to psychotic symptoms has rarely been discussed. Brett-Jones *et al.* (1987) have previously drawn a distinction in delusional beliefs between conviction (how convinced the person is of the truth of their belief), preoccupation (how much time they spend thinking about it) and distress. In many treatment-resistant clients, assessment may reveal chronic and persistent delusional beliefs, which are held with high conviction much of the time. These constitute a dynamic stable factor. What tends to vary from day to day or hour to hour is the degree to which the person's time and attention are dominated by their delusional ideas and how distressed they are by them. These may be said to be the dynamic acute factors. Being clear about the distinction between what is a stable aspect of the person's presentation and what actually represents an increased and imminent likelihood of harm is an important issue.

Currently, there is a lack of published research identifying dynamic indicators of changing violence risk in any high-risk population (Quinsey *et al.*, 2004). Indeed, research studies examining dynamic risk predictors are far outnumbered by those focusing on static characteristics, and scholars are yet to develop a theoretical framework for violence in psychiatric populations (Douglas and Skeem, 2005). This is even more so in the case of dynamic acute factors where triggers and changes in presentation are highly idiosyncratic. However, Craig *et al.* (2008), in their discussion of sexual offending, note common broad examples of acute factors that might be useful as a starting point for assessment. These include:

• access to the victim;
• emotional distress;
• collapse of social supports;
• hostility;
• substance abuse;
• rejection of supervision;
• preoccupation with offence-related ideas.

We might more broadly include preoccupation with psychotic symptoms or beliefs or preoccupation with risk-related ideas (e.g. suicide) as being encompassed within the last factor. Similarly, Boer *et al.* (2004), in their approach to monitoring acute risk in sexual offending, draw attention to:

- *Acute factors involving the staff or environment:* new staff who may lack knowledge of the client or are less able to enforce existing boundaries on behaviour; changes in monitoring of the offender; changes in accommodation, location and access to victims or means.
- *Acute factors associated with the offender:* changes to social support/significant relationships; changes to the pattern of substance abuse; changes in sexual preoccupation; changes in emotional state (e.g. anger/hostility); changes in the ability to manage emotional changes; changes in victim access; preoccupation with selection, acquisition or grooming; changes in attitudes or behaviour towards supervision; changes in the ability to use coping or relapse prevention strategies or recognise high-risk situations; changes to routine and the ability to cope with this; offender-specific factors.

In broad terms, we consider three crucial components that need to be assessed in order to ascertain and monitor the level of acute risk. These are:

- *Recency and frequency:* how recently did the risk behaviour last occur (and if recently with what frequency has it occurred)? Assessment of this component is discussed in more detail in Chapter 9 when we discuss the use of the Challenging Behaviour Checklist for Psychosis (CBC-P). For the moment it is sufficient to note the relevance of behaviours that bear a close resemblance to the offence or risk in question: so-called *offence paralleling behaviour* (Jones, 2004), such as stalking members of staff.
- *Triggering events:* historically, what have been the triggers that have been directly or indirectly implicated in the risk behaviour occurring? Are these triggers (or similar triggers) present or likely to be present in the immediate future?
- *Idiosyncratic early warning signs:* what are the observable signs that this individual's dynamic stable factors are being pushed into a high-risk state (even if the behaviour or similar behaviours have yet to occur). In other words, what does the person say or do that indicates this change in presentation?

It is important to note that dynamic acute factors are by their nature context bound. It is not uncommon to see someone display reduced problem behaviours in an inpatient setting because of the level of supervision, the greater amount of boundaries in place and the enforcing and monitoring of medication compliance. This often presents a dilemma for the Responsible Clinician when considering leave and therapeutic risk taking. It would be a mistake to assume on the basis of improved behaviour alone that the individual was ready to cope with discharge, particularly where the static risk is high and little impact has been made in changing the dynamic stable factors.

Such factors may lead to clients remaining for long periods in residential care (Cowan *et al.*, in preparation). Such findings stress the importance of sound shared risk assessment that can be used to facilitate therapeutic risk taking. Morgan (1998) cites the now well-documented case of Christopher Clunis (Richie Report: Richie *et al.*, 1994) and highlights the importance of detailed individual assessment, efforts to coordinate care and the need to address the early warning signs of relapse.

Table 5.1 offers a format for organising assessment findings and deciding on treatment targets. This can serve as a template for multidisciplinary shared risk assessment and treatment planning for a given (operationally defined) target behaviour.

EVIDENCING RISK FACTORS

Having described the types of risk factors and provided a framework for formulation, it is important, in keeping with the evidence-based principle, to consider the empirical literature on risk factors for specific risks. In the following sections we provide an overview of the risk factors for violence and suicide within the formulation framework (presented in Table 5.1). Before doing so it is important to note a significant conceptual issue. Many studies of risk fail to clarify the described risk factors clearly enough, citing risk factors such as 'substance abuse' for example. It is not necessarily clear whether what is being referred to is a history of problematic substance use, current problematic substance abuse, changes or exacerbations in substance use or attitudes supportive of substance use. In effect, all of those aspects might be risk factors but would be entered into different sections of the risk formulation template presented in Table 5.1. Furthermore, the distinction between whether something is a dynamic stable factor or a dynamic acute factor will vary with the individual concerned. By necessity, therefore, some of the divisions we make below will be somewhat artificial. For example, in the case of a client with ongoing problematic substance abuse, substance use in general will not be a good acute risk indicator (it is a stable dynamic one), but an increase in the amount or frequency of use, or a change in the range or type of substances used, might be very relevant. Similarly, in most clients, current expressions of suicidal intent is a clear acute risk indicator. However, occasionally one encounters clients who frequently voice suicidal intent yet only occasionally make attempts. In such cases, whilst expression of intent should not be ignored or underplayed, it is clearly not of use in being able to identify on which occasions suicide will be attempted or indicate the level or nature of support and monitoring required. Ultimately, deciding whether a factor is a stable dynamic or an acute one will rely on the clinician's clinical judgement and their intimate knowledge of the client.

Table 5.1 A method for organising assessment findings and deciding on treatment targets

Target behaviour	Static factors	Dynamic stable factors	Dynamic acute factors
Operational definition (e.g. setting fire to own room, stabbing other inpatients with a knife, taking an overdose of prescribed medication)	**Demographic factors** (e.g. age, gender, number of offences) **Idiosyncratic historical factors** (e.g. type of victim in previous assaults, lethality of previous suicide attempts) *Unchanging/historical in nature*	**Psychological dispositions** May change slowly over time either through treatment or spontaneously (e.g. trait anger, chronic antisocial attitudes, persistent paranoid delusions, persistent depression)	**Rapidly changing factors** • **Triggers** • **Early warning signs** • **Recency of behaviours** (e.g. increased distress from voices, intoxication, anger)
Care planning process CPA based on structured clinical judgement using actuarial and other assessment tools as appropriate	**Prediction of long-term risk** How likely is this person to repeat the behaviour compared with others? What is the nature of the risk posed and its likely impact/severity? **Use to identify target behaviour for care planning**	**Medium- to long-term treatment targets** Factors responsible for driving the risk behaviour (the function of the behaviour) **MDT-based or individualised CBT to address compliance with command hallucinations, threat control override symptoms**	**Short-term risk management plans** Indicates imminent likelihood of the risk behaviour occurring **Support to use coping strategies/problem-solving skills. Increased supervision and monitoring. Use of hospital-based care**

Risk factors for suicide

The American Psychiatric Association Practice Guidelines for the assessment and treatment of patients with suicidal behaviours (American Psychiatric Association, 2003) provide a comprehensive and detailed overview of the risk factors for suicide in the general psychiatric population. It has been noted by Hawton *et al.* (2005) that many of the risk factors for suicide in schizophrenia are similar to those of the general population. Similarly, suicide attempts by people with bipolar disorder are commonly associated with depressive or mixed episodes rather than hypomania. This latter finding is perhaps unsurprising given the strong relationship between depressive symptoms and suicide risk (American Psychiatric Association, 2003). Clearly, psychotic populations are often not representative of the homogenous groups included in general research studies of suicide and clinicians are frequently dealing with people with a range of diagnoses and co-morbidities. We therefore include the general risk factors below within our risk formulation framework. Some risk factors (based on a number of recent studies and empirical reviews: Powell *et al.*, 2000; Potkin *et al.*, 2003; Hawton *et al.*, 2005; Pompili *et al.*, 2007) have, however, been identified as specific to schizophrenia (denoted in our review as S+) whilst others appear to be less strongly associated (denoted in our review as S–).

Empirically derived static risk factors for suicide

1   Demographic factors

- *Gender:* males are at a fourfold risk increase compared with women (in the general population) and by 1.57 times compared with that of the schizophrenia population in general.
- *Age:* adolescent or young adults (15 to 34 years) are likely to make an increased number of attempts. Older adults have an increased risk of success with fewer attempts, have greater intent and are less likely to communicate intent. Suicide in older people is also associated with increased physical vulnerability and greater social isolation (which may also mitigate against rescue).
- *Race:* being white (S–) is negatively associated whilst young females from the Asian subcontinent are at a greater risk.
- *Marital status:* men who are widowed, divorced or single are at four to five times greater risk than married men (S–), although being a young married couple and conflicted may elevate risk.
- *Professional status:* dentists and physicians, nurses, social workers, artists, mathematicians and scientists are all at greater risk.

2   Diagnoses (having received one at some time)
   Axis I diagnosis

- Diagnosis of depression – 20 times the risk.
- Diagnosis of dysthymia – 12 times the risk.
- Diagnosis of bipolar affective disorder (depressive or mixed episodes).
- Schizoaffective disorder.
- Schizophrenia – 8 times the risk.
- Anxiety disorder (particularly panic attacks and if co-morbid with depression).
- Attention deficit hyperactivity disorder (impulsive type).
- Substance abuse (including alcohol) diagnosis (range and number of substances increases risk).

Axis II diagnosis

- Borderline or antisocial personality disorder.

Axis III diagnosis

- Diseases of the nervous system (e.g. multiple sclerosis, Huntington's chorea, acute brain injury and spinal cord injury, seizure disorders, malignant neoplasms).
- Association with seizure disorders is particularly strong (most evidence for temporal lobe epilepsy).
- Physical illness (S–), particularly if it is terminal or involving pain, disfigurement or dependence upon others.

3   Psychiatric history

- History of past psychiatric treatment (particularly if involving in-patient treatment).
- History of psychiatric illness in the family (S–), especially where there is a history of depression (specifically in the schizophrenia group).
- History of substance abuse in the family.
- History of suicide in first-degree or other relatives.
- Family history of conflict or separation.
- Suicide attempt being the reason for last admission or during the last admission (S+).

4   Psychosocial history

- History of violence or aggression.
- History of other impulsive acts.
- Domestic violence (victim or perpetrator).
- Victim of physical or sexual abuse – 10 times increased risk, with higher risk associated with more severe and multiple types of abuse.
- Higher IQ and higher education (S+).

5   Historical factors (surrounding previous attempts)

- Number of past attempts: single attempt alone increases the risk by 38 times (including aborted attempts: making a noose but not using it, putting a gun to one's head but not firing it).
- Objective lethality or use of violent methods.
- Severity (e.g. requiring medical intervention).
- Person's perception of lethality of means (as important as objective lethality of means).
- Degree of premeditation.
- Degree of intent to die.
- Communication of attempt.
- Preparation made for death (e.g. saying goodbye, suicide notes, making a will).
- How the attempt was averted.
- Attempts to prevent being found.

Empirically derived dynamic stable risk factors for suicide

1   Psychiatric factors

- Depressive symptoms (current): feelings of worthlessness/low self-esteem, anhedonia, insomnia, persistent hopelessness.
- Active psychotic symptoms are less implicated in suicide but may be pertinent in individual cases. Command hallucinations in particular may lead to suicide or self-harm and should be routinely considered (see violence risk factors below for a fuller description).
- Aggression.
- Violence towards others.
- Self-harm.
- Current anxiety symptoms: feelings of anxiety, fearfulness or apprehension (S–).
- Fear of mental disintegration (S+).
- Panic attacks.
- Impulsivity (as a trait factor).
- Current attitudes supportive of substance misuse.
- Current chronic substance abuse interfering with daily functioning.
- Unstable or poor therapeutic alliance with the treatment team/ clinician.
- Non-adherence with prescribed treatment/poor engagement (includes medication and appointment attendance).

2   Personality characteristics and belief factors

- Constricted or polarised thinking (all-or-nothing thinking).
- Closed mindedness (narrowed scope and intensity of interests).

- Perfectionism with excessively high self-expectations.
- Capacity for reality testing.
- Ability to tolerate rejection.
- Subjective loneliness.
- Poor social skills.
- Loss of executive functions (ability to plan, organise, inhibit acting on impulse) (S–).

3 Suicide-related beliefs

- Regret over previous failed attempts.
- Beliefs about after-life, which might support suicide as a viable option.
- Positive views of suicide (means of escape, revenge, ending pain and suffering etc.).

Empirically derived dynamic acute risk factors for suicide

1 Recent behaviour (during the last 12 months)

- Recent suicide attempt.
- Recent deliberate self-harm with unclear intent.
- Recent acts of aggression or violence.

2 Cognitive, emotional and behavioural factors

- Current thoughts and suicidal ideation (if present chronically assess changes in nature and preoccupation).
- Current plans (including consideration of timing and the setting of future attempts, has contemplated means and lethality).
- Degree of current intent to carry out plans.
- Preparatory acts.
- Likely or possible access to means.
- Increased hopelessness.
- Presence of triggers associated with previous attempts.

3 Psychosocial factors

- Recent admission or discharge from hospital (consider if discharged within last one to three months).
- Living alone (S+).
- Recent loss events (S+) or significant anniversaries.
- Recent stresses (financial, housing, interpersonal conflict) or exacerbation of ongoing problems.
- Absence of key support figures.

4   Psychiatric factors

- Intoxication with substances (or if use is chronic then consider increase in amount, type or frequency of use).
- Increased preoccupation with paranoid ideas or increased distress associated with psychotic symptoms (S+).
- Worsening of affective symptoms.
- Agitation (S+).
- Reduction in normal level of medication compliance or worsening of engagement with services.
- Apparent (unexplained) improvement in symptoms.
- Genuine improvement in motivation and decreased apathy (apathy may resolve before low mood and suicidal intent).
- Acute loss of concern for others or by others.
- Acute increase in somatic complaints.
- Absence of key figures.
- Low staffing levels (if an inpatient).

5   Protective factors (mitigating against suicide)

- Children in the home (except those with postpartum mood disorder or psychosis).
- Sense of responsibility to family.
- Pregnancy.
- Religiosity: cultural or religious beliefs that suicide is wrong or sinful. Strength of belief rather than nature of religion *per se* is important.
- Life satisfaction.
- Reality-testing ability/positive coping and problem-solving skills.
- Positive social support.
- Positive therapeutic relationship.

It is important to note that suicide attempts in schizophrenia tend to be more serious and typically require a greater degree of medical intervention compared with suicide attempts in other populations. Many will have contacted professionals in the days or weeks prior to attempting suicide, providing a window of opportunity for risk prevention (Pompili *et al.*, 2007). Powell *et al.* (2000), in a review of inpatient suicides, found that the most common method of suicide was drowning (mainly in rivers but there were three cases involving baths on the ward), followed, in order of occurrence, by hanging, being hit by a train, jumping from a height, taking an overdose, carbon dioxide poisoning, suffocation, cutting one's throat and burning. Notably in inpatients, 72 per cent of suicides occurred outside the hospital site. A large proportion of these were during the weekend and most were on leave. However, overall, 63 per cent of suicides outside of hospital were committed by patients who were absent without leave. It was not uncommon, however, for patients to attempt suicide whilst under staff observation. Powell *et al.* (2000) identified five factors predictive of suicide in inpatients with schizophrenia: planned suicide attempt (thoughts) or actual suicide attempt before or during admission; recent bereavement (in last 12 months); presence of delusions; chronic mental illness (over a five-year duration, not including personality disorder); and family history of suicide (involving a first-degree relative). Of those having all five factors, 30 to 40 per cent would commit suicide but only a small minority actually had the five factors. Statistical prediction of risk was inaccurate due to the low base rate of suicide as noted above.

In summary, the existing literature suggests that suicide risk is best predicted in schizophrenia by affective symptoms, suicide attempts and ideation, recent loss events, substance abuse and treatment adherence. Substance misuse (e.g. opioids, cannabis), excluding alcohol, remains a strong predictor of suicide risk, rather than psychosis-specific factors. However, insight, unemployment, limited education, number of friends and marital status do not appear to reliably predict suicide risk (Hawton *et al.*, 2005); both positive (delusions and voices) and negative symptoms in general show little association to suicide risk (Hawton *et al.*, 2005). This lack of predictive ability of psychotic symptoms seems counterintuitive as most clinicians have encountered individuals who have self-harmed or attempted suicide as a direct or indirect result of psychotic symptoms. The fact that these factors do not play a role in large-scale group studies does not, however, preclude the fact that they may play a role in individual cases. Furthermore, the reader is cautioned to interpret the findings of the Hawton *et al.* (2005) meta-analysis study with some caution. Risk factors were often measured in the studies under review well in advance of suicide attempts. Consequently, dynamic factors (especially acute ones) may not have been evident. Furthermore, studies did not always include clear definitions of symptoms such as the content of command hallucinations or the type of delusion (e.g. persecutory paranoia, threat control override symptoms) and did not include other findings from the cognitive-behaviour literature (e.g. the importance of beliefs about voice power in predicting compliance in some individuals). Finally, the findings across these studies concerning the relevance of psychosis factors were quite mixed. Consequently, we would recommend continued inclusion of psychosis-related factors in the assessment of suicide risk. However, the main focus of initial treatment is likely to be on affective symptoms and day-to-day stressors and problems.

Empirically derived risk factors for violence

The research into risk factors for violence is vast and whilst largely focused on static factors, recent developments have led to a greater understanding of the dynamic aspects of risk. Much of the literature suggests that the risk factors for violence in the psychotic population are similar to those seen in the general criminal population, including a history of violence and antisocial factors. However, consideration is given here to the association between violence and psychotic symptoms.

Static risk factors for violence

The HCR–20 scheme for the assessment of violence (Webster *et al.*, 1997) is a commonly used, structured, professional judgement tool and is useful for prompting the clinician to consider both the frequency and the seriousness of past violence. It consists of ten historical (H) factors, five clinical (C) factors and five risk management (R) factors. The clinician considers a range of risk factors according to pre-defined criteria and makes a final judgement as to whether the individual represents a high, low or medium risk. The H scale includes a number of the items described below. It is useful when completing the scale to draw on additional tools and research findings to support each of the ratings.

I A past history of violent behaviour

This has consistently been shown to be predictive of violence in psychiatric groups and offenders with mental illness (Andrews *et al.*, 2006). Bonta *et al.* (1998), in their meta-analysis, showed that this factor was the strongest predictor of future violence. Phillips *et al.* (2005) examined 346 patients discharged from psychiatric hospital and similarly found greater numbers of previous convictions to be associated with a greater likelihood of recidivism.

2 Psychopathy

Drawing on the earlier work of Checkley (1941), 'psychopathy' according to Hare (2003) incorporates two main factors. Factor 1 consists of superficial charm and grandiosity, lying and manipulative behaviour, a lack of guilt and remorse, shallow emotions and a failure to take responsibility for one's actions. Factor 2 reflects an impulsive, often parasitic lifestyle with a lack of long-term goals, a lack of behavioural control, a history of delinquent behaviour and a proneness to boredom. Psychopathy is a construct measured by the Hare Psychopathy Checklist Revised (PCL–R: Hare 2003). It is a strong predictor of violence amongst criminal populations and offenders with a mental illness (Salekin *et al.*, 1996; Douglas *et al.*, 2006). Monahan *et al.* (2001) found psychopathy to be the strongest predictor of violence. This was largely accounted for by its antisocial factor above and beyond a history of behavioural deviance, the emotional detachment factor being less predictive. However, the majority of mental health patients would not meet criteria for psychopathy and the assessment of psychopathy is a lengthy process and requires specialist training for staff.

3 Antisocial personality disorder

Antisocial personality disorder (ASPD) is associated with a failure to conform to social norms and law-breaking, deceitfulness, impulsivity and a reckless disregard for the safety of self or others, aggression (repeated fights or assaults), an irresponsible lifestyle and a lack of remorse over hurting or taking advantage of others. A diagnosis of ASPD is highly predictive of risk (Bonta et al., 1998), although high rates of criminal males qualify for diagnosis (Cunningham and Reidy, 1998) and so it lacks specificity. Since the diagnosis involves past criminal history and the diagnosis overlaps with psychopathy, not everyone agrees on which aspects are most relevant and many tools (e.g. the Violence Risk Assessment Guide or VRAG [Quinsey et al., 1998]) score both constructs, which can lead to double scoring.

4 Age

Two aspects of age are generally considered to be important. First, being younger at the time of the first offence is associated with an increased risk of recidivism (Harris et al., 1993). The HCR–20 considers less than 20 as a young age for violence onset. Second, the offender's current age or age at release is relevant. The likelihood of violence decreases with increasing age (Swanson et al., 1990; Cunningham and Reidy, 1998) and appears to peak between the ages of 20 and 30 years.

5 A history of substance abuse

Substance abuse is consistently associated with elevated violence risk amongst those with a mental illness (Steadman et al., 1998; Dowden and Brown, 2002) and can be magnified when associated with non-concordance with medication (Swartz et al., 1988). Its use should be of a nature which affects the person's functioning, not just recreational use. Some schemes include in this neurological damage resulting from substance use.

6 Violation of supervision

Violation of supervision, probation, other conditional release (Boer et al., 1997; Quinsey et al., 2006) or escape from custody (Bonta et al., 1998) are well-established factors. We may also think in terms of current service philosophies of engagement as a proxy measure for which instruments have now been developed (e.g. Hall et al., 2001). Escape or elopement from a secure setting, reoffending during probation, revocation of parole and failure to attend for psychiatric treatment as ordered by a court or tribunal would also be relevant to consider here. Less serious acts may include a failure to take medication as prescribed, returning late from leave or using drugs or alcohol when prohibited. Non-compliance with CTOs may also be seen as relevant.

7 Gender

Being male is generally associated with presenting a higher risk than being female (Nicholls *et al.*, 2004) but this is attenuated in psychiatric patients. The evidence suggests that this can mean that potential for violence is often overlooked in female patients who may be more likely to exhibit violence within the home setting. Men, by contrast, are more likely to be violent outside of the home and to commit violence against strangers (Hiday *et al.*, 1999; Robbins *et al.*, 2003).

Dynamic stable risk factors for violence

Douglas and Skeem (2005) provide a useful review of dynamic stable factors for violence. They identify eight main factors likely to be relevant to its assessment:

1 Impulsivity

Impulsivity is the lack of control an individual may have over affect, behaviour or cognition and their inability to keep composed when under external or internal pressure to act. Impulsivity is significantly related to the self-report of violent thoughts and future violence. Importantly, however, so-called non-mentally disordered offenders tend to score higher than controls on impulsivity measures compared with psychiatric inpatients and substance users (Grisso *et al.*, 2000; Monahan *et al.*, 2001).

2 Negative affect

Two aspects of negative affect emerge as important from the literature – anger and negative mood. Anger involves components relating to both emotion and angry thoughts and consists of suspicion, rumination, hostile attitude, somatic tension, irritability, impulsive as well as aggressive reactions, and physical confrontations (Novaco, 1994). It is related to past violent criminality in civil psychiatric patients (Novaco, 1994) and psychiatric inpatients (Kay *et al.*, 1988). Hostility is predictive of inpatient violence and community violence in offenders with a mental illness (Menzies and Webster, 1995). Increases in anxiety and depression are predictive of later community violence (NATO study: Freese *et al.*, 2002) whilst neuroticism predicts violence in civil psychiatric samples (Skeem *et al.*, 2005). It is not clear whether anxiety and depression necessarily cause violence or whether they are an indicator of the presence of other destabilising factors (e.g. interpersonal problems, substance abuse).

3 Antisocial attitudes

Antisocial attitudes have been shown to have a large association with violence (Andrews and Bonta, 2003). They may include anti-authoritarian attitudes and attitudes supportive of crime or the use of violence and extend to a lack of regret or remorse over past actions. Conceptually associated with this risk factor are violent fantasies or thoughts. In the MacArthur sample of civil psychiatric patients, violent thoughts and fantasies predicted violence and six out of ten patients experienced such thoughts in the first year post discharge and two to three out of ten did so persistently (Monahan et al., 2001). A particularly relevant aspect of this risk factor to consider is the degree to which such fantasies are generalised or constitute specific thoughts towards a particular individual.

4 Substance abuse and related problems

Aspects relevant to this domain include ongoing chronic substance abuse and attitudes supportive of it. The use of alcohol and other drugs is strongly associated with violence and mental illness (Swanson et al., 1990; Monahan et al., 2001) and appears to interact with major mental disorder, dramatically increasing risk. Substance abuse increases risk by approximately tenfold, with moderate effects reported for schizophrenia and even greater effects in those with bipolar disorder and depression (Monahan et al., 2001). Alcohol and drug use change over time in high-risk psychiatric patients and the use of these (except marijuana) is predictive of violence two to three days later. The potential destabilising effects of a substance could affect violence risk in a number of ways, by acting as a disinhibitor, worsening mental state, damaging relationships and support, and causing financial difficulties. Substance abuse is also associated with an increased risk of psychotic relapse, medication non-compliance, aggression, depression, suicide, unstable housing and family burden (Drake and Mueser, 2001).

5 Active psychotic symptoms

On balance, the existing evidence tends to support an association between violence and the positive symptoms of psychosis but not for negative symptoms (Conroy and Murrie, 2007). It is commonly accepted that most violence in psychotic individuals is not driven directly by delusions but it may be in a substantial minority (Appelbaum et al., 2000). Junginger et al. (1998) noted that a small proportion (17 per cent) of people with delusional beliefs accounted for a disporporationate amount of violent incidents and reported that a small proportion of individuals described how delusions had motivated at least one act of extreme violence. In some cases (the so-called 'stereotypic delusional offenders') the same delusion appeared to have motivated at least two acts of violence that were separated in time, suggesting the importance of the specific contents of delusional beliefs above and beyond broad typologies of delusion.

Early studies (Buchanan, 1993) suggest that acting on paranoid delusions is more common compared with other delusions. Some studies suggest that acting on persecutory delusions in a range of ways (avoidance, escape, pre-emptive aggression etc.) is relatively common and can be conceptualised as a means to reduce perceived threat (Staznickas *et al.*, 1993; Aziz *et al.*, 2005; Freeman *et al.*, 2007). A particular focus in the forensic literature has been on so-called threat control override (TCO) symptoms: the perception of threat which in reality does not exist or the belief that an outside entity is attempting to take control of one's mind. An association between TCO symptoms and violence has been supported by a number of studies (Link and Stueve, 1994; Swanson *et al.*, 1996; Link *et al.*, 1999). Similarly Hodgins *et al.* (2003) followed up people with a diagnosis of schizophrenia who were discharged into the community from general and forensic mental health units for 26 months. They found that in the first six months severe positive symptoms were associated with an increased risk of violence and in the second six months such symptoms and TCO symptoms increased risk, when antisociality and substance abuse were controlled for. Yet such factors were not found to be predictive of risk in the MacArthur study and Stompe *et al.* (2004) found no difference in the prevalence of these symptoms between violent and non-violent individuals.

A number of explanations for these differences in findings have been offered, including a greater relevance for TCO symptoms in male patients and differences between those who continue to have residual TCO symptoms held with high conviction but are not particularly preoccupied or distressed by them (Conroy and Murrie, 2007). Hodgins *et al.* (2003) also note a failure to control for affective symptoms. Certainly, however, an assessment of TCO symptoms remains an important consideration in risk assessment. The MacArthur study (Monahan *et al.*, 2001) also implicated non-delusional suspiciousness of others (a tendency towards misperceiving others' behaviour as indicating hostile intent) as a factor in increasing violence risk. The ability to identify supporting evidence in the past week, seeking information to confirm or refute the belief and emotional distress (especially anger) may also be important. Belief conviction, preoccupation, systematisation and insight are not, however, associated with a greater likelihood of acting on delusions. Finally, consideration of delusions of misidentification may be important (Silva *et al.*, 1996).

6 Command hallucinations

Voices or hallucinations in general, or indeed command hallucinations in general, do not predict violence risk. However, command hallucinations that specifically command violence do (Monahan *et al.*, 2001). Important factors identified by Byrne *et al.* (2006) and Hacker *et al.* (2008) appear to be:

- whether the commands are subsequently interpreted as innocuous (e.g. punch the wall);
- whether the intention of the commanding voice is seen as benevolent;
- whether there are associated compliance beliefs (e.g. in being punished for non-compliance);
- whether there is a history of compliance behaviour or use of a safety behaviour (which prevents disconfirmation of voice beliefs);
- whether the person believes the voice to be powerful;
- whether they perceive themselves to have little control over the voice;
- whether they have a belief in voice omniscience (e.g. that the voice is all seeing and all knowing);
- when there is voice-related distress.

7 Interpersonal relationships and social skills

Relationships may exert a protective effect or a risk-enhancing effect depending on the nature and quality of relationships available to the person. Poor social skills may result in difficulties establishing and maintaining intimate relationships, peer relationships, therapeutic alliances, stable accommodation and employment (Andrews and Bonta, 1995; Hanson, 1997). These reduce the availability of social support. A lack of social support is related to increased violence as it increases the risk of destabilisation when the person is exposed to external triggers (Webster *et al.*, 1997; Kropp *et al.*, 1999). The feeling of being threatened by friends and relatives has also been linked to violence (Bartels *et al.*, 1991; Estroff *et al.*, 1994).

8 Treatment adherence and alliance

This domain includes compliance with treatment and medication and the quality of the clinician alliance with the client, what we now may term 'engagement'. Non-compliance with medication and the presence of fewer professionals in the client's support network are both associated with violence (Bartels *et al.*, 1991; Monahan *et al.*, 2001).

Dynamic acute risk factors for violence

There is far less research pertaining to acute dynamic risk factors for violence in psychiatric patients. By necessity, therefore, the assessment of acute risk is often idiosyncratic in nature. The issue of identifying triggers and early warning signs is dealt with in more detail in subsequent chapters. In line with Craig *et al.* (2008), relevant factors to consider in broad terms include:

- an increase or alteration in the pattern (frequency, amount and type) of substance misuse;
- collapse of social supports;
- disengagement from and rejection of supervision or medication;
- increased hostility and violent ideation (possibly with a narrowing of focus to particular individuals);
- increased distress or increased preoccupation with paranoid delusions or TCO symptoms;
- increased frequency of positive symptoms (e.g. voice commands).

SUMMARY

In this chapter we have considered a useful framework for risk assessment and formulation, which forms the third of our formulation templates (the first being the WHO shared service level formulation; the second the shared person level formulation). Our aim has been to provide a shared MDT framework for risk assessment, management and care planning that will serve to underpin team working with high-risk clients and foster greater consistency and transparency in decisions that are defensible. It distinguishes risk management from risk treatment and is of use particularly where a judgement must be made regarding the discharge of a client from hospital, a step-down from a secure setting or conversely the need for stepping up supervision or admission to hospital. Since the model incorporates a distinction between long-term and short-term risk and protective factors, it provides a means of facilitating positive risk taking, thereby increasing the range of activities that the person can engage in, reducing barriers to social participation and building hope for recovery. In the next chapter we describe the process of how this framework can be carried out by the MDT and discuss its use as a standalone process or as part of a broader SAFE process. We provide illustrative case examples taken from our own clinical practice.

Chapter 6

Shared risk formulation

INTRODUCTION

In this chapter we focus on the shared process of conducting risk assessment and, in line with the shared understanding of phenomenology principle, we suggest how the different skills and roles of Multidisciplinary Team (MDT) members can best be utilised in this process. We offer guidance on how shared risk assessments can be used to facilitate care planning and treatment by teams and show when management and supervision are needed. Finally, we consider in which settings and circumstances shared risk assessment is most useful and cases where our fuller Shared Assessment, Formulation and Education (SAFE) process may be more usefully employed.

THE SHARED RISK ASSESSMENT AND FORMULATION PROCESS

The risk formulation framework provided in Chapter 5 allows a structured, empirically based assessment of risk to be carried out by a team. It should be used to help identify:

- the likelihood of the risk behaviour occurring;
- the nature of that risk;
- the likely severity of the risk;
- the required medium- to longer-term treatment targets;
- the means of managing the risk in the short term.

In order to complete the shared risk formulation template, we recommend following the stages as set out below. It is a time-consuming process to engage in and is perhaps most relevant for those clients perceived as presenting the most risk.

1 Information gathering

First, the risk behaviour in question needs to be tightly and operationally defined. Each identified behaviour is likely to have its own risk trajectory and will therefore require separate assessment and formulation. Information should be gathered from as many sources as possible. A risk assessment is only as good as the information put into it and small amounts of information may dramatically alter the risk assessment. Information gathering should be tailored to assess the presence or absence of the relevant risk factors for the risk in question.

Taking a full personal and clinical history is an essential starting point to identifying which risk behaviours the person is likely to engage in (e.g. assault with a weapon, parasuicide involving overdosing versus cutting) and who the likely victim/s may be (e.g. strangers, members of the team). It can often be difficult to elicit a detailed and comprehensive personal history from the client. Relatives may be a useful source of early history, but there can be a lack of such informants for assertive outreach clients or long-stay forensic or rehabilitation clients, where relationships with families have often broken down. The rich multiple observations of team members are invaluable here. Corroborative evidence may also be sought from clinical notes and, if relevant, from police and judicial records. Clinical records are, however, often patchy, whilst criminal records can be difficult to obtain especially for instances where only a fine or caution has been issued.

2 Estimation of level of long-term risk

The clinician can, usually by meeting with team members most involved with the client and reviewing the notes, identify the static factors. By subsequently completing relevant actuarial measures with the team members most involved with the client and the client themselves, they may then begin to estimate the level of risk (high versus medium versus low) compared with other groups. However, at this point the MDT should also consider:

- the level of risk in relation to the general population but also to their own client group: someone working in an Assertive Outreach Team (AOT) may wish to suggest that the individual is not only at high risk compared with the general population but also compared with the team caseload as a whole and therefore deserving of more intensive input;
- the base rate for the risk in this population (e.g. the base rate of violence and suicide is low, so even someone deemed to be a 'high risk' will likely fall very short of 100 per cent or even a 50 per cent likelihood of the behaviour occurring);
- using their own judgement to assign a level of risk based on actuarial tool scores, and the information obtained thus far. The individual may be

at very high risk on the basis of one factor alone. Even with no other factors being present, a long and extensive history of violence risk may add sufficient weight to assign the person to a high-risk category;

• the nature of the risk and the likelihood of harm if the risk occurs.

3 Formulation of risk vulnerabilities and identification of treatment targets

The clinician, guided by the evidence with respect to the risk in question (illustrated in Chapter 5), can now assesses (a) which risk factors are relevant in this individual in driving the behaviour and (b) how these factors themselves interact with each other. This will often involve interviewing the client about their view and explanations of previous risk incidents. The team should consider what can be done to reduce risk (e.g. identifying treatment targets) over the next three to six months and which of the dynamic stable factors may be amenable to treatment and who will provide it. Usually this will mean identifying priorities for treatment. The team should decide this together in order to reduce conflict and promote consistency of approach.

The team may wish to consider which behaviour to target (in the case of multiple risks) and which dynamic facts are most likely to respond to treatment. Who is in the best position to do this may depend on the skills of the individual clinicians involved or their level of engagement with the client. The team may also consider dynamic stable factors that are protective in nature. For example, longstanding supportive relationships or pre-existing coping skills are enduring factors that might aid in treatment success.

4 Identification of acute risk factors

Clinicians should initially identify when the risk last occurred and whether any signs of imminent risk are present. This will require careful consideration of what exactly represents an exacerbation of risk in this individual over their normal presentation (dynamic acute versus dynamic stable factors). The clinical history should be examined for typical triggers that may have exacerbated risk in the past and the team will need to consider whether these are currently present. On the basis of this information, decisions can be made on whether the current level of supervision or management is sufficient and what short-term management strategies will need to be put into place. Often this will take the form of protective strategies but in fairness to the individual the presence of acute protective factors should also be considered: the person's current compliance with medication, their tendency to be open and seek help before acting or the presence of other people in the short term who provide a stabilising influence.

5 Sharing the risk assessment and formulation with the broader team

As with the shared person level formulation and Cognitive Approach to Risk Management (CARM) model (or formulation) templates, once the initial risk framework template has been completed (as shown in Chapter 5, Table 5.1 and further illustrated below) a broader MDT meeting can be arranged. This is essential in order to ensure that everyone is on board and a consistent approach is adopted. Here the formulation is presented to the wider team and their reactions elicited. A further meeting may then be required for those involved in the initial risk assessment and formulation to examine the formulation in light of the wider team's input, make any amendments and seek further information if necessary. Some elements may require longer-term validation and require further assessment. A further meeting should then be called in order to present the revised formulation. At this stage it is important to make clear that assessing and managing the person's risk is an ongoing process. People's behaviour and circumstances change over time and so risk assessment should never be considered as a one-off process but rather subject to ongoing revision. Finally, the team, especially those most involved, must consider how this new understanding of the person's risk should be translated into a clear and achievable care plan (for each behaviour), with clearly defined responsibilities. The case examples below illustrate this process.

DECIDING UPON THE RIGHT CARE PLAN STRATEGY

Care needs to be taken when planning treatment and management that the right factors are considered alongside treatability issues. The two cases of inpatients with psychosis presented in Table 6.1 illustrate this most clearly. Key questions to consider are (a) who is the highest risk?, (b) who is the safest to discharge? and (c) who should be given community leave?

The question of who represents the highest risk is misleading. Risk is not an either/or judgement but rather a series of related judgements and questions. According to our framework, Keith's acute (imminent likelihood) of fire setting is too high to allow him to receive community leave or discharge; he requires ongoing inpatient treatment. His level of historical risk of setting fires is in fact quite low, having set only one fire in the context of acute psychotic symptoms. If he could be treated to reduce his symptoms with medication, given cognitive-behavioural therapy (CBT) to address compliance beliefs with his voices and his problem drinking was reduced then leave could be considered. Martin appears to be compliant and the recency of risk is some time ago. His degree of acute risk for fire setting is therefore quite low. However, there has been little change in his dynamic stable factors due to poor engagement and less is known about his symptoms compared to Keith.

Table 6.1 Risk case examples

Keith

Historical static factors	Dynamic stable factors	Dynamic acute factors
Keith has set 1 fire He has no prior arrests There is no evidence of longstanding personality difficulties He has a history of problematic alcohol use	Keith hears command hallucinations telling him to set fires; he believes his voices to be powerful and that he must comply with them He has pro-drinking attitudes and no insight into his psychotic symptoms or treatment needs but will discuss his symptoms openly	He has absconded several times from hospital and recently been found to have been drinking Keith was returned to the ward by police in an aggressive and disturbed state He responds to and is distressed by voices on a regular basis

Martin

Historical static factors	Dynamic stable factors	Dynamic acute factors
Martin has set 5 fires He has a history of weapon use and previous threats of violence as an inpatient.	Keith has poor problem-solving skills and a low IQ He reacts impulsively to stress, minimises previous offences and has delusional beliefs but refuses to discuss them or engage in any treatment	He is currently compliant with medication and care plans and has set no fires or reported thoughts of doing so for 2 years. Generally Martin is pleasant and polite and not preoccupied or distressed by his delusions

Furthermore, his long-term risk of setting fires is higher overall and is not clearly just a function of his psychotic symptoms. Whilst Martin is managing well at present, one would have to suspect that this is in large part due to his structured environment and supervision; when placed under stress his dynamic stable factors might quite rapidly be pushed into a state of high risk and his current mental state is not well understood. He would most likely require gradual testing out on leave prior to discharge but would also most likely require significant ongoing monitoring given that his treatability is questionable.

The risk formulation framework therefore provides a way of organising assessment information to inform different aspects of risk prediction, treatment and management. It also helps to clarify the role of the different professionals involved. Typically, longer-term risk will be assessed by psychiatrists or psychologists often with the knowledge of empirically derived risk factors. Dynamic stable risk factors are intimately linked to the role of the clinical or forensic psychologists with their extensive training in formulation and psychosocial interventions, although increasingly other professionals may also possess these skills or wish to develop them. Management of dynamic acute factors may fit better with the roles usually adopted by nursing staff who often act as care coordinators and will usually have frequent (day-to-day in inpatient settings) contact with clients and thus are better able to monitor signs of acute risk and provide supervision and monitoring.

APPLYING THE FRAMEWORK TO INDIVIDUAL CASES

In this section we consider two community cases, Joe and Winston, to illustrate the process of shared risk assessment and formulation. These are community examples and we view this type of formulation as perhaps better suited to these types of services. Our CARM formulation on the other hand (presented in the next chapter) may be a more appropriate method for use in inpatient or residential settings.

Case study 1: Joe

Joe is a 25-year-old male with a diagnosis of paranoid schizophrenia and a history of violent assault occurring in the context of his mental health difficulties. Joe also writes threatening letters to the Ministry of Defence but has not acted on these. He also has a history of theft and mugging (age 15 years) and it has been suggested that he has some antisocial personality traits (but no formal diagnosis), which involved assault on one occasion (attacking another youth in the street and injuring him with a knife) and for which he spent some time in a youth offending institution. His notes indicate that he has not been involved in any violence since the age of 17, with the exception of the index offence (detailed below). He has never shown remorse for his past actions and has felt that they were fully justified. Joe also has a longstanding history of frequent cannabis use. He has quite positive ideas about this, believing that it does him no harm and serves as a relaxant in social situations. Objectively, his level of cannabis use has been linked to problems maintaining employment, being associated with a worsening of his mental state. At the age of 18, Joe came into contact with psychiatric services having been reported to his general practitioner by his mother. Joe is reported to have claimed that the neighbours were talking to him using an electronic device; he heard them threatening him and his family (voices). This experience is ongoing and he has tended to hide kitchen knives under his mattress just in case the neighbours break in during the night. His emotional response to this tends to be anger. Joe believes that these neighbours are trying to drive him mad and are involved in a conspiracy with the military to cause mental illness and distress to his family. He has tended to play his music loudly when distressed in order to drown out their voices and has got into conflict with the neighbours over this. Joe has no insight into his problems, being 100 per cent convinced of his delusional explanation.

Joe's family describe him as 'hot-headed' and report that he was frequently suspended from school for fighting. He has a history of disengagement from services and poor medication compliance, with frequent relapses leading him to fall under the care of the local AOT. He tends to manage his money poorly, often gets into debt and when placed under stress he tends to drink and occasionally self-harm by cutting his arms superficially (in response to the voices). Joe has recently lost his first real girlfriend and has been turned down for a place on a training scheme. He is usually in when the team visit although sometimes he will not answer the door. He is currently taking his medication but is now drinking a lot more and has been observed to be responding regularly to voices, shouting at them. Joe has also made several complaints to the police about the neighbours over the last month but has not approached them. Attempts have been made by the team to engage Joe in CBT but he has not found this helpful, often getting angry with team members, disengaging from them, and at times he views them as being involved in the conspiracy with the military.

Joe's index offence occurred one month ago and is the focus of the risk assessment. A separate assessment and formulation would be required to address his self-harm and threatening letters (although the same factors may emerge to play a role in these behaviours). The incident involved threatening his neighbour with a kitchen knife. His neighbour ran into his house and called the police. This was followed by a period of increased voice-related distress and attempts to cope with this through excessive use of alcohol and cannabis. Joe's shared risk formulation and management plan is presented in Table 6.2.

Case study 2: Winston

Winston is 50 years old and has a history of depression and mood swings. His primary diagnosis, however, is schizoaffective disorder. He hears derogatory voices, telling him he is worthless and that he would be better off dead. Winston interprets what the voices say as them wanting him to kill himself. He believes that the voices are his deceased ancestors who are spirits and that they are all seeing and all knowing (omniscient). He believes that they are very disappointed in him as he has not made a success of his life and so has brought shame on them. However, at times he also perceives them as caring for him and wanting him to join them in the spirit world and he can present as elated at these times. He is currently not overly distressed by the voices nor is he particularly preoccupied by them. Recently (six months ago) he lost his older sister who was a great source of support to him. This was followed shortly

Table 6.2 Joe's shared risk formulation and management plan

Static factors	Dynamic stable factors	Dynamic acute factors
Diagnosis paranoid schizophrenia Antisocial attitudes? 2 incidents of violence involving the use of a weapon. The most recent was a threat but it is not clear if Joe would have stabbed his neighbour if he had not run back into the house Male Young age at first violence Current age History of early maladjustment History of disengagement from services and non-compliance with medication History of cannabis and alcohol use	100% conviction in paranoid belief that neighbours are the source of his voices, are threatening him and his family and are collaborating with the military (both psychological and physical threat) Trait anger – reacts to perceived threats with aggression and violence Poor financial management skills Poor coping skills/ impulsivity Attitudes supportive of substance use Ongoing cannabis and alcohol use (coping strategy)	Breakdown of romantic relationship Turned down for job training Increased drinking Increased responding to voices and voice related distress **Early warning signs include:** Increased complaints to police about the neighbours Playing music loudly Recent incidents of cutting his arm Recent threats to neighbour **Protective factors include:** Compliant with medication Attends appointments
Moderate level of long-term risk 2 recorded incidents using a weapon, one very recently Majority are less serious acts of violence	**Moderate–high dynamic stable risk Interventions** Alternative medication regimen to reduce psychotic symptoms Team-based CBT to address in-situation paranoid beliefs and the need to act on them Work on substance use and introduce and facilitate development of functional coping strategies for voices Support to manage his money more effectively	**High acute risk Interventions** Support access to employment Debt and benefit advice (tactics to promote engagement with the MDT) Prompt and support Joe to utilise new functional coping strategies for voices Medication review to consider PRN medication to manage increased distress/temporary increase in antipsychotics Respite Increased visits (to monitor and support) Crisis team/home treatment team involvement?

afterwards by a relapse and admission. At this time Winston began to neglect his self-care and stopped taking his medication. He was discharged four months ago and is currently under the care of a specialist community rehabilitation team. He takes his medication regularly and will open the door on most occasions when the team visit. He currently lives alone in a tower block on the eighth floor in an inner-city area of a large city. Winston has been offered CBT and other psychosocial interventions (e.g. psychoeducation, relapse prevention) and has gone along with these but has tended to be a passive recipient, showing no changes in his view of his problems or attempts to cope with them: carry out homework etc. At the time of his recent relapse and admission he did not report any of the early warning signs listed in the relapse plan constructed by his care coordinator.

Winston attempted suicide at the age of 22 shortly after the onset of his mental health problems, by jumping off a bridge, when he broke both his legs (which still cause him pain). He has taken three overdoses (the last of these over five years ago) and has tried to poison himself by ingesting bleach (seven years ago). His previous attempt was precipitated by money problems, an argument with his best friend and by side effects of his medication, which caused impotence and which he was too embarrassed to report. He often discloses feeling suicidal when his voices are distressing him and believes that this is what his ancestors want. Winston's shared risk formulation and management plan is presented in Table 6.3.

Table 6.3 Winston's shared risk formulation and management plan

Static factors	Dynamic stable factors	Dynamic acute factors
Diagnoses of schizoaffective disorder and depression Male 1 incident of attempted suicide by lethal means 3 overdoses (prescribed medication) 1 attempt to poison himself (lethal means) History of medication non-compliance History of psychiatric treatment as an inpatient	Persistent derogatory treatment-resistant voices interpreted as commands, believed to be real and powerful Derogatory content increases depressive symptoms and maintains low self-esteem Positive beliefs about suicide Poor capacity for reality testing Subjective loneliness	Recent loss of sister Recent discharge from hospital – feelings of hopelessness **Early Warning signs include** Increased voice activity and voice-related distress Increased feelings of hopelessness Elated mood (voice driven and associated with increased preoccupation with positive beliefs about suicide) Access to means (lives in tower block, hoards medication) Reading about poisons *(Continued Overleaf)*

Table 6.3 Continued

Static factors	Dynamic stable factors	Dynamic acute factors
Moderate level of long-term risk Number of attempts but none in the past 5 years; but still higher than the general population	**Moderate dynamic stable risk** **Interventions** Alternative medication regimen to reduce psychotic symptoms Focus on increasing social network Refocus on life goals and steps to achieve them	**Low to moderate acute risk** Recency of risk was 5 years ago No current early warning signs of risk (EWS-R) **Interventions** Continue ongoing monitoring of EWS-R, especially mood Twice-weekly visits (give small medi pack doses of medication)

APPLYING THE SHARED FORMULATION TO OTHER RISKS

We have focused in this chapter on risk of violence and suicide with some illustrative examples. The evidence base for other risks such as self-neglect or vulnerability is much less well developed. Nevertheless, the risk formulation framework can still be applied here based on the client's history and the MDT's knowledge of them. For example, one of our clients has a history of being assaulted by others (historical factors would include the nature of the assaults, by whom, in what settings and the number of times this has occurred). The assaults were precipitated by the bizarre content of the client's speech and staring behaviour, secondary to delusions about others communicating with him telepathically (dynamic stable factors). This was particularly prominent when he had been using cannabis, was increasingly preoccupied by delusional ideas and left to go to the pub without support (acute factors). He was particularly helped by behavioural experiments supported by the (CBT) team to challenge his in-situation beliefs as well as increasing activity levels to inhibit substance use (e.g. accompanying him to social events and staff prompting him regarding the content of his speech). As a further example, a client with a history of self-neglect would require consideration of the number of incidences of self-neglect, the type (e.g. not washing, not eating) along with understanding the severity of previous neglect (needing to be hospitalised because of malnutrition). In addition, the team would need to consider the factors driving the neglect. These might include: avoidance and social withdrawal due to positive symptoms; increased negative symptoms and cognitive problems with initiating action and speech; and drug use resulting in worsening mental state and lack of money. Likely triggers (e.g. breakdown of support network, contact with particular individuals, housing issues) and the presence of early warning signs (e.g. decreased engagement, earliest signs of changes in self-care) would also be relevant to consider here.

WHICH SETTINGS TO USE SHARED RISK FORMULATIONS IN

By now it should be obvious that complex risk assessment as outlined here and in the previous chapter is a lengthy process and is unlikely to be an option for busy clinicians in all settings. Our approach has essentially been designed, as in the case for person level formulations, for settings where there is likely to be lengthy involvement with the client and where a team approach is dominant (e.g. assertive outreach services, early intervention teams and other specialist community teams). In these services a good risk assessment is paramount and our risk approach can be used as a standalone method. However, in cases where team splitting regarding the client is evident (our formulation of the team's ABCs of the client provides a useful indication of this) then it is often helpful to carry out our person level formulation. Our CARM model is often best utilised within residential settings (e.g. specialist inpatient rehabilitation units, forensic services and other longer-stay settings), where additional resources are usually available. Applying different aspects of SAFE in different types of psychiatric and care settings is addressed more fully in Chapter 16.

SUMMARY

In this chapter we have illustrated how our approach to risk assessment can be used successfully in a team context to identify clear treatment and management targets. We have indicated potential roles for different team members and suggested the settings and circumstances under which our risk framework may be used as a standalone process or combined within the context of the broader SAFE process. In the next chapter we build on this framework to elaborate on the formulation of acute risk. We provide a clear formulation framework for acute risk, building on models of challenging behaviour and our CARM model and more clearly specify the interrelationship of triggers, early warning signs and dynamic stable factors.

Chapter 7

CARM

An integrative model for understanding problematic behaviour in psychosis

INTRODUCTION

In Chapter 6 we illustrated a framework for risk formulation based on the contemporary risk literature and models of risk. However, this framework is primarily aimed at high-risk behaviours (e.g. suicide or violence) and as we noted in Chapter 1, problematic behaviours in psychosis may take a variety of forms that may more broadly act as significant barriers to participation, preventing the person from engaging in ordinary age-appropriate activities or achieving their life goals. A broader formulation framework is required to encompass information relating to these different types of problematic behaviours and to guide the clinician in selecting an appropriate level of intervention. Our Cognitive Approach to Risk Management (CARM) model provides such an integrative framework. CARM may be viewed as a formulation at the level of the problem behaviour. As such, it builds on the earlier levels of formulation, which essentially help to define which problem behaviours are the main barriers to participation. The CARM model provides a means of focusing more clearly on the factors that drive and maintain the behaviours in question and their interrelationships, allowing clear avenues for intervention. The model is a functional analytic one. By understanding more fully the function that a particular behaviour serves, an intervention plan can be devised that aims to meet those functions in a more appropriate and less damaging way. In this chapter we begin by outlining the development of the various components of the CARM model and their rationale. We subsequently illustrate the process of using the model with two main case studies to show its application to different behaviours.

BACKGROUND TO THE CARM MODEL AND RATIONALE

In examining the current literature on approaches to addressing problematic behaviour in the field of psychosis (Freeman *et al.*, 2001, 2007; Haddock *et al.*, 2004, 2009; Daffern *et al.*, 2006, 2007; Haddock and Shaw, 2008; Meaden *et al.*, 2010), a number of problems are apparent. First, existing methods tend to be based on generic cognitive-behavioural therapy (CBT) models (e.g. Haddock *et al.*, 2004, 2009). Whilst potentially useful, these are really aimed at the level of dynamic stable vulnerability factors and therefore focus on the longer-term treatment targets. They may increase staff understanding of the client and reduce problem attributions in the team to some extent, but they are less readily applicable to acute management. They are also arguably less able to underpin a true Multidisciplinary Team (MDT) approach since they rely on being able to deliver interventions within a mainly individualised one-to-one CBT process. Our experience has been that these approaches also rely on a case conceptualisation at the person level, which is often too vague in specifying the relationship between variables for staff to effectively define a clear treatment target or management programme. Current cognitive approaches also lack a clear behavioural focus and explicit longer-term service and client aims that provide motivation for the client and the team. Furthermore, these individual therapy-focused approaches based on CBT emphasise relatively stable belief factors such as beliefs about the power of the voices. They do not make important distinctions between what triggers the behaviour at a particular point in time or emphasise moment-to-moment interpretations of events that are often driven by more specific in-situation beliefs (usually supported by more stable pan-situational ones).

Case example: Karen

Karen has powerful voices (pan-situational beliefs that the voice is powerful and must be obeyed) but only occasionally acts on them by assaulting other residents when she interprets the specific comments or actions they make as indicating that they are in league with the voices and are about to act against her, on the voices' behalf (Karen's in-situation beliefs).

Finally, these approaches say less about formulating the interaction between different psychotic symptoms. For example, a person with paranoid delusions may avoid situations where they perceive their thoughts to be broadcast to others over the television.

Other authors emphasise more traditional behavioural models (e.g. Beer, 2006) but tend to limit their application to a one-dimensional reinforcement-based approach. They also fail to integrate the relevant belief or symptom factors prominent in a psychotic population. Reinforcement methods alone are particularly problematic when dealing with high-risk behaviours where the aim is not just to extinguish the behaviour but also to actually prevent its occurrence in the first place. Daffern and Howells (2002) and Daffern *et al.*

(2006) offer a more formulaic approach by examining typical triggers and functions for behaviour as perceived by staff. However, their approach relies less on an idiosyncratic formulation of triggers, setting events and maintaining factors. It does, nevertheless, provide a useful and informative addition and suggests areas for assessment and intervention in individual cases which are incorporated below. Finally, functional analytic models such as Emerson's (2001) provide less consideration to the longstanding psychological dispositions of the individual that are implicated in driving their problem behaviours and making clear the distinction between these 'trait factors' (dynamic stable) and 'state factors' (dynamic acute) indicative of an increased imminent likelihood of the problem behaviour occurring. This is particularly relevant to those who have a persistent level of residual psychotic symptoms (e.g. delusions or voices) or other symptoms that do not, since they are generally always present, provide a good means of predicting behaviour.

In the CARM model we have attempted to addresses the shortcomings of these existing approaches and incorporate their useful elements into a single model, which aims to:

- clarify the relationship between dynamic vulnerability factors, setting events, triggers and acute factors;
- integrate environmental, phenomenological/cognitive and team-based factors into a coherent formulation;
- provide a menu of interventions for different types of problem behaviours, which maps clearly onto the CARM model;
- provide a clear distinction between different levels of beliefs and symptom factors relevant to acute rather than stable risk;
- provide a means of illustrating the interaction between different psychotic symptoms and skill deficits in contributing towards the occurrence of problematic behaviours.

THE CARM MODEL

The model is in essence a functional, interactional, cognitive and behavioural one. It is designed expressly to enable staff to have a better understanding of how cognitive and behavioural factors interact and result in problematic behaviours, illustrating both the client's perspective and the broader interpersonal care context. The CARM formulation framework (as illustrated in our two cases below) has five core components. These we propose interact to result in different problematic behaviours and can be used to understand the function of any problematic behaviour in psychosis.

Component 1: Problem behaviour definition

The CARM formulation hinges around a specific problem behaviour, which should be clearly and operationally defined. There is a tendency for those involved in working with the person to apply general labels for a behaviour such as 'self-harm', 'verbal/physical aggression', 'sexually inappropriate behaviour' in their verbal descriptions, in clinical notes and incident reports. Team members, carers and others also tend to jump ahead to describing the function of the behaviour rather than the behaviour itself (e.g. 'attention-seeking behaviour' or 'manipulative behaviour'). This is frequently not based on objective facts or observations but rather on intuition and feelings engendered by the client's behaviour. This is problematic for a number of reasons. First, the nature of the behaviour is not communicated between professionals specifically enough to avoid misunderstandings and inappropriate or inaccurate treatment plans and estimations of risk. Second, team members and others may react towards the occurrence of the behaviour or adopt interventions on the basis of unconfirmed hypotheses about what the function is, which may subsequently prove detrimental or ineffective.

Case example: Joanne

Joanne was perceived to be deliberately cutting her arms superficially as a means of gaining attention. Staff in the group home ignored her, with the rationale (as recorded in her care plan) of 'not reinforcing' this behaviour. It emerged, however, using the CARM model, that the function of Joanne's cutting was to reduce her distress arising from derogatory voices. More crucially, she believed that the voices emanated from the care staff who were in effect threatening to kill her and wanting her to harm herself. Staff withdrawal served to increase this belief and prove to her that this self-harm was in fact what the staff desired in the first instance.

Third, it is well documented that behaviours that appear similar may serve different functions and behaviours that appear dissimilar may serve the same function (Emerson, 2001). If behaviours are then grouped together initially adopting categories such as 'self-harm' then it is likely that subsequent assessment and formulation will be inaccurate.

In considering the first aspect of CARM (the target behaviour), staff are encouraged to move away from terms such as 'self-harm' and be very explicit and concrete about the behaviour in question (e.g. 'head banging against the wall', 'cutting wrists with a razor'). Often, defining a behaviour also includes some measure of its severity based on its impact: whether the behaviour resulted in any bruising or required significant medical attention, for example, act as proxy indicators for severity). We always begin with the behaviour and its definition, which means that we work backwards within the model. Importantly, behaviours that may be functionally different are not grouped together until they have been assessed and formulated and only then if they appear to be driven by the same triggers and factors and maintained by the same factors are they assumed to serve the same function and included within the same CARM formulation. If they emerge as having different functional routes then they are subject to additional CARM formulations.

Useful questions for arriving at a clear operational definition of the target behaviour are:

- 'If I gave your colleague this description and asked them to act it out, do you think it would look identical to the behaviour that you observed?'
- 'Would I know it if I saw it?'
- 'If I walked onto the unit and did not know this person and they displayed the behaviour, would I recognise it from your description?'

The Challenging Behaviour Checklist for Psychosis (CBC-P) is also used at this stage since it encourages clearer definitions of behaviours and also allows staff to prioritise the formulation and treatment of behaviours that are the most problematic. Defining more appropriate desired behaviours clearly is also important since it provides clear guidance for staff and for the client (we provide guidance on this in Part 3 where we consider interventions).

Component 2: Vulnerability factors

Vulnerability factors in CARM constitute the dynamic stable risk factors (Douglas and Skeem, 2005) discussed in Chapter 5. This element of the model highlights the aspects of the person's psychological disposition, including their psychosis, that are most directly relevant to the problem behaviour in question. These might include delusions, poor problem-solving skills and antisocial attitudes. In treatment-resistant clients, such factors (e.g. well-elaborated and systemised paranoid delusional beliefs held with high conviction) may be less amenable to change by traditional CBT. In this instance, risk management and a focus on how the person with such beliefs is tipped into a high-risk state may be the more relevant issue. Prior to becoming violent, for example, the individual might experience an increase in pre-occupation with their delusional beliefs, develop a specific focus to their paranoia and become more distressed as a result. These exacerbations of vulnerability factors prior to the behaviour constitute *internal setting events*. The problem formulation gives a broad overview of the person's symptoms and vulnerability factors from which the clinician can select those that are most relevant to the behaviour in question.

Component 3: Setting events: external and internal

Setting events or distant triggers are factors that may make the behaviour in question more likely to occur but are still distal in time from the occurrence of the behaviour; they represent the build-up to the behaviour in question. These are traditionally described in the challenging behaviour literature (Emerson, 2001) as establishing a motivational basis for the behaviour to occur. We conceptualise setting events as potentially external in nature (e.g. having been let down by family members who promised to visit) or internal (e.g. persistent, derogatory voices, having a poor night's sleep).

Case example: Darren

Darren has high trait anger (a vulnerability factor) and is prone to interpret the actions of staff members (not being allowed to visit the local shops due to low staffing) as malevolent and to react angrily. Darren does not always respond with anger in the face of such provocative situations but may do so if, for example, he is tired (having slept poorly) or has not eaten because he slept in late and missed breakfast (all internal setting events). Having telephoned his girlfriend and asked for money from her and been refused (external setting events), this succession of factors leads to an angry outburst when he is told later by a member of staff that he has no money left for cigarettes (the trigger).

Component 4: Early warning signs of risk

Early warning signs of risk (EWS-R) are a particularly useful aspect of the CARM model. These consist of the external observable signs of internal setting events, combined with external setting events themselves (the distant triggers). In the former case, these are operationally defined, observable characteristics of the client's presentation prior to previous occurrences of the behaviour. The key is in distinguishing between dynamic stable vulnerability factors that are always present and acute early warning signs. EWS-R fall into three key domains:

- *Contextual signs:* these are the triggering factors that push dynamic stable or vulnerability factors into a higher-risk state (the external setting events or distant triggers).
- *Visual signs:* these are aspects of internal setting events that can be objectively observed by others (e.g. increased voice activity might be observed by the person withdrawing to their room and playing the radio noisily).
- *Verbal signs:* these are those aspects of internal setting events that can be

observed only through verbal interactions with the client or from their verbal interaction with others. For example, increases in hostility and suspicion might be observed by negative comments about a particular staff member being made and increased insults to other patients.

The following are typical examples of how vulnerability factors and setting events can be translated into EWS-R:

Vulnerability factors

- High trait anger.
- Paranoid pan-situational beliefs about MI5 plotting to kill him (high conviction).

Internal setting events

- Increased (state) anger.
- Increased preoccupation with threat and increased likelihood of something bad happening (in-situation beliefs).

Contextual EWS-R

- Delay in family arriving.
- Taking leave from the unit to go to busy supermarket.

Visual EWS-R

- Red face, pacing, chain smoking.
- Unplugging electrical equipment.
- Spending more time in room.

Verbal EWS-R

- Speech contains references to police and government.
- Grunts or is monosyllabic on approach (usually very talkative).
- Expresses that particular staff are undercover agents.

Component 4: Immediate triggers

Immediate triggers are those internal or external events that lead immediately, or almost immediately, to the occurrence of the behaviour. These again can be viewed as being both external (e.g. an insult from a passing stranger) or internal (e.g. a voice command). Often they will be an interaction of the two: a delusional misinterpretation of a real-world event.

Component 5: Reinforcers

The final aspect of the CARM formulation concerns those areas that are traditionally the focus of applied behavioural conceptualisations. Reinforcers are a consequence that follows the behaviour and as a result make the behaviour more likely to occur in the future, or maintain its future occurrence. Positive reinforcers are where a consequence is added as a result of the behaviour occurring (e.g. the person gains attention, the person is moved to a different setting). Negative reinforcers are where something is removed as a result of the behaviour occurring (e.g. easing of distress through cannabis use) and this makes the behaviour more likely to occur in the future. This can also include the removal of aversive stimuli (e.g. shouting at staff until they no longer make demands of the individual or encouraging them to do things they do not wish to).

Both positive and negative reinforcers may be either internal or external (e.g. drinking to dampen down or remove voices or to reduce stress [internal negative reinforcement] or hitting another resident to increase one's status [internal positive reinforcement]). We have found that where the internal reinforcement is a relief from delusional distress (e.g. hitting another resident to reduce a perceived threat), then such safety-seeking behaviours (Freeman *et al.*, 2001) are resistant to change by traditional means of behavioural contingency management. This is understandable since people consider it worthwhile or necessary to keep themselves or important others safe, even if this means a loss of leave or movement to a more secure environment. In this instance, CBT interventions aimed at the level of setting events may be more appropriate. It is important to note that not only may behaviours be reinforced but also beliefs. As in our case example above, Joanne's belief that staff wanted to harm her was reinforced by their withdrawal. Similarly, social withdrawal by a client who perceives themselves as socially inadequate or defective (echoed by derogatory insulting voices) may result in others withdrawing from them and reducing their attempts to interact with them. This is likely to reinforce their negative (pan-situational) self-beliefs.

Case study 1: John revisited

In Chapter 4 we described John and constructed a shared person level formulation for him based on traditional models of CBT. This broad formulation was a useful starting point for those working with him and was translated into a service level formulation to identify clear treatment targets. In John's case, one of the clear barriers to participation was his potential violence to other individuals, as an inpatient and in the community. This was severely limiting his access to his desired goals of increased access to the community and moving home with his mother. However, this did not help the team to fully understand the precise relationship between his psychotic symptoms and the relevant internal and environmental factors that were triggering and serving to maintain his problematic behaviours. Using the CARM model we were able to formulate John's violent behaviour towards others. He was assaulting other patients on a regular basis (the focus and target behaviour of our first CARM formulation). This was distressing for everyone and resulted in frequent limits being placed on his leave. In the distant past, John had also made a number of serious suicide attempts including an attempt at hanging himself and another when he ingested bleach (the focus and target behaviour of our second CARM formulation). His paranoid (pan-situational) beliefs about the Killer Queen and her intention to crucify him, remove his eye, cut off his genitals and hurt his mother were noted as important. These could now be reframed as the context for his in-situation beliefs (the focus of subsequent team CBT strategies) that others were acting under the influence of the Killer Queen. Clarifying the setting events and triggers that gave rise to these in-situation beliefs now became the goal of assessment. Once these were understood more fully, attention could then be turned to how the setting events and triggers presented in the form of EWS-R. Finally, the task of the CFT was to elicit and further assess the reactions from others that could be reinforcing these beliefs and this behaviour. The process adopted by John's Case Formulation Team (CFT) for constructing and sharing this CARM formulation are described below.

The process of developing a CARM formulation for John

Typically there are five key stages involved in developing any CARM formulation. These constitute a detailed functional analysis of a given behaviour and include the process of sharing the formulation with the team and using CARM as a means of further challenging any unhelpful staff beliefs.

1 Clearly defining the behaviours and prioritising the behaviours for treatment

Often stages 1 and 2 can be completed concurrently. Problem behaviours identified through using the CBC-P often provide a reasonable first definition of the behaviours to be targeted and help to prioritise which ones are most important to be addressed. Frequency/recency ratings along with ratings of the severity of its impact can be used in order to rank order behaviours. John's CFT used the CBC-P to first generate a list of his difficult problematic behaviours. The team next clearly and operationally defined these target behaviours in order to arrive at idiosyncratic descriptions of them:

- verbal threats of violence to other patients;
- hitting doors and on one occasion putting his fist through a plaster wall;
- breaking a bench outside in the courtyard by hitting and kicking it;
- physical assaults on other male patients involving John punching them repeatedly in the face;
- suicide attempts (a number of years ago): putting a rope around his neck and attempting to fix it to a ligature point, drinking bleach;
- Engaging in repeated delusional speech with others (which made him look odd to others in public and in the past had resulted in threats from members of the public).

In John's case he would typically and most frequently hit other clients or staff in the face with his fist, causing moderate levels of injury; these were typically not life threatening but severe enough to frighten staff and cause injury. This behaviour was clearly prioritised over his other potential intervention targets. Other behaviours such as violence to objects occurred at a similar frequency and were kept in mind as potential early warning signs for John's assaultative behaviour.

2 Introducing the ABC framework

This stage involves both education for staff in the CARM framework (if previous training has not been given) and education about psychosis and the cognitive therapy ABC model. The key points are for staff to understand the framework and the purpose for it. This serves as an important guide for subsequent information gathering.

The ABC model is introduced and applied to both the client's behaviour and linked at each stage to staff beliefs and behaviour: the client's behavioural consequence (Cb) is also the activating event or A for the staff beliefs (B) and their feelings and behaviour (Ce and Cb). This highlights the differing beliefs that staff may hold and introduces some initial doubt and room for change. Importantly, this framework also allows staff to discuss and acknowledge their feelings of dealing with the client. This aspect is more fully described in Chapter 8. In John's case, many staff felt frightened or angry and had mixed views either that he was ill and had no control (and therefore his behaviour could not be changed) or that he had full control and was engaging in the behaviour purposefully. The aim at this stage, however, is simply to allow different views to be expressed without challenging them directly. Rather, it is emphasised that all views are valued. They may have already been addressed by the person formulation and so this stage may not be necessary. Alternatively, they may be addressed by the subsequent sharing of the CARM formulation itself. Staff are, however, introduced to the notion that in CBT the aim may be to alter distress and reduce behaviour but often this involves changing and understanding the beliefs involved. The notion that altering John's beliefs and interpretations of events might reduce his behaviour was introduced in the ABC framework. The need for understanding things from his point of view (the shared phenomenology principle) was emphasised if things were to change. Staff were then encouraged to generate some initial ideas for the CARM template, from their experience of John. The previously completed person level formulation template for John also provided an overview of his broad delusional beliefs and symptoms, which served as a starting point. Staff were less clear, however, regarding what happened in specific situations and had avoided asking him afterwards.

3 Information gathering by John's CFT

CFT tasks for information gathering are now agreed. In John's case, the second author and team psychologist interviewed John regarding recent incidents of violence and threats of violence. The aim was to use the ABC model to elicit John's beliefs about these incidents (this process is described more fully in Chapter 9). The focus of this was to elicit John's 'in-situation beliefs' (detailed in Table 7.1, p. 118) and their triggering events. John's care coordinator agreed to review previous incidents detailed in John's notes, using the CARM framework. The named nurse instigated a behavioural monitoring system with the whole MDT using the Challenging Behaviour Record Sheet for Psychosis (CBRS) (see Appendix 4).

The above sources of information allowed a number of emerging hypotheses regarding the function of John's violent behaviour to be confirmed by combining them in order to triangulate the evidence for each of the CARM model components (following sharing and revising the template with John and the broader team).

The assessment also revealed how in the past John had experienced intrusive thoughts about harming children in the family whom he cared about. He had no desire or intention of harming them but felt that he might lose control and do so. This could lead him to become suicidal as a means of saving the children. This information was retained for use with his second CARM formulation (shown in Figure 7.2, p. 115).

4 Completing the CARM formulation template

The team then met to draft a CARM formulation. The same process as used for the person level formulation to agree the formulation elements was adopted. The CFT also shared the CARM formulation at this stage with John who, whilst lacking in insight, agreed with the reasons for his behaviour as detailed in it. No revisions were made in light of this.

5 Sharing and revising the template with the broader MDT

The CARM formulation was then shared with the broader MDT during a series of team handovers (to take account of shift patterns), again adopting the process used within the team meeting for the person level formulation described in Chapter 4. The two completed CARM templates for John are shown in Figures 7.1 and 7.2.

Case study 2: Adrian

Adrian has an extensive history of violence to others and substance misuse. His main presenting problematic behaviours concern suicide and deliberate self-harm (DSH). Following his CFT's assessment of him, all three behaviours (violence to others, suicide and DSH) emerged as being driven by similar factors and so in his case are dealt with in a single CARM formulation. Adrian also has features of borderline personality disorder (as evidenced by scores on the Millon Clinical Multiaxial Inventory III [MCMI-III]: Millon, 1994), which manifest as a tendency towards black-and-white thinking about others and alternating between dependence on others and feeling rejected or criticised by them. At these times he feels anger towards them. Adrian also has a strong fear of abandonment (as revealed by scores on the Young Schema Questionnaire: Young and Brown, 1990; and the MCMI-III, and tends to react to activation of this schema by DSH. Borderline personality traits are also manifest in a history of impulsivity and polysubstance use along with alcohol binges. Whilst Adrian's DSH is clearly related to underlying traits, it appears to currently function as a means of coping with psychotic symptoms. Adrian's DSH behaviours have taken a variety of forms. The majority have involved suicide attempts by various means, with the exception of cutting, which was formulated as a means of coping with distress resulting from psychotic symptoms. Adrian holds a paranoid delusional belief with near 100 per cent conviction most of the time that a wide range of people (including staff members) are attempting to physically hurt and experiment on him. A related pan-situational belief is that staff members can read his thoughts and speak to him in his head by means of a 'mind machine', although this is not always in operation. This delusion is secondary to experiencing auditory hallucinations, which make derogatory comments about him, threaten him and command him to commit suicide. The voices are not obviously nursing staff but he assumes them to be so by default. He does not feel his psychologist or his psychiatrist are involved.

Figure 7.3 illustrates our CARM formulation for Adrian.

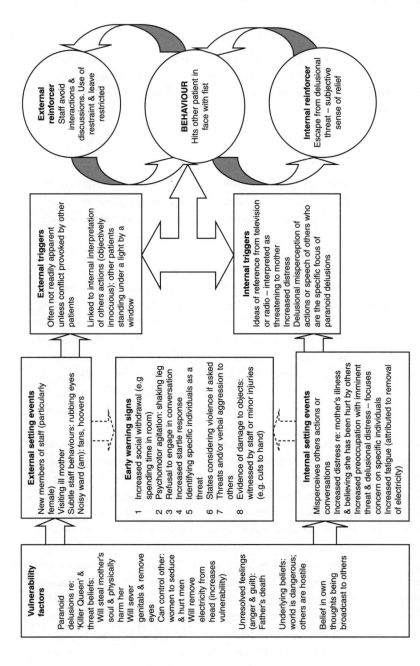

Figure 7.1 CARM formulation of John's violent behaviour.

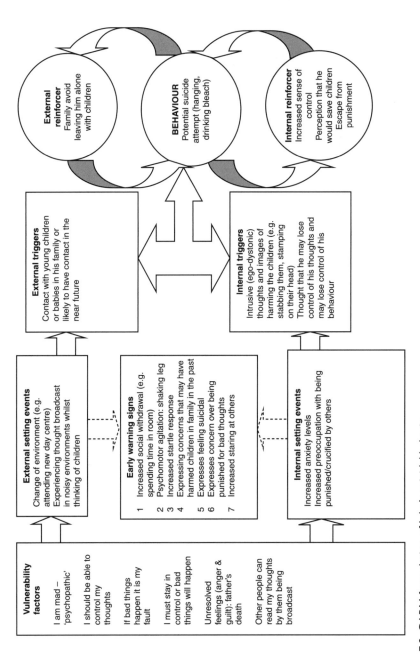

Figure 7.2 CARM formulation of John's suicidal behaviour.

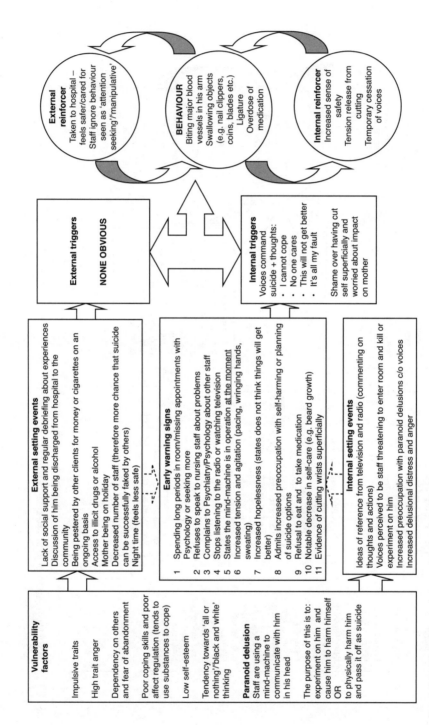

Figure 7.3 CARM formulation of Adrian's self-harm.

A RECONSIDERATION OF CBT FORMULATIONS OF PSYCHOTIC SYMPTOMS IN LIGHT OF CARM

Targeting pan-situational psychotic beliefs (such as beliefs in voice power or persistent delusional beliefs of harmful conspiracies) is the traditional remit of one-to-one cognitive therapy approaches. What we have termed 'in-situation psychotic beliefs' can also be targeted using these approaches but the goal is usually on pan-situational belief change. This is less effective as an intervention strategy in treatment-resistant clients such as John, Winston or Joe. Pan-situational beliefs constitute the dynamic stable or vulnerability factors and apply across a broad range of situations and events. From the CARM perspective, the more useful targets are the in-situation beliefs that often drive daily distress and problematic behaviours. Whilst the client interprets day-to-day events in light of pan-situational beliefs, they are much more difficult to address.

In John's case, the innocuous actions of staff members and other residents (e.g. rubbing their eyes) are interpreted as a specific threat in light of his broad paranoid pan-situational delusional beliefs. John makes situation-specific inferences or interpretations that result (in combination with other setting events and triggers) in an occurrence of the risk behaviour. In CARM the presence of in-situation psychotic beliefs may be indicated by EWS-R, allowing for early intervention by staff. When these signs are observed, staff may intervene with the specific goal of challenging the in-situation belief, preventing the occurrence of the problematic behaviour, without the pan-situational delusional belief being targeted or necessarily impacted upon. This offers a potentially valuable role for MDT members to utilise CBT techniques to reduce problematic risk behaviours; we refer to this as team-based cognitive therapy (TBCT). Table 7.1 details the targets for John's TBCT.

Adopting the CARM model makes explicit the interaction between different psychotic symptoms and beliefs and non-psychosis-related factors. CBT models of psychosis have benefited greatly from a single-symptom approach but clearly this is rarely the clinical reality and teams are left with a complex interaction of factors. The CARM model allows that some symptoms or aspects of them may act as longstanding vulnerability factors, others as setting events and others as immediate triggers. CBT models also take less account of the potentially relevant environmental and interpersonal factors (the external setting events and external triggers) that research has shown are important determinates of inpatient aggression. Overcrowding, ward occupancy levels and space per patient have all been associated with violent incidents (Ng et al., 2001; Chou et al., 2002; Sun et al., 2006). Some studies (e.g. Nijmen and Rector, 1999; Chou et al., 2002; Jansen et al., 2007) have associated increased violence with the use of seclusion (a punishment procedure). Other research has implicated time of day as a relevant factor

Table 7.1 Targets for John's TBCT

As that constitute setting events and triggers	In-situation Bs (the TBCT target)	Emotional and behavioural Cs
Noise from fan or hoover Other noises (e.g. builders)	People can hear my thoughts – they'll find out my weaknesses, know about my mother They're making the noise on purpose to access my thoughts	Increased anxiety Count backwards in head Avoid noise Anger and aggression
Staff rubbing eyes	He wants to remove my eyes	Anxiety Observe staff member suspiciously
Heard the song *Stairway to heaven* on the radio	They're taking my mother from me	Anxiety Assault patient
Voice of father says 'It's done'	My father has made it to heaven	Relief Engage with voice
Feel tired and drained	People have removed the electricity from my mind to make me vulnerable	Anxiety and verbal aggression or violence to other patients
Mother in particular pain with back during home visit	Patient [X] has hurt my mother	Anger towards domicillary staff resulting in violent fantasies

(Ng *et al.*, 2001; Chou *et al.*, 2002). A lack of structured activities and ensuing boredom has also been suggested as environmental setting events by some authors (Shepherd and Lavender, 1999). Triggering events to aggression are often identifiable and are not just a result of underlying psychopathology (Daffern *et al.*, 2007). These latter researchers also found that staff were likely to be the victims of violence because of making demands of patients (demand avoidance), because of refusing requests and the patient using aggression as a means of enforcing staff compliance or because they were the target of venting tension. By contrast, patients were more likely to be the victims for the function of expression of anger, because of compliance with instructions from others (including voices) or as a method of seeking social status. Patients and staff were equally likely to be victims of aggression designed to reduce social contact or to seek attention.

Consequently, when planning any intervention it is important to clearly distinguish between instances when a behaviour occurs as a response to an internal or external trigger in the sequel to an internal or external setting event, or as a means of gaining attention. These may all be factors in the same behaviour, suggesting a different functional route (possibly represented by different EWS-R) on each occasion.

Case example: Alice

Alice believes that she is a member of the medical team on the unit and often attempts to assess other residents by taking their pulse and keeping detailed notes about them. This has frequently resulted in her being assaulted by other residents. Alice has a longstanding belief that she should care for others, she can also get quite bored; prior to her late-onset psychosis she had a productive busy life working for an animal sanctuary. Alice also hears command hallucination telling her that she must care for others and to 'check them'. A final factor to consider is that Alice had an emotionally abusive childhood and never felt cared for by her parents.

When Alice approaches another resident to take their pulse a number of factors need to be considered:

- *Functional route 1:* Is it the case that she is responding to an understimulating environment (a setting event), becomes bored and interprets another resident's voice-related distress in the form of shouting (the external trigger) as them needing her help?
- *Functional route 2:* Alice herself wants attention from staff (a vulnerability factor) and has felt that staff have taken no notice of her that day due to staff shortages (the external setting event). She witnesses them spending time with another resident (the immediate trigger) and has learned that if she approaches another resident and tries to take their pulse, staff will intervene and spend time with her (the external reinforcer).
- *Functional route 3:* Alice hears a voice command (the internal trigger) telling her that she must 'check them', which she interprets as she must check residents' pulse (based on the pan-situational beliefs about the voice's purpose) otherwise she will be sent to hell (the pan-situational compliance belief). When she complies she feels that she has done what the voice asked (e.g. appeased it) and obtains a sense of relief (the internal reinforcer).
- *Functional route 4:* Alice approaches another resident because she sees them sitting in the television lounge (the external trigger), which she interprets as a clinic and that they are waiting for her (the internal trigger in the form of an in-situation delusional inference) and tries to take their pulse. If she succeeds, this meets her own internal standard regarding caring for others (the pan-situational non-psychotic belief) and she feels pleased with herself (the internal reinforcement).

In Alice's case, the team will need to be very skilled at identifying, through carefully observing potentially different patterns of early warning signs, or eliciting from Alice, which set of factors are operating at any given time and consequently deciding on which intervention will be most appropriate. The CARM model helps to identify these different points of intervention.

Another factor to consider is that voice hearers do not always act in response to specific voice commands or even specific beliefs as CBT models might imply. Voice commands or comments may play a role as an immediate trigger or may function as an internal setting event, which contributes to behaviour indirectly by increasing distress or agitation over a longer period (Cheung *et al.*, 1997).

Case example: Lorraine

Lorraine was insulted all morning by malevolent voices (an internal setting event), became increasingly frustrated and distressed, but felt unable to retaliate against them. When insulted by another resident, this served as an immediate trigger, tipping her into violent action.

In this case, voices function as a setting event. Addressing delusional beliefs about them may be less useful than improving coping strategies for Lorraine.

POINTS OF INTERVENTION IN THE CARM MODEL

In aiding the selection of treatment or management strategies, SAFE usefully distinguishes between high-risk behavioural excesses, low-risk behavioural excesses and behavioural deficits. This broad categorisation is a useful start-ing point when care planning as it indicates different types of interventions. High-risk behavioural excesses (as illustrated in the cases of John and Adrian) may involve treatment at the level of the vulnerability factors that are relevant to the risk in question. This might indicate one-to-one therapy or group interventions targeted at the particular risk factors. For violence this might involve addressing longstanding anger-related or aggression-related beliefs, chronic substance misuse and related beliefs, CBT for pan-situational delu-sional beliefs (if possible and not previously attempted) or the development of problem-solving skills. Working with high-risk behavioural excesses will more likely involve working at the level of EWS-R such that staff can detect the potential for high-risk behaviours before they occur and intervene to prevent their occurrence. This might involve staff facilitating the use of cop-ing skills or problem-solving skills in specific situations (the setting events level), building on work at the level of vulnerability factors. Alternatively, as in the case of Alice, it might involve working with in-situation delusional beliefs and interpretations. Finally, working with high-risk behavioural excesses will most likely involve working at the level of reinforcers to positively reinforce the person's use of more appropriate coping skills that result in the absence of the behaviour in question.

Working at the level of low-risk behavioural excesses (e.g. frequent and repetitive demands, verbal aggression, sexually inappropriate speech), we argue, will predominantly involve working at the level of reinforcers by attempting to positively reinforce either the absence of problematic behaviours or more appropriate ones, whilst simultaneously removing the reinforcers maintaining the problem behaviour. However, work may also extend to the level of immediate triggers either by altering the nature of the trigger (e.g. when and in what manner demands are made) or by ensuring that the client does not encounter the trigger in question (e.g. sexually impulsive acts which the person later regrets following being bathed by female staff). Working at the level of setting events may also be relevant. For example, if shouting functions as a means of gaining staff attention then increasing the degree to which the person is engaged in structured activities and given time with others will likely help to reduce the motivation for the behaviour to occur. This may be used alongside the use of differential reinforcement. In some cases, skills building at the level of vulnerability factors may be important.

Case example: Damien

Damien often engaged in sexually inappropriate conversations because of a lack of conversational skills and topics. Intervention involved reinforcing appropriate speech, ignoring sexualised speech and teaching and modelling appropriate skills. EWS-R work would clearly be less relevant to this level of intervention.

Working with behavioural deficits requires a quite different approach using the CARM framework. First, what the person is not doing (the behavioural deficit) should be formulated in the context of the service level formulation so that intervention targets are in line with functional and community-based goals. Second, the desired behaviours the person is required to achieve may need to be operationally defined. Working with behavioural deficits will then involve several aspects of the CARM framework. Vulnerability factors such as deficits in skills, motivation and cognitive factors (problems with planning tasks or initiating actions) will need to be considered (as in Maria's case, Chapter 15). Environmental modification (including inter-personal prompts) at the level of setting events will often be required to remove or simplify the requirements of tasks or to break things down into manageable stages and goals. Finally, successful completion of the stages will involve rewarding the person for their success by incorporating reinforcers, ideally natural ones.

SUMMARY

In this chapter we have described the CARM model in some detail and clearly set out the principles that underpin it together with its advantages over other single model approaches. CARM offers a number of points of intervention, drawing on different models that are linked through our formulation to a shared understanding of the function of each behaviour. In Part 3 these various points of potential intervention will be described in some detail. We fully acknowledge that adopting such a detailed approach is time and resource consuming but would argue that this is justified given the fact that many of our clients have often been in inpatient services or remain under the care of specialist teams for many years, with reduced opportunities to lead a full life.

Chapter 8

Working with staff and carer beliefs in SAFE

INTRODUCTION

The quality of staff and client relationships has been cited as a key determinant in facilitating recovery and reducing the risk of relapse (Penn *et al.*, 2004). This is especially true for people with psychosis as wider social networks can diminish (Randolph, 1998). Good relationships are particularly important when working with individuals who present with problematic behaviours where developing a trusting relationship is often difficult and a whole team approach is needed to avoid team splitting. This is crucial if behaviours are not to be inadvertently reinforced and also to avoid overlapping or competing approaches. In Chapter 4 we detailed how a shared person level formulation could begin the process of achieving a more shared conceptualisation of the client's distress and behaviour in general terms and placing this in the person's life context. A frequently encountered barrier to developing a shared view and consistent approach are the often negative attributions that staff and carers make regarding people who present with what can be very challenging behaviours.

A number of authors have reported on stress and burnout as commonly occurring factors amongst staff working in services for those with problematic behaviours. Burnout, cynicism and a sense of futility (regarding revolving-door clients) were frequently cited in staff working any length of time on a Psychiatric Intensive Care Unit (PICU) (Sambrook, 2008), where high levels of aggression, violence and disrespect were common. High levels of staff turnover were also reported. This latter finding is perhaps not surprising and is likely to lead to problems ensuring consistency and continuity of care and establishing meaningful, trusting and supportive relationships with clients, which are so vital in promoting recovery. A team approach involving all workers acting together, making joint decisions and sharing responsibility for clients is one way of reducing levels of burnout (Navarro and Lowe, 1995) and, we would argue, consolidating the effective management of problematic behaviour. In this chapter we review the literature on staff attributions and show how these can be formulated within a cognitive model that links to the client's behaviour and how in turn this can be addressed through the Shared Assessment, Formulation and Education (SAFE) process.

THE ABC FORMULATION OF STAFF AND CARER BELIEFS

Our person level formulation (described in Chapter 4) summarises knowledge about the client and challenges the team's broad ideas about them and their difficulties. This person level formulation, however, does not provide a ready means for addressing the more specific staff and others beliefs, which follow as a consequence of the person's behaviour. Neither does it generate specific targets for intervention. We utilise the ABC framework (Chadwick *et al.*, 1996) by applying it to the treatment team themselves in the same way that the therapist's own unhelpful beliefs about the clients may be formulated in individual therapy (see Chadwick, 2006). Adopting this framework, the client's problematic behaviours may be viewed as an activating event (A) for the Multidisciplinary Team (MDT) members' beliefs or attributions (B), these then result in positive (e.g. sympathy) or negative (e.g. anger) emotional staff responses (the emotional consequence or Ce) leading in turn to increased or decreased helping behaviour (the behavioural consequence or Cb). The staff response may then become an A for the client as it creates further evidence, in the client's mind, for their delusional beliefs (as well as working at the more traditional operant reinforcement level). Of course, the ABC model can be viewed as 'situation specific' in the same way as in-situation specific client interpretations of events as described in Chapter 4. The ABC model in the general cognitive therapy literature has been used to describe beliefs (B) that occur across a range of situations (what we referred to in Chapter 4 as pan-situational beliefs). An example of this is the belief in the power of a commanding voice (Meaden *et al.*, 2010) that occurs across a range of situations. This broad power belief or schema will drive the interpretation of situations in which the voice is active, leading to situation-specific inferences (B). This notion can be equally well applied to staff and carer beliefs. Their specific beliefs about the client's behaviours or difficulties may be rooted in the staff or carer's broader set of beliefs about the client themselves or other issues such as the nature of care or mental illness.

Before looking further at the use of the staff ABC formulation we examine the literature pertaining to which beliefs or attributions (B) appear to be most pertinent to understanding the reactions of staff and carers. In addition, we discuss some of our own research, which highlights some important distinctions between different types of attributions and also the importance of the behaviour itself in driving staff beliefs and reactions. Interestingly, this latter issue appears to have been largely neglected in the attribution literature;

this is at odds with behavioural theory, which emphasises the importance of triggering events and discriminative stimuli.

THE ROLE OF STAFF ATTRIBUTIONS AND BELIEFS IN PROBLEMATIC BEHAVIOURS: A REVIEW OF THE EMPIRICAL LITERATURE

Attribution theory asserts that attributions, or beliefs, mediate between people's experience of situations and their subsequent behavioural and emotional responses (Weiner, 1985, 1988). Attributions have been categorised broadly in four ways:

- *internality:* where the cause of a behaviour is viewed as being from within the individual (e.g. personality, effort or ability), as opposed to being externally caused (e.g. by the environment);
- *stability:* how constant the behaviour is over time or different situations (if the outcome of an event is ascribed to a stable cause, it will be anticipated with increased certainty in the future);
- *controllability:* how much control an individual is considered to have over their behaviour and its occurrence is particularly important in determining emotional responses.
- *globality:* the extent to which behaviour may occur elsewhere, as opposed to being specific to a certain situation or venue.

Causal attributions are of particular importance as they influence staff's subsequent feelings towards the client and their helping behaviour (Hastings and Remington, 1994). Attribution theory is essentially a cognitive theory stressing the importance of beliefs and appraisals as mediators of emotional and behavioural consequences, which is a basic tenet of cognitive-behavioural therapy (CBT) models. Some empirical support has been found for applying Weiner's (1988) model to staff working with learning disabled populations (Dagnan *et al.*, 1998; Stanley and Standen, 2000; Wanless and Jahoda, 2002). Sympathy and anger have been found to be key emotional responses influenced by attributions made concerning client's behaviour. Where an individual assumes another's need for help is due to uncontrollable circumstances, staff will most likely feel pity and offer help. However, if the cause for the behaviour is attributed to controllable factors, the helper is more likely to experience anger, and withhold help (Weiner, 1985). Therefore, attributions of controllability for challenging behaviour tend to lead to anger in staff and uncontrollability to sympathy. In turn, these emotional responses influence the action that the staff member makes in terms of their intervention (Stanley and Standen, 2000; Wanless and Jahoda, 2002; Rudolph *et al.*, 2004).

Dagnan and Cairns (2005) adopted Weiner's (1988) attributions of internality, stability, controllability and globality and examined the impact of the emotional responses of sympathy and anger on the subsequent intention to offer help in staff working with a learning disabled population. They found that where staff ascribed the behaviour to internal causes and where the client was seen as 'responsible' for the onset of their difficulties, then a sympathetic emotional response was less likely. Increased internality ratings were associated with an angry response by care staff whilst sympathy was found to be the single best predictor of helping intention. Contrary to expectations, this study did not find any significant correlations between controllability (for problem onset) and the emotional response of anger or sympathy, although the correlations found were in the predicted direction, in line with Weiner's theory.

Weiner (1995) has distinguished between 'controllability' and 'responsibility', arguing that whilst a person may have control over an action, they may or may not be held responsible for it. Responsibility is considered a moral judgement regarding the accountability of a person for their actions; mitigating circumstances are seen as diminishing responsibility. Weiner (1995) has suggested that the judgement of responsibility is very significant in influencing responses to negative events. This distinction is often apparent in mental health services. Someone experiencing command hallucinations and engaging in a violent assault may be held not to be responsible, particularly if they held strong conviction in the need to comply with voices perceived as very powerful (Meaden et al., 2010), although arguably they potentially have control over their behaviour. Similarly, a person holding paranoid beliefs that they are being hunted by certain individuals may assault them in the belief that they are defending themselves and have no other choice. Such arguments are often central to pleas of insanity in court. Szasz (1963), however, whilst also discussing the plausibility of 'mental illness' as a concept, has asserted that individuals remain responsible for their actions, and that a diagnosed mental illness is merely an avoidance of the consequences of one's actions, by putting the blame or accountability onto the illness. Other authors have suggested that responsibility can be further subdivided. Brickman et al. (1982) distinguish between judgements made concerning the 'development' or 'cause' of a problem (e.g. a behaviour) and judgements made about responsibility for the problem's future resolution. This is a distinction that is important in order to prevent overly simplistic assumptions regarding problem resolution. It is important in order to prevent therapeutic nihilism: the notion that if the variables that produced the problem cannot be changed, then there is no solution and little point in attempting to support the person to change their behaviour. Four models of helping behaviour have been proposed by Brickman et al. (1982), dependent on whether clients are viewed as having high or low responsibility over the onset and resolution of that problem:

- The *moral model* suggests that individuals are responsible for both the problem and its solution.
- The *compensatory model* suggests that an individual may not be responsible for a problem, but is responsible for its solution and may need support in terms of resources in order to implement change.
- The *enlightenment model* suggests that a person responsible for a problem may be unable or unwilling to solve it and may need discipline to move beyond this point.
- The *medical model* assumes that the person is not responsible for the problem or its solution and is passive and in need of treatment.

Both Weiner's (1988) and Brickman *et al.*'s (1982) models have been examined in a number of studies, of mostly learning disabled clients. Dagnan and Cairns (2005), for example, found that the attribution of controllability increased the likelihood of a judgement of responsibility being made for both the development and resolution of challenging behaviour. On occasions when staff perceive challenging behaviour as controllable, they experience more anger, and are likely to resort to more punitive interventions (Leggett and Silvester, 2003). Weiner (1985, 1988) clearly identifies the judgement of responsibility as an evaluative process. Dagnan and Weston (2006) have suggested adopting a cognitive model to examine how judgements of responsibility could be impacted upon and their relationship with evaluative processes. Dagnan *et al.* (1998) asked care staff to rate how 'bad' a challenging behaviour was alongside their judgement of how 'bad' the person showing the behaviour was. These evaluative judgements were strongly related to attributions, emotions and intended helping behaviour. An approach to research and intervention that distinguishes between the person's control over the behaviour and factors that mitigate the negative evaluation of the behaviour and the person is worthy of further study.

Applying attributional theory to psychosis

Consistent with research on learning disabled populations, Barrowclough *et al.* (2001) studied clients with schizophrenia and staff in a psychiatric inpatient setting. They found that criticism was associated with staff perceptions of symptoms being under the patient's control and stable (unlikely to change). Negative symptoms, such as poor motivation and reduced social functioning, and behaviours such as violence and aggression, were also more likely to be associated with staff criticism than positive symptoms alone. These findings are possibly associated with the fact that positive symptoms are more readily attributed to an 'illness' and therefore beyond the individual's control (Moore *et al.*, 1992; Barrowclough *et al.*, 2001). Markham and Trower (2003) looked at the effect of psychiatric labelling on staff's perceptions (focusing on the same behaviours exhibited by individuals with varying diagnoses). The finding that there was no significant difference between internal attributions for the diagnosis of borderline personality disorder and schizophrenia was contrary to the hypothesis that staff's attributions would be more internal for borderline personality disorder. The authors suggested that this lack of a significant difference may be due to schizophrenia being viewed as a more medicalised condition, and thus more readily perceive the causes of behaviours in this group as more related to external factors.

Optimism on the part of staff (e.g. that change is possible) is a further important factor, since staff are unlikely to invest time and energy in any treatment regime unless they believe that change will occur as a result of their efforts (Hogg and Hall, 1992). Sharrock *et al.* (1990) asked staff to rate behaviours commonly associated with patients with mental illness in a forensic setting. Staff optimism decreased when behaviours were rated as controllable by the client. Higher levels of staff optimism were related to increased helping behaviour, demonstrating that such consequences may be a sequel, which follows from staff's attributions.

The importance of the 'topography' of behaviour

Topography and function of the behaviour also appear to play a significant role, yet there is surprisingly little consideration of this factor in studies to date. Dagnan and Weston (2006) examined the relationship between the topography of challenging behaviour, their subsequent attributions and emotional responses and carers' use of physical interventions and their satisfaction with them. The topography of the aggressive behaviour (whether it was verbal or physical) and intervention (physical intervention or non-physical intervention) were coded from accounts of incidents supplied by carers. Attributions of control and internality were significantly associated with less satisfaction with the intervention. People who presented with physical aggression were evaluated more negatively. However, only the topography of the behaviour (whether the incident was verbal or involved physical aggression) was associated with the use of physical intervention.

Studying a mental health population, Hacker *et al.* (in preparation) asked 80 nursing staff to complete their Attribution Rating Scale (ARS) in relation to four case vignettes, each representing different types of behaviour in a client with schizophrenia. Behaviours were presented that varied in their topography along two dimensions: (a) the likely impact of the behaviour (high versus low risk, e.g. superficial self-harm versus attempts to hang self) and (b) the direction of the behaviour (directed at self or others). The ARS measures a range of attributions, including internality, stability, controllability and globality as well as emotional responses towards the behaviour, subsequent helping intention and feelings of self-efficacy. The scale was designed to separately assess different potential internal factors (symptoms of schizophrenia versus personality characteristics) as well external (environmental versus interpersonal) influences. Unlike previous research, internal and external attributions were not considered to be polar opposites. Indeed, one would not expect staff who knew the client well to necessarily attribute the cause of their behaviour to either internal or external factors but hopefully to understand the contribution and interaction of both types of factors. In support of this notion, high ratings of internality were not associated with lower externality ratings and *vice versa*.

Preliminary findings from this study suggest that different behaviour topographies attracted quite different responses from staff. Staff rated themselves as being significantly angrier in relation to high-risk behaviours directed at others. The target of the behaviour was also influential, with anger rated significantly lower for high-risk self-directed behaviours, than for high-risk behaviours directed towards others or low-risk behaviours directed at self. Sympathy ratings were also influenced by the topography of the behaviour, with higher levels of sympathy recorded in response to high-risk self-directed behaviour and lower ratings given in response to high-risk behaviour directed towards others. Self-harm behaviours, violence towards others and behaviours that sabotage treatment have previously been identified by nursing staff as characteristics of 'difficult patients' (Gallop *et al.*, 1993). These findings suggest that behaviours alone may result in certain attributions being made about a client even in the absence of any client involvement. Staff's attributions of the patient's ability to control the problem behaviour were, however, not significantly related to lower intentions to help them. Correlations between internality in terms of illness factors were significantly and positively correlated with sympathy regardless of behaviour topography and were correlated positively with helping intention in respect of low-risk behaviours.

Internality ratings in terms of personality factors were negatively associated with both sympathy and helping intention in regard to low-risk behaviours. This is important in clinical settings, where presentations are frequently more complex, and where a person may have a number of diagnoses. These findings suggest that staff may attribute behaviours to personality even in the absence of a formal diagnosis of any disorder. High-risk behaviour, however, was an exception, with helping intention positively correlated with personality factors when the behaviour was high risk and directed towards others. The perceived cause of the behaviour seemingly became less relevant here, possibly due to it having a direct impact on other people, increasing staff's motivation to help. Internality in terms of illness was significantly correlated with staff sympathy and higher ratings of helping intention.

Hacker *et al.*'s (in preparation) study suggests that in addition to the topography of a behaviour the perceived function it may have further acts as a mediating variable in influencing staff's attributions. Attributions regarding perceived function have been largely neglected but are implied with the personality and symptom factors here. Our approach to understanding and assessing function (detailed in Chapter 7) and sharing this with the treatment team is therefore crucial.

Carer attributions

Carer attributions of internality and controllability for problematic behaviours in learning disabled populations were associated with a decrease in intended helping in response to aggressive behaviours in a study by Dagnan and Weston (2006). Significant correlations were observed between the attribution of controllability and the judgement of responsibility for both the development and resolution of challenging behaviour. Sympathy was the main predictor of helping intention and was less likely when carers made an attribution that behaviour was internal to the person, and that they were responsible for its development. Sympathy was more likely if carers judged that the person had some responsibility for changing their behaviour. The carer group in this study were reported to have had relatively low levels of behavioural knowledge, which it is suggested may be an important factor.

Links to attribution theory in relation to relatives of people with schizophrenia have been made by Wearden *et al.* (2000), who suggest that patterns of expressed emotion, such as criticism and hostility, can be conceptualised as the carer's attempts to modify or change behaviours. Brewin *et al.* (1991) explored the associated attributions and emotions expressed by relatives towards family members with the diagnosis. They reported that where psychotic symptoms were attributed as internal to and controllable by the individual, a lack of sympathy and greater criticism ensued. However, where causal attributions of externality and uncontrollability were made, associated emotions of sympathy and pity were evoked. More recently, Barrowclough and Hooley (2003) reported similar findings in their study of relatives' beliefs regarding the nature of mental health symptoms. These appeared to play an important role in influencing the emotional climate of relationships, supporting Wearden *et al.*'s (2000) earlier suggestion. Relatives who were critical and hostile were found to be more likely to believe that their relative was responsible for their problems, that they could do more to control their symptoms, and that problems were more likely to endure.

Implications

Even when there are clear procedures in place for dealing with challenging behaviour, staff do not necessarily follow these (Hastings and Remington, 1994). This is possibly because they focus on short-term solutions to difficulties rather than longer-term behaviour change. There is considerable empirical evidence to show that exchanges between staff and clients with a learning disability whose behaviour is challenging, is not uni-directional (Hastings and

Remington, 1994). That is, not only does the behaviour of the client influence staff responses, but also the staff's responses will have further influence on the client. This highlights the importance of gaining an understanding of the factors that influence staff responses. Staff attributions are an important part of this understanding since they appear to mediate often punitive and unsophisticated approaches to the management of problematic behaviour in schizophrenia (e.g. being locked in a room, or secluded, given excessive sedative drugs or having privileges withdrawn: Leggett and Silvester, 2003). Use of punishment often reflects staff's frustrations rather than an effective and suitable method of problem management. These approaches can be counter-productive in addition to being unethical (Hogg and Hall, 1992). Examining attributions and beliefs about the client's behaviour may then help identify the source of such frustrations and provide an opportunity to target them. We begin this process in SAFE by first formulating staff beliefs in ABC terms and then developing the various interlocking shared formulation templates. These beliefs, together with the SAFE formulation process, become the intervention or D (disputation) in cognitive terms. This in turn may facilitate a decrease in staff burnout by reducing feelings of hopelessness and negativity and increasing staff perceptions of their own efficacy. This can be complimented through supervision, which can further focus on more broadly unhelpful beliefs regarding care and as necessary educate staff with respect to both problem behaviours and psychosis. Ultimately, this process aims to improve staff engagement with clients, create more consistency in implementing care plans and decrease the use of aversive interventions

FORMULATING STAFF AND OTHERS BELIEFS

We described above a rating scale we have developed for measuring staff attributions. This can be a helpful and practical way of conducting research in this area. However, in terms of working more directly with staff teams, we have found that the process of formulating idiosyncratic ABCs of carers and staff as described below more helpful. This is a collaborative process usually working with several staff together (the Case Formulation Team: CFT). It further helps staff to better understand the cognitive model since it is applied to themselves as well as serving as a useful process of change, since eliciting staff beliefs and explanations is itself a form of disputation, challenging the different and often contradictory beliefs that staff often hold about their clients and their behaviour.

Stage 1: Agreeing the A

As described in Chapter 7, those involved in working with or supporting the client are asked to detail the person's problematic behaviours and arrive at an operational definition of them. This is the focus of the staff ABC formulation since the behaviour provides a clear A from which to formulate. It is also important to elicit such behavioural definitions since it illustrates the distinction between the A (in this case the client's behaviour) and the B (in this case the staff belief or attribution), which is a crucial distinction in cognitive therapy.

Stage 2: Eliciting staff and carer Bs and Cs

Staff and carers are now asked about their emotional reactions to the behaviour identified (formulating the A–Ce link). This provides an opportunity for team members and carers to express the frustrations of working with or supporting the client and the difficult emotions these evoke. We adopt a non-judgemental approach and often share our own initial beliefs and feelings about the client's behaviour. We encourage them to discuss their own differing, personal theories (staff and others' Bs) about the possible function of the client's behaviour. Eliciting differing views (Bs) helps them to adopt a metacognitive view of their own beliefs, another key process in cognitive therapy (Chadwick, 2006). Staff are also encouraged to be honest about how they typically respond to the behaviour in question (the Staff Cb) and, as a team, to give opinions about what is effective and what is not. This conversation allows staff to see that there are different approaches and to model good practice. It also serves to help staff see that they may sometimes react in ways that may be less helpful and to understand the links between their own (unhelpful) beliefs and their responses. Finally, this stage serves the purpose of introducing the idea that staff may react to manage the situation as best they can at the time but that this can often be driven by their own emotional reactions (e.g. frustration). The facilitator can then begin to usefully draw a distinction between short-term management (which might in the longer term reinforce the behaviour) and making longer-term changes in behaviour and link this back to the client's longer-term recovery-oriented goals.

Stage 3: Informaton gathering: staff and carers as scientists

Staff and carers are encouraged to view subsequent information gathering and assessment (e.g. as part of the Cognitive Approach to Risk Management [CARM] formulation) as an examination of the evidence supporting or refuting their own beliefs. By examining triggers and potential reinforcers, some hypotheses and beliefs can be disputed and others supported. Previous discussions of the staff's own ABCs can now be helpful since they can more clearly understand the ABC framework and how it can be usefully applied to the client (in separating out actual triggers and client interpretations). In addition, formulating using the CARM approach helps to shift the focus towards reducing the client's behavioural response (C) rather than their symptoms (A), which is traditionally the focus in psychiatric management. Staff, and where appropriate carer, beliefs and reactions are then formulated explicitly as shown in Table 8.1.

Staff beliefs in John's case

John (first described in Chapter 3) demonstrated repeated violence towards other residents: punching them in the mouth (the operational definition). This was chosen as the formulation focus: the A for staff. Staff were then asked how they felt with regard to this behaviour, what they did when it occurred and what were their beliefs about it (its purpose or function): what did they think on the last occasion it happened to which they were a witness or in which they were involved in the subsequent restraint procedure. These were then formulated to establish the staff ABC and illustrate the cognitive model. The typical process, in this case occurring in the context of a CFT meeting, is illustrated below:

DH: So, I'm sure most of you have at some point witnessed John assault one of the other service users. What's your take on what's going on?

STAFF 1: Well I think it's just attention seeking [*internal and controllable*] to get what he wants.

STAFF 2: I don't agree, the poor guy is just driven demented by his psychosis [*a responsibility attribution of not being responsible*]. He's been like this for years, there's no way he's going to change [*stability attribution*]. It's not really his fault, is it?

STAFF 3: Usually when something happens it's because John thinks the other person is trying to harm his mum. I usually try to reassure him that we won't let anyone harm his mum or him and let him phone his mum and that seems to work.

DH: It sounds like if I understand what you're saying that you all agree on the behaviour that is the problem. Let's call that the A for you and draw it on the flipchart, okay?

STAFF: (COLLECTIVELY) Sure.

DH: You all though seem to have different ideas about why. One idea is that it's to get attention or to ensure John gets what he wants, another idea is that he's ill and has no control, and another idea is that it's because of a specific threat that John perceives to his mum and chooses to take action. You [to staff member 3] mentioned that you use reassurance and let him check his mum is okay, right? What do the rest of you try to do?

STAFF 2: Well I tell him that it's not real and that he is ill and offer him some PRN medication.

STAFF 1: I tend to ignore what he says. It doesn't make sense most of the time

Table 8.1 Staff attributions about John, pre and post formulation

Pre and post CARM	Staff A (Client's Cb)	Staff B	Staff Ce and Cb (potential subsequent client A)
Pre formulation	Punches other patient	He's aggressive and has no remorse He's ill and can't control himself	Frightened Try to avoid Sympathy Provide PRN medication Don't discuss incidents with him
Post formulation	Punches other patient	He does this to save himself and his mother It must be awful to live being that afraid John can control this – he chooses to do it for logical reasons	Sympathy Try to reassure re: threat Try to discuss incidents and defuse problems early
Pre formulation	John engages in delusional talk about the Killer Queen	He's bizarre and makes no sense – it's jibberish You can't understand him	Confused Ignore what John says
Post formulation	John engages in delusional talk about the Killer Queen	John's delusions are bizarre and complex but are consistent and understandable	Sympathy Attempt to engage in conversation and empathise
Pre formulation	Puts fist through the wall	He's done it again Nothing works	Hopeless Invest more time in other patients Stop leave
Post formulation	Puts fist through the wall	He's done this because he's afraid, he's trying to avoid hitting someone by frightening them instead	Hopeful

and I'm not going to reinforce that sort of behaviour by letting him phone his mum.

DH: Okay, let's put these on the flipchart and call them your Cs (the staff Cbs): how can you manage the behaviour?

The psychologist then goes on to draw out the different ABCs of the staff concerned. Themes within staff beliefs (B) showed that John's behaviour was attributed to personal characteristics or uncontrollable illness with little perceived opportunity for intervention or hope for change. Emotional reactions emerged as quite mixed and care responses focused on restraint, avoidance (if possible) and increasing restrictions. An initial suggestion was made at this point that symptom reduction itself may not be necessary and better management might be possible as increased understanding emerged during the formulation process.

DO FORMULATIONS HAVE AN IMPACT ON STAFF BELIEFS AND EMOTIONAL CONSEQUENCES?

Berry *et al.* (2009) conducted a pilot study to examine the impact of a team case formulation on psychiatric staff's perceptions of mental health problems caring for people with psychosis. Staff perceptions were measured before and after the intervention using the Brief Illness Perception Questionnaire (Brief IPQ: Broadbent *et al.*, 2006) and the Illness Perception Questionnaire for Schizophrenia (Lobban *et al.*, 2005). Individual scale items concerned perceived causes and control over mental health problems, as well as their stability. Measures of staff understanding of problems, negative feelings towards clients and confidence in their work were also included. Significant changes were reported in all of these domains, with increases in staff perceptions of clients' control over problems. Decreases in negative feelings were also reported in line with positive changes in relation to cognitive appraisals. (Service users are often aware of staff negative feelings towards them [Barrowclough *et al.*, 2001]. This is likely to reduce engagement and further reinforce delusional and other beliefs, in turn exacerbating or maintaining problematic behaviour.) It is unclear, however, how long term these benefits were, the study being carried out over a relatively short period of time. As acknowledged by the researchers it is also unclear whether it was the formulation itself that was responsible for change or simply the demand characteristics of the study as no control group or baseline was established.

As part of our routine work with other colleagues we measured (employing a single-case experimental design methodology) the impact of asking staff about their beliefs, treating them as working ideas and subsequently performing the tasks of a CFT as described in Chapter 4. Staff (who themselves constituted the single cases) reported marked shifts in their attributions (as measured by scores on the ARS), which were sustained up to nine months later. Change was, however, idiosyncratic, with each CFT member reporting a unique change in their beliefs and emotional reactions about the client's behaviour (e.g. improved sympathy). Subsequent levels of SAFE formulation had further differential impacts for some staff on some attributions and emotional reactions (e.g. further changes in reduced responsibility and controllability). One member of the CFT, however, showed no significant change on any ratings. Where change occurred, it was mostly associated with the ongoing implementation of SAFE (e.g. responding to subsequent person level and problem level or CARM formulations).

Our case study of John (as as shown in Table 8.1) shows how constructing a shared problem level formulation using our CARM template can produce clear changes in staff beliefs in relation to a specific target behaviour. Examining and testing out specific staff beliefs and emotional and behaviour consequences in relation to specific behaviours is important since this may differ for each behaviour (or other attribute) and will likely be unique in some way to each staff member when assessed idiosyncratically. This is the strength of utilising both the SAFE approach and the CARM model. We again illustrate this process from a CFT meeting facilitated by the second author:

DH: So if we look back now to our initial meeting and the ABCs we did of your explanations for John's behaviour, what do you make of that now?

STAFF 1: Well I can see that there are specific triggers to John's paranoia. Although one of the setting events is being left alone I don't think he does it to seek attention . . . I just think when he's on his own he gets more preoccupied without anything to distract him. The one formulation we did [at the person level] helped me to understand that John does make sense in his own way.

STAFF 2: I can see that John is ill but sometimes talking to him and sympathising with how he feels can help sometimes and I haven't always had to give him PRN [medication].

DOES BELIEF CHANGE LEAD TO A CHANGE IN HELPING RESPONSE?

As discussed previously, optimism and sympathy are linked to a positive intention to help as well as the perceived function of the behaviour and the behavioural topography. However, these studies have mostly employed vignettes in their methodology. Meaden *et al.* (in preparation b) asked staff about their emotional and behavioural (care) reactions in relation to an actual client and a recent episode of 'demanding that immediate needs were met' (a low-risk behavioural excess). Staff identified this as a problematic behaviour in management terms and found it difficult to cope with and mange effectively due to its very high frequency. Staff reported feeling annoyed and frustrated but the most strongly rated emotional reaction was sympathy. Controllability, changeability and optimism were reported but were not clear predictors of wanting to help. Actual helping was quite varied and did not relate clearly to attributions in some staff whereas in others (especially those reporting sympathy) they did: showing a corresponding helping behaviour, attempting to resolve the 'demand' in a more functionally helpful way. This is perhaps not surprising considering the attitude behaviour consistency literature. People may hold attitudes that are in conflict with their behaviour especially if it is considered unwise, immoral or objectionable in some way (Swanson *et al.*, 2001). Cognitive dissonance theory (Festinger, 1957) remains an influential and well-researched theory, which suggests that people will attempt to alter their beliefs, attitudes and values in some way so as to make their behaviour seem more acceptable: to reduce the amount of cognitive dissonance. Behaviour amongst staff towards clients may thus be influenced by a range of factors, including peer pressure, established (poor) working practices, staff stress and burnout. Addressing staff and carers' or relatives' beliefs is therefore important if care responses are to be improved but other factors will also need to be considered and addressed, including service initiatives such as those described in Part 4 of this book, especially those described in Chapter 18.

Research with relatives has suggested that when they believe their relative to have high levels of control over their problems they demonstrate greater criticism and hostility, but become over-involved when they themselves believe that they have high levels of control over problems (Barrowclough and Hooley, 2003). In addition, relatives with a more coherent understanding of their relative's mental health problems are more optimistic regarding treatment and report feeling better able to manage them (Lobban *et al.*, 2005). Previous research has also found a link between perceptions of illness being stable and criticism in both relatives (Barrowclough and Hooley, 2003) and staff (Barrowclough *et al.*, 2001). Any intervention that increases optimism regarding change may therefore bring about reduced levels of criticism. Research with relatives also suggests that the alternative perspective offered by formulation could enhance staff knowledge and increase their sense of efficacy and build optimism for change. Such change is likely to facilitate better engagement and inspire hope in the client. An essential ingredient in promoting recovery is to create a hope-inspiring environment (Perkins, 2001), which is especially important for those residing in inpatient settings for long periods.

ELICITING PAN-SITUATIONAL STAFF CARE BELIEFS

As well as developing beliefs about clients' behaviours, staff will also have developed a broad set of beliefs regarding how they should care for and support others. These will have been influenced by training, policy and guidelines, their own moral standards and personal values and possibly their own experience of mental health problems. These constitute what we have termed 'staff pan-situational care beliefs' and may constitute dysfunctional or incorrect beliefs about the nature of mental illness or represent very skewed views of mental illness based on personal experience encountered in their own lives. Psychoeducation for staff can therefore be a useful endeavour. As a useful illustration of this, during a recent training session the first author

(AM) noted how a staff member stated that she would not be able to ignore a client lying on the dining room floor in apparent distress even if it was clearly established that their behaviour was an inappropriate way of obtaining attention. This staff member explained that she could not ignore her as she [the client] "is like my mom" and "I could never ignore someone in distress". Another staff member stated that "We have got them stable and should not rock the boat".

Low frustration tolerance beliefs (typically expressed in terms of 'I can't stand it': Dryden, 1995) are, we propose, another type of pan-situational staff care belief and worthy of attention. One member of staff reported in a recent CFT meeting that they "could not stand it" when a client frequently made requests for them to rush round and deal with seemingly minor domestic crises on a regular basis. Instead, they would attempt to ignore telephone calls from the client or would visit them as requested as it was "just easier". Maintaining a boundaried team approach was thus thwarted and the client's excessive requests were reinforced, with the longer-term consequence that the client became less and less able to cope independently.

These beliefs are often difficult to elicit and require the development of a trusting relationship and non-judgemental enquiry style. However, if they are not tackled (directly or indirectly) they can serve as major obstacles to changing staff care responses and achieving consensus and consistency in managing problematic behaviour in clients.

Training, supervision and reflective practice groups can be usefully adopted here. These issues are discussed in detail in Chapter 18. However, it is worth noting here that these are often effective processes for addressing pan-situational care beliefs held by staff. Training is also very useful for addressing staff beliefs about behaviour. Surprisingly, those working in services dealing with clients with the most problematic or risk behaviour often lack in-depth knowledge regarding its possible causes in clients with psychosis. This is perhaps not surprising as it is only recently that more sophisticated understandings have been achieved regarding behaviour, such as acting on command hallucinations (e.g. Byrne *et al.*, 2006).

SUMMARY

Staff and carers working with individuals presenting with problematic behaviours, poor engagement and minimal response to standard care may develop unhelpful ways of understanding their behaviours and subsequently managing them. Staff and carers are also themselves vulnerable to stress and burnout. The process of developing shared formulations to better understand both the client's problems and behaviours and those involved in their care may be an effective process for changing these beliefs and interactions. This individualised approach may also be more successful than traditional standardised training packages in the same way that successful family interventions require idiosyncratic tailoring of the approach to meet each family's unique needs (Barrowclough and Tarrier, 1992). Formulating staff and others' beliefs using a cognitive model facilitates the development of a cognitive understanding that can then be generalised to understanding the client. It is also a more precise means of assessing specific beliefs about specific behaviours. These as we have noted earlier are idiosyncratic to each person involved in a client's care and (as we have described in relation to our CARM model) may be different for each different behaviour or type of behaviour. This process also allows those involved to become scientists themselves in being able to treat their own beliefs as testable hypotheses. This helps to move away from blaming staff or carers for their beliefs to seeing them as understandable in the face of often complex and bewildering difficulties that may be quite frightening, to working more collaboratively, developing optimism for change and beginning to hold hope of some recovery.

Part 2

Assessment

Chapter 9

Assessing problematic behavioural excesses in psychosis

A Multidisciplinary Team-based approach

INTRODUCTION

In this chapter we return to the Cognitive Approach to Risk Management (CARM) model and use it as a guide to conducting a functional analytic assessment of problematic behaviours in psychosis and provide a number of useful tools and methodologies for conducting such an assessment. It is not uncommon for staff to make assumptions about the function of a behaviour (e.g. deliberate self-harm being seen as a form of 'manipulation') without gathering sufficient information. These assumptions regarding function are often implicit in the way in which behaviours are described and recorded by staff. They may, for instance, record that an individual was being 'manipulative' or was just 'attention seeking', without a clear operational definition of the behaviour itself. Emerson (2001) has noted that behaviours that appear similar may actually serve markedly different functions. Conversely, those behaviours that look dissimilar may serve quite similar functions. Hence, at the assessment stage it is particularly important to (a) be clear about the behaviours being described and (b) treat them as separate until the setting events, triggers and maintaining factors have been assessed. Function should be derived from an analysis of such factors.

Previous authors (Emerson, 2001) have also noted that the 'pathological approach' (Goldiamond, 1974) to behavioural change can frequently predominate. The pathological approach emphasises the elimination of the problem behaviour with little consideration of the functional aspects for the person involved. By contrast, the 'constructional approach' emphasises the need to establish ways in which the individual can meet their needs or respond to the situation more appropriately. The aim, therefore, is to understand the function of the individual's behaviour and to meet that function in alternative, more prosocial and less activity-limiting ways in line with the World Health Organization (WHO) model, service level formulation described in Chapter 3. This may involve encouraging the use of skills used in other situations or at other times, or the development of new skills and behavioural repertoires.

The end result of the assessment process should be to produce a CARM formulation that provides a clear and shared understanding of the client's behaviour. CARM serves both as a framework for functional analysis and as a means of conceptualising the individual's cognitive phenomenology. This facilitates team problem solving, enabling them to decide on a care plan emphasising the teaching of alternative behaviours or skills that can meet the function in alternative ways, take into account cognitive processes that mediate distress and behaviour and work towards increasing social participation.

DEFINING AND PRIORITISING BEHAVIOURS

A number of methods exist for assessing problematic and risk behaviours, including the use of structured interviews with staff, recording using Antecedent, Behaviour, Consequence charts, questionnaires, experimental analysis (by manipulation of triggers or reinforcers) and informal interviews with the team, carers and client themselves. All of these methods rely on an initial clear definition of the behaviour in question. This is the starting point, which can sometimes be difficult to achieve. One sticking point at this early stage of assessment is that clients with psychosis often present with a range of risk and problematic behaviours. Therefore, teams and families must be able to develop some sort of consensus regarding which ones are a priority for change. The Shared, Assessment, Formulation and Education (SAFE) approach offers a clear methodology for prioritising and targeting behaviours for change. First, in light of the service level formulation, behaviours that reduce social participation or the achievement of valued goals are clearly a priority. Other important considerations are the degree of risk posed to self and others, and the likely level of burden on carers or staff in terms of the effort required to effect meaningful change.

A clear, operational definition is one in which the behaviour is observable. In other words, in devising the description one should ask:

- Would one of my colleagues be able to re-enact the behaviour accurately from my description alone?
- Would new staff, unfamiliar with the client, be able to agree, when observing the client, whether the behaviour is present or absent based solely on the definition provided?
- Could the description I've given be applied to a range of behaviours which actually might look quite different?

Zarkowska and Clements (1994) contrast 'fuzzy' descriptive terms, which may be emotionally laden, pejorative or include hypotheses about function, with clear 'behavioural terminology'. Examples of poor descriptions and behavioural definitions are provided in Table 9.1.

Table 9.1 Fuzzy and behavioural description examples

Fuzzy descriptions	Operationally defined behavioural description examples
Physically aggressive	Attempts to stab fellow patient in the chest with a knife Punches staff member in the face with their fist once and then walks away Repeatedly punches staff member until they fall to the ground and then kicks them whilst on the ground and requires restraint in order to make them desist
Verbally aggressive	Shouts racist comments to members of the public Threatens to kill family members by burning down their houses Tells staff to 'fuck off' when they call at his house
Paranoid	States that other patients on the ward are talking about them in a derogatory way Fails to leave their flat even for basic needs and covers their windows with tin foil Does not trust their family to buy or cook food for them
Attention seeking	Dresses in inappropriately in revealing clothing Makes frequent complaints about physical symptoms with no apparent cause Exposes genitals when in public places Hits walls and doors
Distressed	Sits with their head in their hands, crying and talking to themself, claiming voices are threatening them Paces and wrings their hands with constant seeking of reassurance that their family are okay
Manipulative	Superficially scratches their arms with a can ring pull and threatens suicide when their demands are refused Makes repeated, unfounded accusations of sexual activity against male staff who enforce boundaries When refused a request by one family member they will ask other family members for the same thing
Impulsive	Spends money on non-essential items and runs into debt frequently Walks out in front of traffic without looking when they have argued with their family Attempts to touch female staff sexually when they are aroused despite previous sanctions resulting from this

As can be seen, fuzzy descriptions might refer to a wide range of behaviours with a wide range of functions. Subsequent assessment and formulation based on these will be unlikely to lead to successful treatment and management and may in some circumstances lead to an increase in the behaviour or emergence of another (if the function is not addressed). Training is important but should also be supported by more structured standardised measures to better ensure consistency. A pre-defined checklist may be more useful for monitoring and assessment purposes. The Challenging Behaviour Checklist for Psychosis (CBC-P: see Appendix 1) is a 116-item measure (and has room to add further challenges in the boxes below). It removes the onus on staff to be clear in their initial definitions and descriptions. We devised the CBC-P from a questionnaire completed by staff across three High Dependency Units for people with psychosis alongside those derived from the empirical risk literature. In line with Emerson's (2001) definition of challenging behaviours and the WHO model described in Chapter 3, behaviours are accordingly rated on a severity/risk scale, which ranges from 'no challenge' to 'social exclusion' through to life-threatening physical impact. A behaviour scoring a 4 may also cause emotional distress and social exclusion since a high score can encompass those below it. Some behaviours are clearly going to involve high levels of physical risk by their very nature (e.g. 'attempting to remove sense organ') whilst others are more ambiguous in terms of their risk (e.g. 'banging head against objects'). Therefore, some items have only a limited range of possible risk scores. By using these ratings behaviours can be prioritised for further assessment and construction of a CARM formulation on the basis of the level of risk that they present.

The frequency with which the behaviour occurs is also an important factor in prioritising assessment and intervention. The recency and frequency rating on the CBC-P is designed to capture behaviours that are historical as well as those that are more recent and more frequently occurring. The CBC-P thus also provides a measure of acute risk by examining recency and frequency. If behaviours have not occurred recently then the frequency becomes a less important consideration, whilst those that are more historical may be assessed through a systematic review of case notes and using our Personal, Social, Developmental and Psychiatric History Assessment (see Appendix 3). Those occurring more recently and frequently may require the use of more observational methods as detailed below.

The CBC-P therefore provides a useful starting point for generating a profile of the client's problematic behaviours for subsequent intervention using the CARM framework. It can also be used to inform the shared risk formulation in conjunction with our Early Warning Signs of Risk (EWS-R) methodology, discussed in the next chapter. The CBC-P can be further used to monitor change over time and to help determine the level of supervision or monitoring required. We have developed a simple computer scoring package that automatically eliminates any behaviours that score a '0' on risk or severity (since by definition they are not problematic) and eliminates any behaviour scoring a '0' on frequency/recency (since the behaviour in question has never been exhibited by the client). The program then orders behaviours from high to low risk and then by recency/frequency. It highlights any that have occurred in the last month which are especially relevant when making decisions regarding the granting of leave for inpatients or adjusting the frequency of visits or level of supervision required in the community.

Behaviours associated with the highest risk will, generally, automatically be the primary target of treatment. However, if they are historical (e.g. assault with a weapon) and do not present an imminent risk, then they may not form the basis of the team's current efforts for assessment. In which case, other behaviours that are more of an immediate management problem but of lower risk may become the main focus of assessment efforts and intervention plans. Nevertheless, historical high-risk behaviours will at some point require a care plan that takes into account the circumstances under which they occurred and whether these may occur again in the future and, if so, what action should be taken.

The team will also need to agree whether to target other less risky behaviours or those that may be easier to change first. The rationale here is that this will increase the team's motivation for change and raise hope that things can improve (thus further addressing staff beliefs regarding optimism for change). Such change may also promote optimism in the person displaying the problematic behaviour and build hope for future recovery.

It is important to note that sometimes staff can struggle with how to define a 'unit' of behaviour. A 'unit' of behaviour is the behavioural definition in the CARM model used to assess the triggering and maintaining factors. What constitutes that 'unit' will vary across behaviours and clients. For example, there may be different forms of self-harm (as in the case of Adrian in Chapter 7), or there may be a series of behaviours which occur in rapid succession: shouting at staff, hitting walls, threatening staff and then punching a member of staff. In Adrian's case the forms of deliberate self-harm served two different functions and were not part of the same behavioural category. In the second example, however, the chain of behaviours occurring in one incident in rapid succession might be usefully considered a single unit for intervention purposes. It would still, however, be important to define the elements of that behavioural chain clearly. Where the co-occurrence of behaviours is unclear (e.g. whether a behaviour forms part of a chain or is a unit) then monitoring of each behaviour and the degree to which they correlate will need to be conducted, as described below.

ARRIVING AT A CARM FORMULATION

Having agreed the target behaviour for intervention and arrived at a clear operational definition, the next step is to conduct a shared formulation with the staff using the CARM framework. This process was detailed in Chapter 7 but a few key points are worth noting here. The process will typically include the identification of setting events, early warning signs, triggers, and potential reinforcing or maintaining factors. This can be done by:

- reviewing previous recorded incidents of the behaviour;

- interviewing the staff who have witnessed the behaviour in question;
- initiating structured recording by staff;
- interviewing the client about their behaviours.

In addition to the process carried out by the Case Formulation Team (CFT) we commonly employ the CARM framework for group sessions with inpatient staff at handover times. The staff with whom we work will have had some training in the CARM framework in order to be able to understand the model and terminology used. The framework is then used to structure a discussion based on the team's shared experience of the client. It is often useful prior to this meeting for the most involved clinician to have reviewed incidents from notes using the elements that comprise CARM as a guiding framework. It is not uncommon for staff to disagree on triggers, setting events and potential reinforcers and they are encouraged to openly hypothesise about these. Operational definitions will again be important to clearly describe triggers and setting events and to give reasons for their ideas about potential reinforcing factors. As noted in Chapter 7, working with behavioural deficits requires a somewhat different use of the CARM framework and this is discussed at length in Chapter 11.

USING THE CHALLENGING BEHAVIOUR RECORD SHEET

Once some initial hypotheses are generated, it is useful to carry out structured recording of occurrences of the behaviour. This can serve to confirm or disconfirm ideas about triggers, setting events and reinforcers. Staff are typically used to filling out Antecedent, Behaviour, Consequence forms that in our experience are often confusing, with the result that they produce poor-quality information. The Challenging Behaviour Record Sheet for Psychosis (CBRS) maps directly onto the CARM framework and is more explicit about what needs to be recorded (see Appendix 4). It also importantly provides an opportunity for the observer to interview the client about their behaviour when it occurs, thus potentially providing information regarding the cognitive phenomenology of the person as it relates to the target behaviour. Information gleaned from the CBRS can also be used to clarify the CARM formulation with the team at subsequent meetings as required. It is particularly useful where behaviours occur relatively infrequently, as is often the case when working with individuals with psychosis, particularly where those behaviours are high-risk behavioural excesses. It is less useful, however, with ongoing behavioural deficits (which typically have few immediate triggers or early warning signs) or if behaviours are occurring with very high frequency. In the latter case, a frequency checklist may prove to be more practical.

USING THE IDIOSYNCRATIC BEHAVIOUR
MONITORING CHECKLIST FOR PSYCHOSIS

Using a frequency checklist such as the Idiosyncratic Behaviour Monitoring Checklist for Psychosis (IBMC-P) (see Appendix 5) involves observing the client over an agreed period of time and recording a code each time a particular pre-defined behaviour occurs. Behaviours can be recorded more quickly when they are of high frequency compared with the CBRS and the checklist allows the co-occurrence of behaviours to be clarified. The time of the recording period should be noted to observe differences in the frequency of behaviours at different times of the day or during different shifts (which may then indicate the relevance of environmental setting events or triggers such as the presence of certain staff, particular mealtimes etc.). Additional factors such as hypothesised triggers or reinforcers can also be coded as trigger codes (T) or response (from others) codes (R) (which may act as reinforcers):

- being asked to do something or not to do something (T1);
- being refused a request (T2);
- the presence of a particular staff member or type of staff member (T3);
- staff member taking them for a walk when they begin shouting at other residents (R1);
- another resident giving them a cigarette (R2);
- being left to stay in bed after telling a member of staff to get lost (R3).

The exact nature of the codes for behaviours, triggers and responses as well as the frequency of recording will be dependent on the client's presentation and the resources available. Staff may record every 15 minutes or every hour or even every shift may be more appropriate depending on the frequency of the behaviour in question. Alternatively, if the behaviour occurs very frequently then time sampling may be required: for example, the client is observed for a 15-minute period every hour and recordings are not carried out outside of this time unless for serious incidents. Similarly, if potential Early Warning Signs of Risk (EWS-R) have been identified these can form their own coding system on the IBMC-P in order to determine their validity in predicting the behaviour in question.

The information obtained from the CBRS or the IBMC-P can be used to determine which behaviours co-occur as a behavioural unit. It also allows a clear determination of which events or triggers typically precede or follow the behaviour and may be important in determining its function and devising subsequent intervention programmes. However, at this stage of assessment we are simply monitoring and recording, leaving hypothesising about function to the shared formulation meeting with the CFT. Requiring team members to fill in measures such as the CBRS or IBMC-P can also be useful as a means of establishing their commitment to working with the client. We might conceptualise this as staff homework. If staff members do not complete the forms then we might ask what will be their motivation to work with the client to achieve, often difficult to obtain, behavioural change.

INTERVIEWING THE CLIENT: OBTAINING THE CLIENT'S ABC

Interviewing clients about their risk or problematic behaviours is a crucial element of assessment but not one that is always possible. Research evidence suggests that clients may give a more accurate account of the actual frequency of risk behaviours than official records, which tend to provide an underestimate (Monahan *et al.*, 2001). Furthermore, interviewing the client will most likely be the only way of understanding the psychotic phenomenology involved and engaging the client in a change process. Clearly, clients with psychosis may not share the view of the Multidisciplinary Team (MDT) that their behaviour is either a problem or indeed unreasonable. The client's goals agreed as part of the service level formulation (Chapter 3) and completion of the Recovery Goal Planning Interview (see Appendix 2) can be drawn upon here to support the client and motivate them to see that engaging in such a change process is aimed at reducing the barriers towards them achieving their recovery goals.

It is helpful for staff to develop and adopt a curious, collaborative and non-confrontational style with the client whilst not condoning their inappropriate behaviour. It is usually important to intersperse normal conversations about day-to-day events with discussion of the problem behaviour in order to prevent the client from disengaging from the conversation too early by feeling overly pressured. The emphasis should be on striking a balance between expressing concern over the consequences of the problem behaviour for the client and for others, whilst showing a desire to understand, from the client's perspective, why they feel the need to engage in the behaviour in question. It is crucial to adopt the stance that the client must have had a good reason from their point of view. The emphasis should be on highlighting the inappropriateness of the behaviour, NOT the badness of the person (another cognitive therapy technique). Open-ended questions will be more useful in eliciting accurate information than closed ones:

- What prompted you to do that?
- When did that happen?
- When did you first notice that?
- How did you figure that out?

It may also be useful to enquire about times when the client has encountered the same problems but have managed them or responded in a different way.

This introduces the notion of choice and responsibility for the behaviour even in the presence of a subjectively justifiable trigger. Whilst acknowledging the positive result of their behaviour (from their perspective) it is important to enquire from the client's point of view about any downsides to their behaviour, which might be used as a motivation for change. This might include being unpopular with others, guilt over harm caused (even if it is seen as necessary by the client to protect themselves) or the risk of jeopardising their freedom and independence. Whilst interviewing the client it is important to remember that clients will vary in their willingness or indeed ability to give an explanation for their behaviour. The clinician should be attuned to potential limits in the client's ability to communicate or label feelings, express motives or indeed the ability to recall the events in question.

The cognitive ABC framework discussed in earlier chapters is particularly useful when examining psychotic reasons behind problematic or risk behaviours. In this instance, the C is the client's behaviours (Cb) and emotions (Ce). The B is their belief or interpretation of events and the A is the antecedent, activating event or trigger. When interviewing clients to obtain information regarding triggers it is important to note that on many occasions the client will provide a B–C explanation. Interviewing John soon after he had punched another patient in the face demonstrates this clearly:

JOHN: He was going to cut off my penis so I hit him.

Here we have a belief: the (delusional) threat of castration from a fellow patient, with a behavioural response of physical assault. What we do not know is the actual trigger from John's point of view that led to that interpretation. The assessment interview continued as follows:

DH: That must have been terribly frightening. I can understand why you felt that you needed to protect yourself. Unfortunately you have now lost your leave and hurt someone you thought was a friend. What did Adam do to let you know that he was coming to hurt you?
JOHN: God told me he was going to do it.
DH: What did God actually say to you?
JOHN: He said to look out.
DH: Oh . . . okay, did Adam do anything himself to indicate that he was out to get you?
JOHN: No, not really but I'm sure he was.
DH: So let me make sure I've got this right . . . you heard God say 'look out' [the actual A from the client's point of view] and you took that to mean that Adam was coming to castrate you . . . understandably you felt frightened and ended up lashing out at him [Ce and Cb]. The result of that was that you felt safer but now you've lost your leave and Adam isn't talking to you?

Note how in this example the actual A or trigger is an internal psychotic experience. In this case, the cognitive-behavioural challenge might occur at the A–B link: the voice saying 'look out' may not have referred to the potential castration and so the behaviour may have been an inappropriate response. This challenge can occur without challenging the broader beliefs about the power of the voice, its purpose or the need to comply. Alternatively, the staff member might challenge the credibility of the voice: whether the voice was lying or had malicious intent to ruin John's friendship with Adam and get him into trouble (intervening with the broader beliefs about voices). Finally, the staff member might explore alternative responses to the threat even if the threat was real (the B–C link), which might carry fewer consequences for the client, for example seeking help from staff. We revisit the intervention possibilities in later chapters. In other cases, the trigger may be observable in the real world but may not be immediately obvious without an understanding of the client's internal world.

On another occasion John assaulted a staff member without any obvious immediate trigger. The following one-to-one session focused on clarifying the presence (prior to the assault) of EWS-R identified as indicating increased preoccupation and distress (associated with his paranoid delusions about the Killer Queen):

DH: John, I've heard from the staff that you've been very distressed this morning and about half an hour ago you hit Mary [staff nurse] in the face. Can you tell me what happened?

JOHN: Mary is in league with the Killer Queen, she was going to blind me and then go after my mother.

DH: So I'm guessing you felt. . . .

JOHN: Terrified . . . and angry, yeah.

DH: So, you believed Mary was going to blind you and then hurt your mother . . . and . . . you felt terrified and angry . . . [John's B–C explanation].

JOHN: Terrified . . . and angry, yeah.

DH: Tell me, what did Mary do to indicate this was her intention?

JOHN: I don't know what you mean.

DH: What did you notice about her that warned you?

JOHN: She was rubbing her eyes like this [gestures].

DH: I see . . . so you saw Mary rubbing her eyes [the actual A or trigger] and that meant that she was coming to blind you [belief or interpretation of the A] so, feeling angry and frightened [Ce], you hit her [Cb].

JOHN: Yeah!

In both examples DH uses the ABC framework to elicit the actual A, from the client's point of view. Eliciting the A clarifies whether or not the behaviour is being driven by objectively understandable triggers (e.g. actual provocation by other clients or staff) or whether the behaviour is being driven by psychotic interpretations of innocuous events (in light of broader delusional ideas). This process can be summarised using a CAB framework:

1   Ask about the behaviour (Cb).
2   The client gives a B–C explanation (belief and behaviour).
3   If the emotional consequence is not clear, clarify it (obtain the Ce).
4   Enquire about the actual A that led to the interpretation or belief.
5   Establishing the A–B link: 'So A happened and you took that to mean B?'. This is important as it constitutes the basis for staff intervention: team-based cognitive therapy (TBCT). The intervention is then targeted at the in-situation beliefs: challenging the interpretation of events, rather than more traditionally targeting the pan-situational belief (members of staff, in this case Mary, are in league with the Killer Queen). If this belief is challenged, greater resistance is likely to be encountered.
6   Reflect back the information gleaned from the CAB process as an A–B–C chain: 'So A happened and you took that to mean B and you did/ felt C)?'. This serves to socialise the client into the model, making them more receptive to TBCT.

The same CAB framework can be used to elicit both immediate and distant triggers (setting events) but requires separating out the As further. The eliciting of early warning signs is discussed in more detail in the next chapter.

SUMMARY

In this chapter we have outlined a number of methods for assessing behaviour and its possible function/s. These methods include interviewing staff and clients and structured behavioural recording. All aim to elicit information related to the components of the CARM model for a particular client's specific behaviour. The approach emphasises establishing clear operationally defined definitions of the behaviour. Ideally, information should be triangulated across different sources to increase the validity of the subsequent CARM formulation. In reality, this is not always possible if the client engages poorly or is unable to offer an explanation for their behaviour. Early warning signs, however, may compliment this approach. By carefully defining these signs and observing them, a picture can be built up over time of which factors when present reliably predict a given behaviour. We turn to this methodology in the next chapter.

Chapter 10

Identifying early warning signs of risk

The notion of early warning signs has been most commonly applied to the prediction of psychotic relapse. A widely accepted method described by Birchwood *et al.* (2000) seeks to identify an idiosyncratic relapse signature, which comprises the unique set of signs and symptoms for an individual that warn of an imminent likelihood of psychotic relapse. Interview-based techniques, checklists and card sorts have all been developed to elicit these early warning signs of psychosis (EWS-P) with both carers and patients. These signs once identified can be used to construct the relapse signature; essentially the order in which idiosyncratic signs and symptoms occur over a particular time period. Whilst utilising this approach to predict risk has been discussed anecdotally in the literature (Collins and Munroe, 2004), there has been little attempt to develop a systematic reliable method for compiling early warning signs of Risk (EWS-R). We have drawn on current best practice methods employed for identifying and intervening to prevent psychotic relapse to devise an acute dynamic risk measure. Using checklists and monitoring forms, a risk signature can be devised that can subsequently be used to help predict, in this case, the imminent likelihood of the specified risk behaviour occurring and offers potential points of intervention for clinicians to enable them to better manage risk. In this chapter we describe how to devise a EWS-R signature for individuals with problematic behaviours.

EARLY WARNING SIGNS OF RISK

EWS-R form part of our Cognitive Approach to Risk Management (CARM) formulation and support both team-based cognitive therapy (TBCT) and risk management in general. The importance of avoiding 'fuzzy' definitions (as described in Chapter 9) is particularly important here. Monitoring EWS-R is most relevant to high-risk behavioural excesses where the frequency of occurrence is relatively low, and the impact is high (a score of 3 or 4 on the Challenging Behaviour Checklist for Psychosis: CBC-P). The aim is to prevent any occurrence of the behaviour if at all possible. Unlike EWS-P,

EWS-R may fluctuate more rapidly and over a shorter time period and can then resolve quickly after the occurrence of the risk behaviour. They may relate to transient changes in psychotic symptoms or mental state that do not amount to an actual psychotic relapse (indeed many treatment-resistant clients might be seen as almost always 'relapsed'). They may also involve non-psychotic or environmental triggers. A useful working hypothesis, unless evidence emerges to the contrary, is that different behaviours may have different sets of triggers and setting events and hence potentially different warning signs. Therefore, a single client may have a defined set of early warning signs for potential assault, and another quite distinct, but potentially overlapping set for an increased risk of suicide.

The construction of an idiosyncratic EWS-R signature provides a method for Multidisciplinary Team (MDT) staff to carry out short-term monitoring of high-risk behaviours within an inpatient or community setting. It may also be of use in helping relatives or carers to know which particular signs to bring to the attention of services. It is important to remember that when identifying EWS-R for a specific behaviour, signs may sometimes occur without being followed by the risk behaviour. In other words, their presence may indicate a raised probability of occurrence but does not guarantee it. Furthermore, what may be an early sign for one client may be a daily occurrence for another and thus serves no useful indication of acute risk for them. In line with the CARM model, the EWS-R must represent a change in the client's presentation above and beyond their own baseline: they must indicate in some way the presence of setting events as opposed to ongoing vulnerability (dynamic stable) factors. It is for this reason that the main focus when completing the EWS-R plan is to identify visible changes in the individual's behaviour, thinking and feelings and distinguish how they differ from their normal daily functioning. It is therefore important to be detailed and specific when describing any signs and associated behaviours.

TYPES OF EWS-R

In devising this method we have identified three types of commonly occurring early warning signs that require assessment:

- *Contextual signs* are the distant triggering events that can be reliably associated with an increase in the likelihood of the problematic behaviour occurring in the past. On this basis, if present, they may represent an increased level of acute risk. Such factors might include visits from family, levels of disruption on the ward, conflict with neighbours or team members and social discrimination in the community. These are the triggering factors that push dynamic stable or vulnerability factors into a higher risk state (the external setting events or distant triggers).

- *Visual signs* are those aspects of internal setting events that can be object-ively observed by others. They are the behavioural manifestations and may take a variety of forms: withdrawing to one's room (due to increased perceptions of threat), playing the radio loudly (to drown out derogatory voices), pacing (due to increased anxiety), talking to oneself (in response to voices), crying (due to low mood), staring fixedly at staff (hypervigi-lance to threat) or wearing particular clothes (to disguise oneself in order to fool voices about their whereabouts).
- *Verbal signs* constitute those aspects of internal setting events that can only be observed through verbal interaction with the client or from their verbal interaction with others. For example, increases in hostility and suspicion might be observed by the client making negative comments about a particular staff member and increased insults directed towards other patients.

IDENTIFYING THE CLIENT'S EWS-R

Ideally, staff should be able to agree on what the EWS-R are and identify whether they are present or not over a given period. The presence of early warning signs should be associated with the occurrence of a clearly specified high-risk behaviour. When compiling EWS-R for an individual client, we ask those most involved with the client (usually the Case Formulation Team [CFT]) to consider the three types of signs described above. As a first stage, team members complete the EWS-R Checklist (see Appendix 6). This serves as a semi-structured interview and is designed to act as a set of prompts organised around the three types of EWS-R. These signs are those we have found to be most commonly identified by team members in both inpatient and community settings to be associated with the behaviours that make up the CBC-P. It is not an exhaustive list and team members are encouraged to offer other suggestions for early signs at this point. EWS-R can also be derived from nursing or case notes along with information from the Challenging Behaviour Record Sheet (CBRS) distal trigger section. Each of the signs on the checklist are generic descriptions and further refinement in line with behavioural principles will subsequently be required in order to operationalise each sign as it occurs for that individual in relation to the specified target behaviour. For instance, contact with family (a contextual sign) may relate to contact with a specific family member and be defined as 'being telephoned by sister instead of a visit'.

Once each sign has been clearly defined then the order in which they occur should be considered. This is the 'signature' aspect of the process and may require several attempts before the process can be reliably identified. The purpose of ordering signs into what is in effect a timeline is that there will be a greater chance (especially in community settings where observation will be less frequent) to intervene. For some individuals, their signs may all occur together or occur very closely in time, making a timeline less relevant, but usually a process unfolds comprising of early, middle and late signs. EWS-R should be at the level of setting events and should represent a potential build-up to the high-risk behaviour in question. They should not be something that is always present as a symptom or behaviour since this will be of little use in predicting risk behaviours (this would be at the level of vulnerability factors in the CARM model).

Case study 1: Kate

Kate has a diagnosis of schizoaffective disorder and co-morbid features of borderline personality disorder. She regularly uses a variety of substances in attempts to both elevate and lower her mood. She has experienced frequent inpatient admissions often for lengthy periods. These usually revolve around suicide attempts (hanging, cutting her throat and ingesting poisons) or episodes of self-harm, being sexually disinhibited in public and threatening members of the public and the team. Kate has never disclosed an abuse history and remains closed about much of her past. A number of attempts to engage her in psycho-logical work have failed and she remains erratically engaged with her Assertive Outreach Team and their interventions.

Following both CARM and shared risk formulations the target behaviours (for monitoring and intervention) were agreed as being sexually disinhibited (the focus of the CARM formulation) and self-harm (as this, if poorly managed, resulted in 'attempted suicide'); the topic of the shared risk formulation. Kate's EWS-R for both behaviours are detailed in Tables 10.1 and 10.2 and are

Table 10.1 EWS-R for Kate's target behaviour 1: wearing minimal clothing and approaching strangers in the street for sex

	Type of EWS-R	Typical presentation	Operationally defined EWS-R
Earliest signs	1 Increased speech and flight of ideas (verbal sign)	Kate usually talks little about her personal life and goals or plans for the future	Kate talks rapidly, expressing great (unrealistic) plans for the future
	2 Increased use of alcohol (visual and contextual signs)	Kate usually drinks only when going out with friends	Operationally defined EWS-R: drinks 1–2 bottles of wine daily (may present as intoxicated), empty

(Continued Overleaf)

Table 10.1 Continued

	Type of EWS-R	Typical presentation	Operationally defined EWS-R
			bottles are apparent in her flat (visual signs) and will often still be in bed at midday when the team visit (contextual sign)
Middle signs	3 Buying lots of new clothes (verbal and visual signs)	Kate only buys new clothes occasionally and only one or two items	Operationally defined EWS-R: Kate begins buying several items of clothes from teenage fashion shops
Middle signs	4 Kate begins wearing inappropriate clothes (visual sign)	Kate normally wears casual clothes such as jeans and T-shirts	Kate presents wearing minimal clothing (e.g. very short skirts)
Late signs	5 Talking openly about sex (verbal sign)	Kate usually talks very little about her personal life	Kate talks openly about sexual matters (e.g. people who she thinks want to have sex with her including members of the team)

Table 10.2 EWS-R for Kate's target behaviour 2: cutting the underside of upper and lower arms with a kitchen knife

	Type of EWS-R	Typical presentation	Operationally defined EWS-R
Earliest signs	1 Break-up of a relationship (contextual sign) *Kate finds it very difficult to cope following the end of a relationship*		
Earliest signs	2 Increased distressed calls to the team base (verbal sign)	Kate contacts the team infrequently (usually only when she has problems with her benefits or her flat)	Kate calls the, team in an agitated state, crying and asking for visits most days (where she asks for reassurance about relationships)

Middle signs	3 Increased substance use (visual sign)	No evidence of substance misuse	Daily cannabis use (evident on visits from the smell in her flat)
	4 Emergence of psychotic symptoms (visual and verbal signs)	No evidence of psychotic symptoms	Actively responding (talking back) to voices (visual sign) and expressing paranoid ideas about ex-partners trying to kill her and steal her soul (verbal sign)
Late signs	5 Increased distressed calls to the team (verbal sign)	In an agitated state, crying and asking for visits most days (asks for reassurance about relationships) *Typical presentation in early phase*	Kate calls the team in an agitated state, crying and asking for visits every day (where she asks for reassurance about relationships)

contrasted with her normal presentation in order to facilitate clear monitoring and identification of the emergence of EWS-R from what is relatively good social functioning.

Constructing these EWS-R for Kate has enabled the team to intervene earlier. There has subsequently been a reduction in the number of reported incidents of both behaviours. These have in turn reduced her use of hospital-based care.

Case study 2: Paul

Paul has a diagnosis of paranoid schizophrenia although it has been questioned whether in fact he has a paranoid personality disorder, as reflected in his scores on the the Millon Clinical Multiaxial Inventory III (Millon, 1994). He also presents with anger control problems and has a long history of behavioural problems and relationship difficulties. During the past five years, Paul has deliberately set six fires (usually in bins). In Paul's case the CFT completed a CARM formulation having agreed to focus on fire setting as the key barrier to participation. Paul's EWS-R for this behaviour are detailed in Table 10.3 and are contrasted with his normal presentation in order to facilitate clear monitoring and identification of the emergence of EWS-R from, in Paul's case, ongoing chronic symptoms and poor social functioning.

Constructing these EWS-R for Paul has enabled staff to prevent further instances of fire setting.

Table 10.3 EWS-R for Paul's target behaviour: fire setting by dropping lighted matches into bins

	Type of EWS-R	Typical presentation	Operationally defined EWS-R
Earliest signs	1 Discussion of move on at CPA review (contextual sign) *Paul copes poorly with the thought of move on since he feels safer on the unit and has some outstanding debts with local drug dealers*		
	2 Increased reporting of symptoms (verbal sign)	Paul rarely talks about his actual symptoms of mental illness or paranoia in general	Paul will tell his psychiatrist in ward round that he is hearing voices telling him to harm others and that he is feeling angry much of the time
Middle signs	3 Decreased medication compliance (verbal sign)	Paul demonstrates erratic compliance with regards to accepting medication but can always be persuaded by nursing staff to comply even if this is an hour later	Paul's compliance with medication declines. He will refuse consistently over days and will swear and shout at staff if approached
	4 Decreased self-care (visual sign)	Paul maintains an acceptable level of personal hygiene and a good self-care routine, with little to no prompts	Paul's personal hygiene decreases as observed by his hair being poorly groomed and being unshaven. He needs prompting to wash and may begin to have slight body odour
Late signs	5 Checking bins for lighting fires (visual sign)	Paul does not check the bins	Paul walks around the unit checking bins to see what they contain

RELIABILITY AND VALIDITY ISSUES

The starting point for ensuring reliability and validity is to be clear that one has a behavioural definition of the early warning signs that can easily be observed by others without substantial disagreement. We recently undertook a pilot study to determine the validity and reliability of the EWS-R methodology (Meaden et al., in preparation a). We investigated specifically whether nursing staff could agree on the relevance of early warning signs to the client and their behaviour. We were also interested in whether the EWS-R identified by the named nurse, once behaviourally defined, could be accurately stated to be present or absent by other nursing staff with day-to-day contact with the client. If staff cannot agree on which signs are important or whether they are being displayed at any given time then the methodology will be of little use in risk prediction and prevention. EWS-R signatures were compiled on 24 inpatients with chronic psychosis and problematic behaviours residing at two High Dependency Units (HDUs). The checklist was initially completed by the researcher and the named nurses or most-involved clinicians. They were then asked to construct operational behavioural definitions of these signs with the guidance of the researcher, who was a trainee clinical psychologist (a member of the research team). This was done in relation to one high-risk behaviour for each client. Other staff were then presented with these signs along with 'dummy' ones that were not relevant to the client in question but had been relevant to other clients. Staff were then asked to rate how relevant they thought each EWS-R was for the client and risk behaviour in question. In addition, they were asked to rate whether the EWS-R and the behaviour in question had been present over the preceding week and, if so, how frequently.

The findings indicated that staff not initially involved in constructing the EWS-R signature (e.g. they were blind to which items were rated by the named nurse as dummy or real) rated real EWS-R as more relevant to the client and their behaviour than the dummy signs. However, when staff (excluding the named nurse or most involved clinician) were asked to rate the relevancy of 'real' items compared with each other, staff reached only a 'fair' level of agreement on which items were more relevant than others ($\kappa = 0.25$–0.29; 'fair' agreement as determined by Landis and Koch, 1977). The most commonly occurring EWS-Rs were increase in demands being made by the patient (n = 14), increased swearing or bad language (n = 13), social withdrawal (n = 13), staring (n = 12), pacing (n = 11), refusal to take medication (n = 9) and responding out loud to voices (n = 9).

In summary, nursing staff appeared to be able to agree on relevant versus non-relevant early warning signs. However, when subjectively rating which were the most important or predictive, staff reached some level of agreement but this was not high. When nursing staff were asked to rate whether the pre-defined EWS-R were present over the last week (present or absent), staff rating the items independently reached a 'moderate' level of agreement

(Landis and Koch, 1977) with a Kappa value of 0.42 ($p = < .01$). When asked to rate the more subtle aspects such as how frequently the EWS-R had been present in the last week, the agreement was only 'fair' ($\kappa = 0.296$; $p = < .01$).

It would seem then that there is some evidence that staff can agree with each other and with the named nurse on which EWS-R are relevant and if behaviours are pre-defined clearly then they can agree on whether they are present or absent over a given time period of around one week. The results of the study also showed that staff can reliably rate the presence or absence of the problem behaviour itself over the last week. Unfortunately, no relationship was found between the occurrence of the EWS-R and the occurrence of the risk behaviour in our study. This may be for a number of reasons. First, there was a relatively low base rate of the behaviours in question (only nine out of 24 clients displayed the behaviour in question over the time period) and with a small sample and rating only over one week it is difficult to conclude an absence of a relationship. Second, staff may have intervened to prevent the behaviours as the client was in an inpatient setting, which would mean that EWS-R may be present but not the behaviour due to staff intervention. Third, the relationship between the presence of EWS-R and risk behaviours over time is not likely to be perfect in that EWS-R may only occasionally lead to the behaviour. In fact in the clients who displayed no behaviour in the time period there was between one and nine early warning signs present. The predictive validity of the methodology, therefore, has yet to be fully established and will be the aim of further studies by our group. However, the methodology does appear to have face validity with the MDT staff with whom we have worked. Furthermore, qualitative examination of the data revealed that all clients who displayed the behaviour over the past week had at least three of their idiosyncratic EWS-R present with a mean number of EWS-R of just over six. Therefore, there was no instance where the behaviour occurred and it was not preceded by the presence of EWS-R.

DEVISING ACTION POINTS

A frequent question once the EWS-R have been identified is 'what to do next?'. As illustrated in Chapter 6 on shared risk formulations, clear action points should be tailored to guide intervention following the detection of EWS-R. We illustrate this process in the case of Jim.

Case study 3: Jim

Jim is a man with schizoaffective disorder and co-morbid mild learning disabilities. He has a history of attempted rape and sexually inappropriate behaviour, including rubbing his penis against females and exposing himself. The target behaviour chosen was exposing genitals (which itself may be construed as a EWS-R for more serious sexual behaviours). The typical signs and the order in which they occur are given below along with actions to be taken.

EWS-R: Increase in sexualised speech

The nature of verbal interactions is marked by repeated sexual content.

Action to be taken:
Staff to encourage Jim to participate and engage in non-sexualised speech, not attending or responding neutrally to any sexualised speech and conversing with him when he talks about non-sexual matters (this will also assist in improving his interpersonal skills more generally).

EWS-R: Developing fantasy relationships with female staff

Referring to specific female members of staff as his girlfriend.

Action to be taken:
Staff to gently but clearly remind Jim that they are a member of staff and that it would not be appropriate for them to be his girlfriend but also to explore his reason for thinking this and utilise cognitive-behavioural therapy (CBT) techniques to gently challenge the evidence offered in support of this belief.

EWS-R: Being overly intimate

Stroking, attempting to hold hands, attempting to kiss or hug staff members or visitors.

Action to be taken:
Staff to gently but firmly physically intervene to prevent such contact.

EWS-R: Stalking

Closely following specific females around the ward and invading their personal space.

Actions to be taken:
Staff not to positively reinforce Jim's over-familiarity with specific staff by hugging or providing close personal contact.

Jim to be placed on level 3 observations immediately if he is following specific female staff around the ward and continually invading personal space. Level 3 constitutes close supportive observation (within arm's length) applied when a patient is assessed and demonstrates imminent risk.

This action plan proved effective in terms of reducing Jim's sexualised speech, and his stalking and inappropriate touching behaviours. However, he continues to develop fantasy relationships about female staff.

SUMMARY

In this chapter we have outlined in detail a methodology for assessing clients' EWS-R for use with high-risk behavioural excesses. The aim is to help staff predict such behaviours in advance of their occurrence and to intervene at an early stage. Such intervention will be the subject of later chapters. The EWS-R methodology appears to be reliable and can be used by multidisciplinary staff although its validity warrants further investigation. The EWS-R methodology can be usefully used with the CARM or shared risk formulations, as required.

Chapter 11

Assessing behavioural deficits

INTRODUCTION

Behavioural deficits are defined as behaviours that the individual does not display which one would reasonably expect to be present in someone of their age and cultural background. In other words, what is the individual not doing that one would reasonably expect them to do? For example, they may fail to attend to hygiene or personal safety, may be unable to cook for themselves, may be unable to use public transport or may fail to engage in conversation with others.

There is, as discussed in Chapter 1, an additional distinction to be drawn between those behavioural deficits that might pose a high risk to self and those that pose a lower risk. A failure to take prescription medication for a physical health problem such as diabetes, for example, can have serious cognitive and physical effects for the individual involved. Indeed, issues relating to physical health are particularly pertinent since the physical health of people with schizophrenia and other types of severe mental illness can frequently be poor (Phelan *et al.*, 2001) and they may have higher rates of morbidity and mortality compared with the general population (Harris and Barraclough, 1998). Problems such as poor memory or lack of insight may also impact on the individual's ability to maintain good self-care and their engagement with multidisciplinary care plans relating to health issues. Self-neglect may extend to the neglect of children or other dependants, which may require the prompt input of social services. The Shared Assessment, Formulation and Education (SAFE) approach does not aim to meet all of these needs but clear assessment processes employed as part of SAFE can aid in identifying such needs. Other behavioural deficits (e.g. not speaking or communicating) may be more or less risky depending on the other issues present (e.g. poverty of speech might be associated with a failure to report physical pain or may simply be a barrier to engagement). Issues relating to skill in managing money may be worked on over time but if there are issues of exploitation then assessment of mental capacity under the Mental Capacity Act 2005 may need to be implemented to safeguard the individual.

The assessment framework presented in this chapter and the interventions described in Chapter 14 will apply to a broad variety of behavioural deficits and attempts to elicit longer-term change. There is still an issue with respect to the level of risk and the timescales and urgency of dealing with the problem. The timescale over which an absence of the desired behaviour is acceptable and the urgency of intervention required will vary with the behaviour involved: someone not brushing their teeth for several days may be acceptable as part of a care plan. However, sporadic compliance with anti-epileptic drugs will likely increase the risk of seizures. Here, closer monitoring and prompting by staff might be required.

In this chapter we focus on a rehabilitation approach to assessing behavioural deficits using the service level formulation and the Cognitive Approach to Risk Management (CARM) formulation. We draw heavily on ideas from the field of rehabilitation of people with acquired brain injury since it has much to offer to the rehabilitation of people with psychosis in a number of respects. First, neurorehabilitation is generally very goal focused and targeted at maximising independence and social participation. Second, in acquired brain injury, impairments or symptoms cannot often be changed but rather the focus of intervention is at the level of increasing the person's independence even with persistant impairments; this approach is therefore particularly pertinent with highly treatment-resistant clients. Third, as we shall see shortly, there is evidence that people with negative symptoms/behavioural deficits frequently have co-morbid cognitive problems not dissimilar to those seen in patients with neurological conditions. Before considering the assessment of behavioural deficits it is worth giving brief attention to the relationship between negative symptoms, behavioural deficits and cognitive impairment.

NEGATIVE SYMPTOMS AND BEHAVIOURAL DEFICITS

In discussing behavioural excesses we have largely focused on the positive symptoms of schizophrenia such as voices or delusions. As discussed in earlier chapters, the reason for this is that existing evidence suggests a greater association between risk behaviours, such as violence and attempted suicide, and positive symptoms. By contrast, the negative symptoms of schizophrenia have shown less association with risk behaviours. They are, however, very relevant to understanding and working with behavioural deficits. Negative symptoms include flattening of affect (including poor facial expression of emotion, reduced eye contact and body language), decreased fluency and content of speech (alogia) and an inability to initiate and persist in goal-directed activities (avolition).

These are quite clearly deficits in normal behaviour. However, other behaviours evident in people with schizophrenia that are not typically thought of as negative symptoms may also be viewed as representing behavioural deficits. The *Diagnostic and statistical manual of mental disorders* (4th edition, text revision) (DSM-IV-TR) (American Psychiatric Association, 2000), for example, describes 'grossly disorganised behaviour' as a symptom that can include behavioural deficits, such as 'appearing dishevelled', 'problems in preparing a meal' or 'maintaining hygiene', as well as behavioural excesses. Since negative symptoms are expressed essentially as changes in behaviour and behavioural deficits are present in the description of other symptoms of schizophrenia, we prefer for the purposes of psychosocial interventions to focus on the term 'behavioural deficits'. Such deficits represent barriers to participation or 'activity limitations' in our service level formulation described in Chapter 3 and are inherently linked into the client's goals as part of the rehabilitation process. Furthermore, in terms of the service level formulation, it is not clear whether negative symptoms represent an impairment or an activity limitation. This is also reflected in the negative symptoms literature where it has been proposed that negative symptoms may reflect variously: a neurological deficit, a reaction to positive symptoms, a result of trauma or a loss of motivation. Whatever the cause, negative symptoms and behavioural deficits are often rated as very distressing by service users and carers (Barraclough and Tarrier, 1992). They can also be the most frustrating for members of the Multidisciplinary Team (MDT) to work with since engagement and motivation are often poor and progress slow. It is not uncommon, perhaps understandably so, for these behaviours to be attributed to 'laziness' by staff or carers. This, of course, can have implications for the amount of effort people are willing to put into helping the individual (as noted in Chapter 8). In our service level formulation, behavioural deficits are clearly represented at the level of activity limitations. Of course, the impairments underlying such deficits may vary. The existing literature, however, suggests that behavioural deficits or negative symptoms have been associated with significant cognitive impairments in at least some individuals.

Cognitive impairment in psychosis

There is evidence that people with schizophrenia can show deficits across many neurocognitive domains and recent reviews suggest that there are most likely specific cognitive deficits in the context of generalised cognitive impairment (Sharma and Antonova, 2003). Estimates indicate that around 70 per cent of individuals with schizophrenia may have significant cognitive impairment with a lack of insight being the only symptom of schizophrenia that occurs more frequently (Harvey and Sharma, 2002). However, it is important to note that the degree of cognitive impairment present will vary depending on the person's pre-morbid intellectual functioning. Cognitive impairments show a greater relationship to negative symptoms than to positive symptoms such as voices and delusions. Cognitive impairments, however, do not appear to be caused by negative symptoms. Negative symptoms may improve or remain stable whilst cognitive impairments may remain stable or worsen (Leff *et al.*, 1994).

Harvey and Sharma (2002) note that the most severe deficits in groups of schizophrenic patients are in the areas of learning new verbal information, sustained attention or vigilance as well as executive functions, verbal fluency (the ability to generate words within a given time limit) and motor speed. The term 'executive functions' is an umbrella term referring to a range of higher-level cognitive functions, including attentional inhibition and attentional switching, initiation of action, planning, error monitoring etc. So-called 'dysexecutive' symptoms can include lack of ability to initiate action or thought, problems with planning, flattening of emotion, being perseverative in thought or action, being impulsive or disinhibited and being socially inappropriate. Such problems show some association to damage to the frontal lobes of the brain. Harvey and Sharma (2002) also note that there can be moderate deficits (defined as 1–2 standard deviations below the population mean) in areas of distractibility and working memory (the ability to hold information in mind for a short time and mentally manipulate that information to perform a task). Moderate impairments have also been noted in visuo-motor skills and recall of information.

Executive deficits tend to show more association with negative symptoms but cognitive deficits in patients with negative symptoms are, interestingly, not distinguishable from those in a cognitively disorganised group (Donahoe and Robertson, 2003). This is perhaps not surprising since, by definition, cognitive disorganisation symptoms also overlap with behavioural deficits. However, not all authors are convinced by a specific deficit in executive problems above and beyond deficits in general intelligence or more basic problems with psychomotor speed (Laws, 1999; Henry and Crawford, 2005).

THE ASSESSMENT OF BEHAVIOURAL DEFICITS

There is a well-established literature on the assessment of negative symptoms (e.g. Wykes and Reeder, 2005) along with a number of well-developed tools such as the Positive and Negative Syndrome Scale (Kay, 1991) and KGV scale (Krawiecka *et al.*, 1977). These scales seek to establish the presence of negative symptoms and their severity. In this section we are concerned with assessment of behavioural deficits and the potential underlying processes that can be meaningfully translated into clear care plans. Our aim remains consistent: to reduce problematic behaviours that serve as barriers to social participation, to leading an ordinary life and to recovery.

Assessing the behavioural deficit

This is the starting point. Information from psychiatric assessment (e.g. of negative symptoms) and occupational and nursing observations is useful and helps in identifying potential behavioural deficits. The Challenging Behaviour Checklist for Psychosis (CBC-P) is our main tool and offers a reasonably comprehensive (although not exhaustive) set of deficits, which are rated in terms of their frequency and recency along with their impact/ level of risk. CBC-P ratings can subsequently be used to set specific care plan goals and monitor progress, with each item representing a potential care plan goal.

Assessing cognitive impairment

Cognitive impairments have been shown to be a significant predictor of outcome in terms of social and occupational functioning and independent living (Green, 1996; Sharma and Antonova, 2003) as well as predicting success in acquiring daily living skills and in work rehabilitation (Bell and Bryson, 2001). Knowledge of such cognitive impairments is useful in planning the rehabilitation of individuals with psychosis and particularly helpful in challenging some of the attributions staff or carers may make about the function of the individual's behaviour. However, we believe that the focus of work should still be on addressing behaviour and social participation. It is not uncommon, in our experience, that multidisciplinary staff will request neuropsychological assessment for individuals with psychosis. However, the questions being asked are often poorly formulated and not easily answered directly by an assessment of cognitive function alone. Furthermore, the cause of any cognitive impairment is usually difficult if not impossible to disentangle given the complex history of many of our clients who may have co-morbid organic conditions such as epilepsy, learning difficulties and disabilities, poor education, history of significant substance misuse and other psychiatric conditions as well as the potential long-term effects of antipsychotic and other medications. In later sections of this chapter we propose an assessment and goal-setting framework for behavioural deficits, which, whilst taking into account cognitive impairment, is not driven solely by it but rather by an overarching approach to rehabilitation. Since part of this process can involve assessing the nature and severity of any cognitive impairment, this issue is addressed briefly below.

The assessment of cognition is a specialist task arguably best undertaken by clinical psychologists who have, ideally, undertaken further specialist training in neuropsychology. Occupational therapists will also be able to assess cognition but generally more with an emphasis on functional abilities. Such functional assessment (using tools such as the Model of Human Occupation Screening Tool [MOHOST]: http://www.moho.uic.edu/assess/mohost.html) is invaluable often in monitoring progress and assessing the functional impact of cognitive impairment and should be part of a comprehensive multidisciplinary assessment process. As we described in Chapter 4 (and summarised again here), when assessing cognitive problems in people with psychosis, a vast number of tools are available. The Wechsler Adult Intelligence Scale (4th edition) (WAIS-IV) provides a useful measure of current intellectual functioning and problem solving; the Wechsler Memory Scale (4th edition) (WMS-IV) provides a useful measure of memory function. One of the key areas to assess in schizophrenia is executive functioning, encompassing a range of higher-level cognitive tasks including planning, multitasking, self-monitoring, and divided and selective attention. Useful tools in this regard are the Delis Kaplan Executive Functions System (DKEFS: Delis et al., 2001), the Hayling and Brixton (Burgess and Shallice, 1997) and the Behavioural Assessment of Dysexecutive Syndrome (BADS: Wilson et al., 1996). In addition, it is often important to assess whether the person has declined from their pre-illness abilities and the Wechsler Test of Adult Reading (WTAR) can be useful in this regard. It should be noted, however, that tests of pre-morbid abilities tend to be heavily influenced by educational attainment and opportunities and this may be compromised in clients with psychosis. Finally, it is essential that clinicians consider the validity of their test results obtained in these and other instruments by considering the degree to which the individual has applied themselves to the test situation (Bush et al., 2005). A number of tools exist but the Test of Memory Malingering (TOMM: Tombaugh, 1996) has been shown to be relatively insensitive to the symptoms of schizophrenia and so is valid for use in this population as a symptom validity test (Duncan, 2005).

Assessment of physical health

As noted above, behavioural deficits can pose a high risk if they are associated with physical health issues. Since a failure to engage in normal activities can affect both physical health and compliance with attempts to address physical health issues, this particular area of assessment requires special mention. Guidelines for the treatment of schizophrenia (National Institute for Health and Clinical Excellence, 2009) heavily emphasise the assessment of physical health complications such as endocrine disorders, cardiovascular risk factors, diabetes, medication side effects, cancer and lifestyle factors (e.g. alcohol use, smoking, obesity). It should be emphasised that regular physical health checks with the client's general practitioner are essential. Usefully, Cormac et al. (2004) provide a comprehensive review of physical health assessments and possible interventions for long-stay patients, which also have direct application to those clients not in inpatient services.

THE ASSESSMENT PROCESS

The formulation frameworks most relevant to working with behavioural deficits include the CARM and service level formulation frameworks. As noted in Chapter 7, working with behavioural deficits requires a somewhat different use of the CARM framework. First, what the person is not doing (the behavioural deficit) should be formulated in the context of the service level formulation so that intervention targets are in line with functional and community-based recovery goals. Second, the desired behaviours that the person is assessed as needing to achieve for successful living may also need to be operationally defined since often there is a skill or more appropriate behaviour that needs to be acquired. For example, a client may only wash twice a week and even then with at least five prompts from staff. The desired behaviour might be for the client to wash every morning with only one verbal prompt from staff. Such goals or definitions of behaviour are far more specific and clear than those seen in the majority of mental healthcare plans (e.g. improve personal hygiene).

Having defined the behavioural deficit (refining the CBC-P items) and the desired behaviour, working with behavioural deficits may then potentially involve several aspects of the CARM framework. Vulnerability factors such as deficits in skills, motivation and cognitive factors (problems with planning tasks or initiating actions) are often the primary focus. Environmental modification (including interpersonal prompts) at the level of setting events will often be required to remove or simplify the requirements of tasks or to break them down into manageable stages and goals. In other words, setting events are considered not for the problem behaviour but for ones that might facilitate the new or desired behaviour. Finally, the intervention should include positive reinforcement for the more desirable behaviour.

The assessment of behavioural deficits can usefully be thought of as consisting of a number of stages, which show considerable overlap with the setting of goals to improve function and participation:

1 *Define long-term goals.* These should be collaboratively arrived at if possible (using the Recovery Goal Planning Interview, see Appendix 2) but also be realistic or at least potentially feasible in the eyes of the care team as well as the client. A long-term goal might be to live in an independent flat within supported living accommodation or attend college in order to obtain a computing qualification.

2 *Identify required tasks* that the individual would need to be capable of in order to reach their long-term goal. These might include:

- using public transport;
- cooking meals independently;
- being able to independently tidy and maintain their own room;

- learning the route to local shops and being able to shop with a list that staff will help the client to plan beforehand;
- maintaining personal hygiene without prompting.

3 *Identify current behavioural deficits (activity limitations on functional tasks)*. This will typically involve an assessment of the client's current engagement in the above tasks, the degree of prompting required and, if the person is not doing the task at present, an assessment of their ability to do so. Here it is best to call on the skills of an occupational therapist who is highly skilled at breaking a task down into functional units and assessing where in the performance of that task the client is struggling or failing and specifically where points of failure lie (assessment of functional skills and task analysis).

4 *Identify cognitive impairment, if relevant*. Whilst the focus should remain at the level of functional skills and tasks, it may sometimes also be important to clarify the symptoms or impairments impacting upon the client's functional skills. At this point, it may be useful to undertake a cognitive, neuropsychological assessment of the client as described above. In our opinion this assessment should have a clear focus and question, embedded within the task analysis and long-term goals. Frequently, neuropsychological assessments are requested by MDTs that are too focused at an impairment level (e.g. 'does this person have executive dysfunction?', 'are this person's memory problems a function of alcohol abuse or schizophrenia?'). Little thought is often given as to what use the results will be put. In our opinion a goal- and task-based focus is crucial in making cognitive assessment both relevant and useful. Often, a cognitive assessment is not essential and strategies can be put into place in relation to the task and their success evaluated. Clinicians should carefully consider:

- Will the client benefit from simplification and repetition of information, for instance at college or the use of visual aids? If not, will they need to rely on external memory aids?
- Can the client plan and sequence steps in a task independently or will they need to have the steps of the task listed for them in the order they are to be performed?
- Is this a function of not being able to plan *per se* or not being able to hold the information in mind long enough to monitor progress (working memory)?

5 *Set SMART goals* (small, measurable, achievable, relevant and time limited[1]). Shorter-term goals can be set to clearly define what steps will

---

1 Typically in the acronym SMART the 'R' refers to 'realistic'. In our usage we have used the word 'relevant' to reflect the fact that short-term goals are set in the context of longer-term life goals and aspirations (the social participation principle described in Chapter 2) by embedding goal setting within the service level formulation.

need to be reached in order to achieve the long-term goal. Examples of SMART goals would be:

- Mark currently only showers once a week with repeated prompts from staff. In the next three months Mark will be showering twice a week, with only two verbal prompts from staff on each occasion.
- Jane (who currently needs escorting by staff in the car from her accommodation to her computer course at college) will, in the next two months, be attending college on the bus shadowed by staff but with her taking the lead. She will return by taxi.

6   *Devise methods and strategies* by which the SMART goals will be achieved. It will be important to be clear who will provide the intervention, and be very clear about the method by which this will be achieved. This clarity is particularly important if the intervention is to be provided through unqualified staff or support workers. Without such clarity the intervention may be delivered inconsistently or by different means, which will inhibit the client from learning new skills or behaviours. Methods and strategies are discussed in Chapter 14. For the present purpose, consider a client who cannot explicitly remember things taught to them or told to them but who can learn through skill repetition. The goal might be to teach the client to plan and cook a meal independently. If guidelines are not clear, however, each member of staff may support this in a different way, altering the steps or elements, making developing the skill more complex for the client.

7   *Implement, evaluate and revise short-term goals.* This will need to be done on a regular basis either when the SMART goal is achieved, or if the client is not achieving the goal. An analysis will need to be carried out of the goal and where the task is breaking down. The steps or elements of the task may then need to be altered. This might be done by altering the goal itself (reducing steps, increasing support level etc.) or by altering the method or strategy used to achieve the goal if this is not working.

SUMMARY

In this chapter we have considered the nature of behavioural deficits and their relationship to cognitive impairment and negative symptoms in people with psychosis. A functional approach to assessment and defining goals is emphasised, drawing on neurorehabilitation technology to promote social participation. A seven-stage process of defining behavioural deficits and setting goals for care planning was outlined. In Chapter 14, interventions targeting behavioural deficits are discussed in light of the service level formulation and CARM frameworks.

Part 3

Interventions in SAFE

Chapter 12

Working with low-risk behavioural excesses

INTRODUCTION

Addressing low-risk behavioural excesses is all too often not a priority area for services or clinicians. A number of components of the Cognitive Approach to Risk Management (CARM) model provide opportunities to address such behaviours. The aim, however, is not simply to reduce these behaviours for their own sake or make management of them easier (although the latter may be desirable as it will likely engender better engagement with the treating team or carers), but rather to increase the use of more prosocial or functional behaviours thereby enabling the individual to lead an ordinary life and achieve, what for them, is some level of recovery. These are the guiding principles under which we employ the behavioural techniques and other strategies outlined in this and successive chapters.

Low-risk behavioural excesses do not pose an immediate high risk of physical harm to self or others, or a very high level of emotional trauma or distress to self or others. They may, however, be associated with potential annoyance or milder forms of distress to others or may cause embarrassment for carers or indeed for services. Examples of behavioural excesses include:

- bizarre speech or bizarre behaviours;
- verbal aggression directed towards others;
- inappropriate or sexualised comments;
- self-exposure (intentional or otherwise);
- making false accusations against others;
- overly frequent and excessive demands (e.g. for cigarettes);
- property damage (not including arson, which has the potential for inadvertent or intentional physical harm);
- urinating in inappropriate places;
- frequent somatic complaints with no organic basis.

Most importantly, these behaviours tend to limit the individual's access to normal community activities and facilities and may, in some cases, render the individual with psychosis vulnerable to harm or victimisation from members of the public. Hiday *et al.* (1999) found that patients with severe mental illness had an increased risk of 2.5 times that of the normal population for violent victimisation and Brekke, *et al.* (2001) found that they were 14 times more likely to be victims of crime, with 91 per cent becoming victims of violence.

Cognitive approaches have traditionally had less to say about such behaviours. In our experience teams often struggle with how best to manage them and may adopt methods loosely based on behavioural principles with little proper assessment of function. In this chapter we draw on such principles but utilise them within the CARM model.

LEARNING THEORY AND THE MANAGEMENT OF PROBLEMATIC BEHAVIOUR IN PSYCHOSIS

Behavioural management approaches derive from learning theory (Skinner, 1953). They are premised on the two broad generalisations of learnt behaviour. The first principle, the *law of effect*, asserts that the frequency of a behaviour is determined by its consequences or effects. The second principle, the *law of association by contiguity*, asserts that two events will become associated with each other if they occur together.

There are two main types of reinforcement that tend to maintain human behaviour or increase the likelihood of it occurring again in the future. They are defined not by how pleasant or unpleasant they are but rather by their impact on the behaviour. Positive reinforcement involves a consequence being added as a result of the behaviour occurring and that consequence increasing the likelihood of the behaviour occurring again. The term 'positive' does not refer to the quality or characteristic of the reinforcer itself (e.g. whether it is pleasant or even desired) but rather the fact that something is added in as a consequence of the behaviour. Negative reinforcement is said to occur when something is removed as a result of the behaviour occurring and the result is an increase in the likelihood of the behaviour occurring in the future. Both positive and negative reinforcers maintain or increase the likelihood of occurrence of the behaviour that preceded them and may be internal (reducing the threat of punishment from a voice) as well as external (gaining attention from staff).

For the purposes of care planning, since a behaviour can be seen as being maintained by the consequences that follow it, then in effect the behaviour serves a function for the individual since it exerts some impact on the environment. A behaviour may, for example, serve as a means of avoiding demands or aversive situations (negative reinforcement) or of obtaining tangible rewards or attention (positive reinforcement). However, just because a behaviour serves an important function for the individual does not mean that it is the most functional option. The individual who engages with benevolent voices and derives a grandiose sense of self-esteem from being told that they are chosen and special and will attain wealth and power in the future is clearly obtaining something from engaging with their voices. However, they may subsequently fail to invest in real-world relationships or make realistic plans for the future.

Of course, it is not just the behaviour of the client that may be reinforced. Staff may avoid a client who is abusive to them and thereby avoid complying with care plans. Staff, by escaping or avoiding the client, may feel a reduction in stress and a sense of relief, leading them to be more likely to avoid that client in the future. Alternatively, as in the example above, a well-meaning relative may end up helping the client too much, with their behaviour being reinforced either by reducing the likelihood they will be shouted at or by reducing a subjective sense of guilt. These patterns have been described as the 'avoidance trap' and 'benevolence trap'. Changing these patterns may mean simply educating staff or relatives about the negative effects of their behaviour on the client or providing alternative strategies or methods for dealing with the client. However, on occasion, altering the behaviour of staff or relatives may mean needing to address their underlying beliefs about the client's behaviour or indeed more general beliefs about mental health or care, as discussed in earlier chapters.

Intervention strategies based on the manipulation of operant reinforcement contingencies have been used to treat a range of overt behaviours that may be termed behavioural excesses, most notably to decrease the rate of delusional speech. In a multiple baseline design, the delusional speech of a male inpatient with chronic schizophrenia was significantly reduced by the selective reinforcement of so-called more appropriate responses (Foxx *et al.*, 1988). This reduction was found to generalise across settings and was maintained at 15-month follow-up. Similarly, in a case series of four schizophrenic patients with chronic schizophrenia (Liberman *et al.*, 1973), social reinforcement was contingent upon the amount of time that the participant engaged in 'rational talk' during a daily ten-minute interview. Compared with the baseline rate, improvements of between 200 per cent and 600 per cent were observed in the amount of time patients engaged in so-called rational talk during the contingent reinforcement condition. However, delusional speech returned to baseline levels when the patient was confronted directly with their delusional ideas. This might suggest that there was an increase in rational talk but no alteration in delusion preoccupation and/or conviction overall.

In a case series of ten schizophrenic patients (Wincze *et al.*, 1972), the efficacy of token reinforcement was compared with the effects of feedback with respect to delusional speech. Verbal feedback was effective in reducing delusional speech in approximately 50 per cent of participants but produced adverse reactions in approximately one-third of participants. In contrast, the token reinforcement reduced delusional speech in 78 per cent of participants and was not associated with adverse reactions. The reduction in delusional speech consequent on both token reinforcement and verbal feedback did not generalise to novel situations. Jimenez *et al.* (1996) reported on a behaviourally based treatment package to decrease the frequency of verbal responding to auditory hallucinations and to increase attention to important external stimuli, rather than to the hallucinations. Social and token reinforcement was contingent on the absence of overt behaviour consistent with the experience of auditory hallucinations. Compared with baseline conditions there was a significant reduction in auditory hallucinations and an increase in the subject's ability to attend to external tasks. Similarly, Belcher (1988) reported a single-case experimental design of the treatment of verbally aggressive hallucinatory outbursts by contingent reinforcement of other behaviour. This intervention resulted in a 92 per cent decrease in the number of outbursts at the end of the 20-week programme.

These approaches have, however, fallen out of favour in being applied to people with psychosis. A number of reasons can be identified for this. First, such programmes may simply have encouraged patients just to not talk about their symptoms and experiences rather than actually reducing them in any meaningful way. Second, cognitive therapy has clearly demonstrated the utility of engaging clients in discussion about their beliefs about these experiences. Third, we would argue that even when such benefits cannot be obtained from discussing voices or delusions, it may still help lessen distress in the short term and is important for understanding the person's distress and problematic behaviour.

Behavioural approaches that are more appropriately targeted have been used as part of the RAID approach (Reinforce Appropriate [behaviour], Ignore Difficult or disruptive [behaviour]) for the management of problematic behaviour in people with psychosis (Beer, 2006). Behavioural management principles have also been most successfully applied in the field of learning disability to working with individuals with challenging behaviour (e.g. Donnellan *et al.*, 1988; Zarkowska and Clements, 1994; Emerson, 2001). Unlike in RAID, these approaches typically stress the importance of interventions based on functional analysis methods to construct individualised treatment plans, with the aim of facilitating not just the elimination of problem behaviours but also the development of new skills. We argue that these principles need to be further combined with a more integrated model that takes into account the cognitive phenomenology of psychosis such as that represented by our CARM model.

MEDICATION

Medications such as antipsychotics or mood stabilisers can be effective treatments for reducing distress and behaviour. However, adherence is often an issue and by definition is less effective when employed with highly treatment-resistant clients such as those described in this book. Clozapine is recommended for treatment-resistant clients and along with adjunctive medical treatment can be helpful if an appropriate treatment process is adopted, such as that described by Beer (2006). However, medication is only likely to be successful if behaviours are purely mediated through active symptoms that can be effectively managed through medication and adherence can be fostered, or through the effects of sedation (which may be short term or be so sedating that continued use is not practicable in the long term).

WORKING AT THE REINFORCER LEVEL

A useful first step is to understand which reinforcers may be maintaining the behaviour in question. This can be examined by the use of monitoring forms or shared formulation meetings, as discussed previously. As for other components of the CARM model, reinforcers are inherently linked to the function of the behaviour. A behaviour that is followed by removal of an aversive or difficult task is clearly serving the purpose of demand avoidance, a behaviour resulting in obtaining desired tangibles from staff is serving the purpose of forcing staff compliance. In order to effect change in behaviour, therefore, a number of options are available:

- Attempt to discourage the inappropriate behaviour.
- Attempt to encourage more appropriate behaviours (ideally, the appropriate behaviours should in some way address the function or need for the client that was previously being met by the inappropriate behaviour).
- Use a combination of the two.

Discouraging the inappropriate or problematic behaviour

Once the current maintaining factors or reinforcers for the behaviour are established, then the simplest possibility for reducing the behaviour is to remove the current reinforcers. In the absence of the reinforcers the individual will eventually desist with the behaviour; this is known as 'extinction'. For example, consistently ignoring a client who lies on the floor outside the staff room in order to gain attention may lead to extinction of this behaviour. Of course, this does not really address the function of the behaviour (the need for attention), which the client might, for example, experience in the context of a neglectful childhood (a vulnerability factor).

Case example: Alex

Alex's aggressive verbal behaviour results in increased attention from staff or other clients. He is removed from all potential attention at these times (a 'time-out' procedure) for a short period following the behaviour and receives minimal interactions from staff. If the reinforcer is escape from demands (e.g. attendance at group sessions) then staff would need to ensure that the demand was not removed by Alex's verbal aggression (this is known as 'escape extinction'). One of the problems with extinction is that as the reinforcer is removed or reduced, the client may temporarily escalate their behaviour under the assumption that the reinforcer will be reinstated (a so-called 'extinction burst'). This could potentially be difficult for Alex's carers to tolerate and on occasion may place him and others at risk if it escalates to physical aggression. A successful extinction procedure requires a great deal of consistency in its application amongst staff or carers, which can be difficult to achieve.

Punishment procedures are often adopted as default procedures either where other methods have proved ineffective or where the ethical considerations of implementing a punishment programme are outweighed by the risks to the client or others of not intervening. *Negative punishment* or 'response cost' involves the withdrawal of a positive reinforcer contingent upon the occurrence of the problem behaviour, which then serves to decrease the rate of that behaviour as with negative reinforcement something is removed. Unlike extinction, the removed positive reinforcer might not be the reinforcer maintaining the behaviour initially. For example, access to trips out may be withdrawn if the client exhibits the problem behaviour even though this is not the initial reinforcer maintaining the problem. *Positive punishment* involves the presentation of a stimulus, which results in a reduction in the frequency of the behaviour. As with positive reinforcement, positive punishment involves the addition of a consequence to the behaviour. This is typically something aversive, for example being shouted at or reprimanded, or being made to complete an unpleasant task. Punishment procedures can be effective in reducing behaviours in the short term (Emerson, 2001) but as Donnellan *et al.* (1988) have noted, they have several problems:

- they can produce social withdrawal (the punishee avoids the punishers);
- they can result in aggression (retaliation);
- they can become addictive to the punisher as they often produce short-term effects;
- they suppress but do not eliminate behaviour in the longer term;
- they do not build replacement behaviours;
- they can inhibit behaviours in general other than the one being targeted;
- their effects do not generalise (they are often situation specific).

Introducing positive reinforcers (either the reinforcer already maintaining the behaviour or other salient reinforcer) for (contingent upon) the non-occurrence of the problem behaviour is likely to be much more effective as well as more ethical. For example, if a behaviour (shouting at staff) is being maintained by gaining attention, shouting at the person (punishment) will not help the person meet their needs in a more functional way. Instead, additional one-to-one time with staff doing something constructive and meaningful with the client might be provided on the basis that the client has not displayed the behaviour for a specified period of time. This clearly disrupts the relationship between the reinforcer and the behaviour and is known as 'differential reinforcement of other behaviour' (DRO). The 'other' behaviour required for reinforcers to be provided is not specified but rather reinforcement is provided for the absence of the target problem behaviour over a specified time period. A related method is 'differential reinforcement of low rate of responding (DRL): the client is reinforced by staff or carers if their behaviour does not occur above a threshold level set by staff. For example, the client might be rewarded if they have attempted self-harm less than three times in one week.

Encouraging more appropriate behaviours

Ideally, the aim of behavioural intervention should be to encourage the client to engagement in more prosocial functional behaviours, thereby reducing barriers to social participation and successful community living. Differential reinforcement of alternative behaviours (DRA) is a means of increasing the likelihood of the client displaying more appropriate, more functional and less problematic behaviours. The client is rewarded for the presence of a specified behaviour, which is not the problem behaviour, but which is, ideally, functionally equivalent to it. For example, the client may be rewarded for displaying assertive negotiation with staff rather than verbal aggression or threats of physical aggression. Alternatively, the client may be reinforced for their use of relaxation techniques and distraction as an alternative means of coping with distress as opposed to superficial scratching of the skin and hair pulling. In effect, the behaviour to be avoided is defined, as is the behaviour which is to be reinforced. Reinforcement is withheld for the problematic behaviour and only provided for the more functional behaviour. A more specific form of differential reinforcement is differential reinforcement of incompatible behaviour (DRI). To return to an earlier example, if a client lies on the floor outside of the office (in order to gain attention), reinforcement in the form of one-to-one interaction can only be given when the client is either standing or sitting (a physically incompatible behaviour). Alternatively, the client may be rewarded for engaging in conversation with other clients as opposed to talking to their voices (since vocalising to other clients is likely to suppress voice activity by occupying the speech areas of the brain).

Of course, one of the problems with DRA or DRI schedules is that the client may lack the skill or ability to perform an alternative, more functional behaviour. Hence, some work may be required to help them build an alternative behavioural repertoire, coping skills or the ability to challenge their beliefs about events to allow them to use an alternative behaviour. This requires reinforcer work to be combined with work involving other elements of the CARM model (vulnerability factors) in treating low-risk behavioural excesses.

To summarise, interventions aimed at the level of reinforcers can be achieved through a number of different methods:

- withholding the reinforcer for a problematic behaviour;
- providing reinforcement for a more appropriate behaviour (potentially combined with teaching new skills);
- providing reinforcement for the absence of the behaviour;
- providing reinforcement irrespective of the behaviour (e.g. an increase in attention generally);
- providing rewards for lowered frequency of the problem behaviour.

WORKING AT THE LEVEL OF EXTERNAL AND INTERPERSONAL SETTING EVENTS

In addition to working at the level of reinforcers, using the CARM formulation highlights other areas of potential intervention employing a number of methods. Intervening at the level of setting events can be useful either in isolation or in conjunction with reinforcer-based interventions.

Environmental enrichment involves increasing the availability of reinforcement in the person's environment, particularly of the reinforcer that currently maintains the behaviour in question. For example, if the behaviour is driven by attention and the behaviour tends to occur when the client is alone, bored or there are few staff available, then staff might schedule more interaction time with the client. This increased attention will not be based around the absence of the problem behaviour or around the presence of any other behaviour. However, since the person has more access to attention, attention becomes less salient as a reinforcer for the problem behaviour and also the setting event of loneliness and boredom is curtailed.

An alternative might be to focus on reducing the aversiveness of the environment if this appears to act as a setting event to the problem behaviour. For example, one of our clients, when the ward environment was noisy, where there was little room for personal space and other clients were in conflict with each other, became increasingly agitated and paranoid and engaged in pacing and verbal aggression. In this instance, then, the client might be given increased access to a quiet space with more privacy to engage in an enjoyable and distracting activity.

There may be other simple means of altering setting events and assessing their potential contribution should be part of any good functional analysis of the problem behaviour. For instance, ensuring that the client has an adequate diet and healthy sleep routine may reduce the motivation for problem behaviours (many of us are grumpy in the morning or if we have not eaten properly). In addition, where there is conflict with other clients or family (or family fail to visit), the client might be helped to resolve these issues in a more constructive way. If the client is refusing medication because of beliefs about being poisoned or a lack of understanding, then they may require some explanation of the purpose and costs and benefits of taking the medication. Of course, sometimes working with setting events involves working with fluctuations in mental state, which might include increased anger, increased voice activity, increased preoccupation with delusions or increased delusional or voice-related distress. We discuss the use of the CARM framework and techniques to address these in the next chapter in light of high-risk behavioural excesses. In some instances, however, such techniques may be also of use with low-risk behavioural excesses. For the present purpose, it is relevant to note that working with setting events may involve staff encouraging the use of coping skills that may be taught to the client by means of group programmes or one-to-one work. Such skills teaching would of course be addressing underlying skill deficits at the level of vulnerability factors in our CARM model. In the next chapter we also examine how a staff-based approach to using cognitive-behavioural techniques might be of use in addressing setting events for challenging behaviours.

WORKING WITH IMMEDIATE TRIGGERS

Where there are clear immediate triggers, intervention may usefully be targeted at disrupting their relationship to the target behaviour. Clients are not passive recipients in their environment. They will learn to distinguish which triggers or stimuli signal the need for the problem behaviour or the likelihood of that behaviour being reinforced in some way. For example, clients may learn that certain staff are more likely to accede to demands than others or that one staff member may be more easily intimidated and give up on making demands in the face of being ignored or verbally abused. Clients will learn which environments or aspects of their environment are signals for the behaviour to come into play, although this will not always operate at the level of being a conscious decision or indeed intentional. Working at the level of triggers may involve a number of different approaches or techniques, as described below.

Removing the trigger

If an immediate trigger is apparent then clearly the most straightforward option is to ensure its non-occurrence. If the client's paranoia is provoked by key staff then those staff may not be involved in the direct care of the client. If female staff being in the client's vicinity (as in the case of Jim in Chapter 11) triggers attempts at sexually inappropriate behaviour, then perhaps the client requires nursing by only male staff. If taking particular tablets leads to fears of being poisoned and medication refusal, then the appearance of the medication might be altered, an alternative liquid form given or the medication may need to be administered by particular staff who the client trusts. Of course, removing the triggers does not always resolve the issues in a constructive way: if certain staff are removed from working with the client due to paranoia then clearly this serves to maintain the client's paranoid beliefs in the longer term and it is likely that those beliefs will eventually generalise to other staff. However, occasionally, removal of the trigger may be useful to control the frequency of the behaviour, allowing other interventions to be attempted, and the trigger can be gradually reintroduced combined with other interventions.

Disrupting the relationship between the trigger and the behaviour

The second approach to working with immediate triggers is to disrupt the relationship between the trigger and the behaviour such that the stimulus no longer triggers the behaviour in question. For example, if a paranoid client trusts one particular staff member but not other members of the team, then other members of the team might be introduced gradually. Initially, another team member might go out on visits with the trusted team member but take a very passive role. Gradually they may take over some of the activities involved in the visit but still in the presence of the trusted team member; this can be faded gradually so that the new staff member increasingly takes the more active role in the visits. This approach can then be generalised to other members of team in a graded fashion. Furthermore, once this has been done with one or two members and the client learns that no harm has come to them, this direct experience of the client can be used to gently challenge the accuracy of their paranoid beliefs about the team. Sometimes environmental stimuli rather than interpersonal ones trigger the behaviour.

Case example: Gary

Gary had schizoaffective disorder. In addition to having marked negative symptoms, he also had a fear of water, which had generalised to a fear of being in the bathroom with staff. If staff provided too much encouragement he would lash out at them. This, coupled with poor motivation, would lead to an avoidance of bathing and poor personal hygiene, which would limit his leave off the unit and make other clients reluctant to spend any time with him. Gradually, introducing Gary to the room without initially encouraging washing but pairing the room with a pleasurable stimulus (playing his music on a CD player) was used to increase the amount of time spent in the bathroom without obvious distress. A graded approach to exposure to water was then introduced, beginning with only washing his hands and face and gradually moving on to other body parts.

Altering the nature of the immediate trigger

Sometimes there is a need to alter the trigger itself. Staff can vary, for example, how they make requests or demands of clients with some staff eliciting good compliance and a positive response and others eliciting refusal and problem behaviours. As we noted in earlier chapters, a belittling interactional style is particularly likely to trigger problems. In such instances it is useful for an independent observer to observe the interaction styles of different staff and the key successful elements to be extracted and modelled to other staff involved in the client's care. Occasionally, clients may have co-morbid cognitive or communication problems, which means that they fail to understand why demands are being made of them or why they are being refused something at a particular point in time. In such circumstances, staff may need to ensure that they adapt their communication appropriately and that they provide clear explanations of why demands are being refused or when demands can be met as a compromise. One useful technique that is often used with learning disabled clients is that of 'behavioural momentum' for non-compliance. For clients who frequently refuse a particular request or instruction it is often helpful to make a series of requests beforehand that have a far higher probability of compliance and then to request the typically refused action.

In some instances, of course, triggers can be internal such as command hallucinations or ideas of reference about everyday people or objects. Here, environmental control of triggers can be harder and may need to be supplemented with staff-based cognitive therapy to challenge the clients in-situation beliefs.

Case example: Susan

Susan was particularly prone to staring threateningly at others and making verbal threats when attending the local day centre. This was often triggered by the sound of car or house alarms nearby. She believed that this indicated that special agents were on their way to harm her. She benefited from staff members acknowledging that they could hear the alarm but that she was safe and had not been harmed in any way when previously at the day centre alarms had gone off.

In practice, these techniques will often be used in combination with each other in a way uniquely tied to a CARM formulation of the client and their difficulties. They will also often be used in combination with skills teaching, psychoeducation and traditional cognitive-behavioural therapy (CBT) techniques that are targeted at the client's vulnerability factors. Below we illustrate a number of case examples in the management of low-risk behavioural excesses in psychosis.

Case study 1: James

James had a longstanding diagnosis of paranoid schizophrenia and mild learning disabilities. He had been hospitalised for 15 years and had no desire to leave the unit. He was lacking in self-esteem and his conversational skills were poor. Over the years he had developed inappropriate bizarre and sexualised speech, which others found humourous and responded by engaging with him and laughing. He also experienced both malevolent and benevolent voices, the former having been previously associated with high-risk behavioural excesses: compliance with commands to self-mutilate and assault others. James tended to lay the responsibility for his sexualised speech on the voices, stating that they told him to say these things. However, an analysis of James' behaviour using the CARM framework revealed that at the time of his inappropriate speech, James was not responding to voices or distressed by them. Rather, the setting event seemed to be when he was not engaged in social interaction and was bored. Some staff appeared to be acting as triggers whilst others did not. Those who did were those who tended to engage with him and laugh at his comments; those who did not, often told him not to 'be so stupid' and ignored him. As James was generally quiet and would not be assertive in asking for activities or interaction, he was often left to one side. It was hypothesised that James' inappropriate speech was being maintained by positive reinforcement in the form of attention and social interaction with staff and not by voice activity. A variety of interventions were used to address this:

1   First, the amount of social interaction and activity available to James was increased. Time with staff to do pleasurable activities, such as having them read film magazines with him and discuss the content, watching favoured television programmes, playing games and cooking, were timetabled in on a daily basis.

2   These activities also provided a structure for conversation with James on particular topics; this took the onus away from him to generate topics of conversation as he found this difficult to do and would typically resort back to inappropriate speech. This intervention was therefore targeted at the level of setting events.

3   James was provided with social skills training sessions by Psychology (a vulnerability factors intervention), which involved role-playing conversations and videotaping appropriate and inappropriate conversations for direct feedback.

4   James was also provided with cue cards of standard conversation topics or openings to conversations that he could refer to on a day-to-day basis.

5   These interventions were supplemented by a DRA programme. When James was speaking inappropriately to staff, they were told to consistently say to him that they did not wish to talk to him like this and that they would talk to him when he was saying more appropriate things, referring him if necessary to his cue cards. When displaying the appropriate behaviour, staff were instructed to spend at least two minutes talking to him. Finally, if he managed to go for a period of time each day (longer as the programme progressed but initially only two hours) without behaving inappropriately then he was given positive verbal praise.

6   Over a period of several months there was a noticeable improvement in the range of topics James would discuss without cue cards. Also, the frequency of his inappropriate speech decreased and on those occasions where he was still inappropriate he was more responsive to prompts to engage in alternative topics of conversation.

Case study 2: Adam

Adam had diagnoses of paranoid schizophrenia and antisocial and borderline personality disorders. He made frequent verbal threats of aggression to staff and their families, would expose his penis to staff and also make false accusations of sexual activity by female staff being directed towards him. Since these behaviours tended to occur as a cluster of behaviours and were considered to be part of the same behavioural unit, they were formulated together. The trigger for the behaviours appeared to be conflict with his family over the telephone or their failure to visit him. In addition, he would frequently buy gifts for female staff ranging from perfume to crisps, which in the past staff had occasionally accepted. This would lead to him believing that he was having a relationship with these staff and when they did not reciprocate by agreeing to his demands on the unit or by paying attention to other clients, he would display the behaviours noted above. This was particularly crucial as this sequence of events had also led up to his index offence where he had threatened a vulnerable woman with a kitchen knife. His current low-risk behavioural excess might therefore be seen as an 'offence paralleling behaviour'. Adams behaviour was dealt with in a number of ways. First, it was decided that Adam would not be alone with a sole female staff member at any point on the inpatient unit in order to protect them from the consequences of false accusations. Staff were also educated about the problems of accepting gifts and that, whilst this appeared to be a positive behaviour, it was not to be encouraged. Female staff were to reinforce explicitly that they were not in any form of relationship with Adam other than a professional one and that any such relationship would be inappropriate and could not happen. In order to deal with the triggers, a programme of visits was agreed with Adam's family, which they felt they could maintain regularly, preventing further disappointment. Following his telephone calls home when Adam could feel rejected if the call did not go well, he was offered time with staff to engage in a choice of pleasurable activities. When staff observed Adam engaging in self-exposure or verbal threats or insults on the unit, other clients were removed from the situation (since attempts to remove Adam could result in physical assault and the need for restraint) and Adam was observed at line of sight by one staff member who provided no verbal interaction to reinforce the behaviour (an extinction paradigm). Adam was provided with a token for each half day where he had not displayed the aggression, accusations or self-exposure and if he had sufficient tokens by the end of the week he was offered a choice of trips off the unit with staff (DRL programme). In this case, reinforcer interventions were incorporated on two levels: first, reinforcement contingencies were altered immediately following the behaviour (short-term use of reinforcers); second, reinforcement was used over a period of days or weeks (longer-term use of reinforcers) aimed at providing positive reinforcement for the reductions in the problem behaviour or increases in the socially appropriate behaviour.

Over a period of six months, Adam showed some significant degree of reduction in his accusations against female staff and his self-exposure. However, difficulties in his relationship with his family continued as the family still responded to his problem behaviours on home leave by acquiescing to his demands on many occasions and there were marked difficulties in supporting them to respond differently as they had been this way with Adam for many years prior to the onset of his psychosis. Furthermore, Adam remained at high risk of recidivism as he was unremorseful about his index offence and continued to minimise his actions, externalise responsibility and to state that, if released, he would do the same again. Adam therefore remained on the inpatient unit but his behaviour was more manageable and his quality of life improved.

Case study 3: Liz

Liz had a diagnosis of paranoid schizophrenia. She was continually concerned that people were staring at her and thinking negatively about her when in public areas such as restaurants and pubs. She believed that she was being persecuted because of her special gift, which involved being able to heal other people by channelling power through her eyes (by staring) or by touching others. She felt extremely pressured to help others and believed that it was her duty to do so. Liz was poor at picking up on social signals that others were uncomfortable with her staring and would often invade others' personal space or touch them on the arm when they were not known to her. Liz would also talk at length about Jesus and her special gift to the exclusion of other topics of conversation. Her behaviour was driven both by delusional ideas but also by a lack of social skills. Liz was provided with more general training in social interactions such as maintaining an arm's length distance, turn taking and length of appropriate eye contact. It was also discussed that, as for most people in the helping professions, it was important to take breaks from helping or healing and that Liz's trip to the local pub or restaurant was to be a rest for her when she should not feel pressured into helping others. This gently challenged the appropriateness of her behaviour in the particular settings most likely to make her more vulnerable but left her delusional beliefs unchallenged. It was also agreed that other people may not share her beliefs even if they were true and that this had been her experience in the past. Team members accompanied Liz to the pub and restaurant to model appropriate social interactions and to prompt and reinforce more appropriate topics of conversation and to avoid behaviours such as prolonged staring. These prompts were gradually faded over time. Liz's delusional beliefs had been resistant to traditional CBT techniques but her history revealed that she had been valued for caring for others as a child and had felt guilt and responsibility for the death of her sibling in her early life. Liz was therefore given help to find a volunteer post where she might fulfil a useful role, which she saw as giving her value and helping others. This served to reduce the time solely preoccupied with her delusions, which had been preventing her from making more constructive plans and making real social contacts. In addition, it was hypothesised that this might in some way meet the function of her delusional beliefs in an alternative fashion.

After 12 months, Liz still continued to hold her delusional beliefs with high levels of conviction and preoccupation. She was, however, able to manage her expression of this far better and could go to local pubs and cafes for around

an hour to an hour and a half with only occasional comments (and not pro-
tracted conversations) about her delusions and without invading the space
of others. Longer periods tended to result in a deterioration in her behaviour.
Liz maintained her volunteer work and found this to be a valuable source of
self-esteem.

SUMMARY

In this chapter a number of methods for working with low-risk behavioural
excesses were examined. These include working primarily at the level of
reinforcers, using a variety of techniques. In addition, however, interventions
can be targeted at the level of immediate triggers, setting events and skills
teaching as well as including CBT elements. In the next chapter the issue
of working with higher-risk behaviours is addressed, which necessitates a
somewhat different approach.

Chapter 13

Working with high-risk behavioural excesses

INTRODUCTION

In contrast to low-risk behavioural excesses described in the previous chapter, behavioural excesses that are high risk (e.g. those involving violence to self or others) frequently raise significant concern amongst professionals, carers and members of the public. This should not mean that they are the only behaviours focused on although they may be the focus of initial targets. This is not just because they may have serious or lethal consequences but also because merely the possibility of their occurrence often means that such behaviours are focused on to the exclusion of the client's other needs and life goals, with significant restrictions or barriers being likely to be put in place. Current practice, as we have noted in earlier chapters, focuses on the use of restrictions, medication, monitoring and supervision and individual cognitive-behavioural therapy (CBT). Working at the level of reinforcers or utilising punishment strategies is a further common approach, but is problematic since ideally efforts need to be focused on prevention. Our approach draws on utilising both a shared risk formulation and the Cognitive Approach to Risk Management (CARM) model. This functional-level understanding incorporates working at the level of both case-specific cognitive phenomenology, utilising behavioural methods, and a dynamic, acute process in the form of early warning signs of risk (EWS-R). We may also integrate other approaches to risk management such as de-escalation as required.

CARM ELEMENTS IN WORKING WITH HIGH-RISK BEHAVIOURAL EXCESSES

A useful starting point for working with high-risk behavioural excesses is to develop a shared risk formulation as described in Chapter 6 since this will enable the team to arrive at a shared understanding of the pertinent risk factors and devise a risk management plan. However, it is also helpful when planning treatment to have a functional level of understanding of how these risk factors result in the target behaviour. This will aid considerably in devising intervention strategies rather than simply, as we have often observed, suggesting broad treatments such as CBT when delusions are a factor or social skills training where social skills deficits are apparent. As should be clear by now, we argue that a more detailed understanding of, in this case, beliefs and skills, and how these specifically mediate the risk behaviour in question, is needed in order to work with highly treatment-resistant clients. The CARM model is our chosen means of this analysis. The primary components most relevant to high-risk behavioural excesses are as follows.

Vulnerability factors

Where possible, the client's vulnerability factors or stable dynamic risk factors known to be connected to the risk behaviours should be targeted based on the evidence base, and assessment and shared formulation findings. This might include working with delusional beliefs driving the risk behaviours such as beliefs about the power of voices implicated in compliance with command hallucinations (Meaden *et al.*, 2010) or using cognitive approaches to substance misuse (Graham *et al.*, 2004) and anger (Haddock and Shaw, 2008). For many of the clients described, vulnerability and stable dynamic factors such as delusions are not amenable to change and they often struggle to independently self-monitor and apply the strategies or methods they have been taught without additional support. Working with such individuals may more usefully involve other components of the CARM model that facilitate staff-based interventions.

Early warning signs and setting events

For the purpose of preventing high-risk behavioural excesses, behaviourally defined early warning signs and setting events are the most useful. In the absence of self-reported changes by the client, those working most closely with the individual will need to be able to identify when such signs are present and which tend to precede the risk behaviour and intervene to prevent the occurrence of the behaviour. They signify that the individual has been pushed into a high-risk state. The assessment and development of an idiosyncratic early warning signs signature was described fully in Chapter 10 and the reader is referred to that chapter for more guidance. In terms of working with delu-sional beliefs, the focus at the setting event level is to challenge the specific interpretation of the specific situation and not to address the overall delu-sional belief. The purpose is to prevent the occurrence of the risk behaviour; it is not anticipated that the broad, pan-situational delusional belief will alter, although over time the distress and the need to act on it that it engenders may lessen. Ongoing monitoring and support will therefore be required. This is the level at which team-based cognitive therapy (TBCT) may be most useful either as an alternative or a supplement to traditional one-to-one CBT.

Reinforcers

Whilst we have argued that work at this level will be less useful because of safety reasons, reinforcement can be employed to consolidate longer-term change, helping to facilitate the adoption by the client of more prosocial, barrier-reducing behaviours. The aim of utilising reinforcers with high-risk behaviours is not necessarily to alter the contingencies immediately following the behaviour but to devise a reinforcement schedule to be adopted over a longer period, to reinforce the appropriate use of strategies and the absence of the problematic behaviour.

These elements of CARM can be successfully combined to address high-risk behavioural excesses. In line with our evidence-based principle, we draw on evidence-based interventions where relevant but also measure the impact of care plans through the Challenging Behaviour Checklist for Psychosis (CBC-P), reformulation with the team and (as described in Chapter 15) Goal Attainment Scaling.

Case study 1: John

Our main case study of John illustrates the use of TBCT in working with high-risk behavioural excesses. As an inpatient with a history of violence to others on a long-stay High Dependency Unit (HDU) he had been in hospital for many years. A key factor in John's violence towards others, operating at both the vulnerability and setting events levels, were his delusional beliefs. A number of interlocking methods were adopted, guided by the CARM framework, as illustrated below. The process was underpinned by completing the shared formulation frameworks with staff as described earlier in this book.

Component 1: Early warning signs

The Multidisciplinary Team (MDT) on the HDU compiled a set of idiosyncratic warning signs of violence, as described in previous chapters:

1   Increased social withdrawal (e.g. spending time in his room).
2   Psychomotor agitation; shaking leg.
3   Refusal to engage in conversation.
4   Increased startle response.
5   Identifying specific individuals as a threat.

6   States considering violence if asked.

7   Threats and/or verbal aggression to others.

8   Evidence of damage to objects: witnessed by staff or minor injuries (e.g. cuts to hand).

These signs were subsequently reframed into three domains, as described in Chapter 10, so that they could be easily identified. These we later shared with his family and staff at a local day centre.

Environmental changes that might be important

1   New female staff or residents or rapid turnover of these.

2   Particularly middle-aged females with blue eyes and dark hair.

3   People wearing purple.

4   Being left alone for long periods (where misinterpretations of conversations, radio, television or actions of others go unchallenged).

5   Family stresses (e.g. worsening of mother's health).

Changes in the way John appears from the outside

1   Increased social withdrawal: spending time in his room.

2   Refusal to engage in conversation when approached.

3   Increased startle response (rapid turning of his head and appears jumpy) to benign events: noise.

4   Signs of motor agitation (e.g. pronounced shaking of leg often accompanied by chain-smoking representing an increase over normal amounts).

5   Evidence of damage to objects through either direct observation or minor injuries to John (e.g. cuts to hand).

6   Threats or verbal aggression to others; gesturing with his fist.

7   Staring at individuals for a long period in a suspicious manner.

Changes that might be observed in interacting with John

1   John identifies particular members of staff or other patients as making threats to himself or his family or believes them to be in league with the Killer Queen.

2   If asked, John acknowledges that he may need to fight or be violent toward these individuals.

3   If very distressed John will not respond to challenging of these ideas and becomes very rigid in his thinking and insistent that he is right (this change is indicative of an increase in risk).

4   John becomes concerned that his father may not be in heaven, because he has not heard the voice for a while.

Component 2: TBCT

Despite being slowly engaged over a long period and a large number of individual sessions of cognitive therapy for psychosis, there was limited sustained impact. These sessions did, however, help to inform John's SAFE formulations drawing on the ABC framework. Typical thought chains or inferences were identified in which John tended to make specific in-situation inferences, which would lead to an increase in distress or preoccupation (as indicated by the presence of internal setting events and early warning signs). In other words, the ABC formulation was used to describe the process occurring for John at the level of internal setting events that would normally lead to the problem behaviour. Typical ABCs for John are presented in Table 7.1 (Chapter 7, p. 118); an example from which is given below:

A   Feel tired and drained.
B   People have removed the electricity from my mind to make me vulnerable.
C   Anxiety and verbal aggression or violence toward other patients.

In essence this provides a psychological conceptualisation of a temporarily worsening 'mental state', as distinct from a full relapse. This approach differs from the more typical approach in CBT of formulating more general beliefs such as power beliefs about voices, which are present across a broad range of situations and yet may be expressed differently in different situations. Formulating such broad beliefs would, in our model, equate to constructing ABC chains at the level of vulnerability factors. We see this more as the role of highly trained cognitive therapists than the broad staff team. By using a CBT formulation in this rather novel manner, staff can be engaged as co-therapists in their ongoing interactions with clients, with an explicit aim of managing risk and problematic behaviours, utilising cognitively based interventions. The ABC framework is, in this instance, guided closely by the formulation of the problematic behaviour developed at an earlier stage, and allows staff to identify the A for the client (increasing their understanding of the client's internal world) and possible avenues to challenge the client's ongoing inferences.

This understanding was used to guide the day-to-day interactions of staff with John and combined with his EWS-R; in other words TBCT. The focus of this was to diffuse specific in-situation delusional interpretations of events to prevent John from engaging in violence. Team members were assigned the task of monitoring his EWS-R (the when to intervene), using a formalised checklist. The question of how to intervene was then addressed in two ways: first, by sharing the ABC formulation (presented in Table 7.1, Chapter 7); second, by providing guidance and modelling on how to deconstruct ABC chains in the presence of early warning signs.

DECONSTRUCTING ABC CHAINS IN THE PRESENCE OF EARLY WARNING SIGNS OF RISK (EWS-R)

As a first stage, team members were taught basic techniques for eliciting, and empathising with John's emotional responses: the use of reflection, paraphrasing and suspension of disbelief. They were then taught how to identify the actual A for John were they to observe his EWS-R to be present. As is typical, John would often present a feeling and delusional belief (B) as if it were an A (fact). Team members may then ask:

- What did [X] do to indicate that he was doing this?
- How did you figure this out? (Avoiding words like 'think' or 'believe', which discredit the client's experience)

They were thereby taught to clarify the actual A and feed this back as an ABC framework to John: the real event (A), his interpretation (B) and his feelings/behaviour (C).

The team were then shown how to elicit alternative explanations or interpretations of the A from John or, if he was particularly distressed and unable to focus, to provide these for him. This re-interpretation of the A utilises traditional cognitive therapy procedures:

- eliciting supporting evidence and weighing it;
- examining alternatives;
- exploring logical inconsistencies;
- testing out beliefs: encouraging John to speak to the person perceived of as a threat; allowing him telephone access to reassure him regarding his mother's health (meeting the function of the violent behaviour).

Whilst the primary aim here is to reduce problem behaviours, even in cases where more formal CBT might be applicable such a team-based approach might add to the process of belief change and encourage generalisation of this outside of therapy sessions.

Component 3: Reinforcement of appropriate behaviour

Finally, John was provided with increasing levels of leave to home, the day centre and the local pub, contingent upon him not displaying the target behaviour or verbal threats to others (a differential reinforcement of low rate of responding [DLR] programme).

Component 4: Generalising the approach to other settings

Once it was established that this approach was useful (see outcome below), a plan was devised to enable others to utilise the same management principles. Often it is not possible (due to time and resources or level of staff or carer skill) to fully train others involved in supporting the person with the relevant techniques and models. In John's case the TCBT approach and EWS-R were simplified so that they could be adopted by staff in the day care centre. This stage of intervention is designed to further promote social participation and inclusion.

WHAT TO DO

Step 1: Monitoring

Monitor John by casual observation and interactions with him – look out for the following early warning signs (reproduced from above).

Step 2: One to one

If John expresses ideas or appears distressed then ask him what has been happening and try to give him some one-to-one time to provide reassurance and time to check out his ideas and get some perspective.

Step 3: Tackling John's concerns and providing reassurance

If John is concerned about the actions of a member of staff:

- Try to get from him what that member of staff did or said that worried him: what did they do and what did it mean? Examples John has given are . . .
  'X was wearing a purple jumper and was writing in a black book in the office – it meant that he was ordering a hit on my mother.'
- The meaning of these actions can be gently challenged by getting

---

> John to talk more openly to the member of staff concerned (in this
> case talking to X and allowing John to read the contents of the
> black book).
>
> • It is also sometimes useful to draw John's attention to contradictory
>   evidence about the member of staff (e.g. Is there anything which X
>   has done which might make you think they are okay?). Often this will
>   result in a change in John's own attitude.
>
> • Finally, it can be useful to reassure John about staff (e.g. they are
>   there to help; they have undergone police checks and they mean him
>   no harm).
>
> If John is concerned about the actions of another service user:
>
> • Again, try to clarify what it is specifically that John has noticed and
>   then attempt to provide an alternative explanation for this, which
>   will not be so threatening.
>
> • For example, if another service user is being disruptive, you might
>   want to remind John that this is part of the person's illness and that
>   it is not directed specifically at John.
>
> In all cases you are challenging or providing reassurance about events and
> John's interpretation of them, NOT at any point trying to convince John
> that the Killer Queen or their powers are not real (this will not work).
>
> *Step 4: Engaging in normal activities/conversations*
>
> If John responds to reassurance then try to engage him in normal
> activities or conversation but continue to monitor (step 1). If unable to
> de-escalate, contact HDU.

Outcome

The number and frequency of incidents of violence committed by John reduced
rapidly from eight per week to one per week over the subsequent 12-month
period. Unfortunately, EWS-R consisting of verbal aggression to others (threats
of violence) and damage to objects were consistently recorded in notes by staff.
These might be considered problematic behaviours in their own right. These
showed a similar reduction over the same period from 31 per week to six per
week. Clinically, the other less challenging EWS-R continued to be present in
the context of ongoing paranoid delusions, demonstrating that only the

behaviour targeted was impacted upon and suggesting that reduction in the target behaviour was not due to general changes in treatment during this period, supporting the efficacy of TBCT + EWS-R + differential reinforcement.

This approach enabled John to have increased leave for extended periods, which had an additive effect in that contact with his mother on a more frequent basis reassured him of her safety. John was subsequently discharged from his Mental Health Section after 16 years of hospitalisation, became an informal patient supported by an Assertive Outreach Team (AOT) and went to live in supported accommodation. This progress was achieved without any changes in neuroleptic medication and with no apparent decrease in John's symptoms. His conviction in his delusional beliefs remained high but he was less preoccupied and distressed by them and dealt more appropriately with them by questioning others about their actions and motives; he now appeared to take their answers as evidence against his beliefs. The added benefit of the shared formulation approach was that the AOT were already engaged, had a good understanding of John and furthermore had clear and written formulations, which could be passed on to others, including John's family, to aid in risk management.

Case study 2: Adrian

Adrian (first described in Chapter 7) had an extensive history of violence to others and substance abuse, although his main presenting risk at the time of the author's involvement was of deliberate self-harm and suicide attempts. These were driven by traits such as impulsivity and fear of abandonment associated with characteristics of borderline personality disorder. He also experienced psychotic symptoms in the form of ideas of reference from the television and radio as well as persecutory, derogatory and threatening voices, which he believed came from nursing staff (and occasionally his family). Adrian believed that the source of these voices was nursing staff operating a 'mind-machine' to transmit their thoughts or comments to him even when they were not in the room. He also believed that they had access to his thoughts. The voices would either threaten to kill him or suggest to him he would be better off dead (an implied command). As seen in his CARM formulation (Figure 7.3, Chapter 7, p. 116), signs of depression such as hopelessness and withdrawal as well as pent-up anger featured heavily in the build-up to Adrian's self-harm and suicide attempts in addition to increased voice frequency.

Component 1: Monitoring of EWS-R

Staff were provided with a list of idiosyncratic EWS-R to monitor Adrian's mental state and behaviour.

Environmental changes that might be important

1   Discussion of him being discharged from the unit back into the community.
2   Being pestered by other clients for money or cigarettes on an ongoing basis.
3   Access to illicit drugs or alcohol.
4   His mother being on holiday.
5   Decreased number of staff (therefore subjectively he believes there is more chance that his suicide can be successfully faked by others).
6   Night time (feels less safe).

Changes in the way Adrian appears from the outside

1   Begins to spend long periods in his room.
2   Misses appointments with Psychology or seeks additional ones.
3   Refuses to speak to nursing staff about any problems (even day-to-day ones).
4   Increased tension and agitation (pacing, wringing hands, sweating).
5   Refusal to eat and take medication.
6   Notable decrease in self-care (e.g. beard growth).
7   Evidence of cutting wrists superficially.

Changes that might be observed in interacting with Adrian

1   Complaints to Psychiatry/Psychology about other staff.
2   Stops listening to the radio or television and/or complains that they are making comments about him.
3   States that the 'mind-machine' is in operation.
4   Increased hopelessness (states that he does not think things will get better and there is no point).
5   Admits increased preoccupation with self-harming or planning of suicide options.
6   Increased frequency of voices (only reported to Psychology).
7   Increased preoccupation with the idea that staff are threatening to enter his room and kill him.

One-to-one observations were implemented as required based on the estimated risk of serious self-harm or suicide. Ironically, Adrian found this to be a source of some reassurance as he believed that it would be less possible for people to fake his death as a suicide if he was on one-to-one observations in the ward documentation.

Component 2: Individual psychology sessions

Adrian had one-to-one sessions with his psychologist (DH) on at least a weekly basis and only rarely became paranoid about him. However, at times when he became increasingly paranoid and suspicious of staff, Psychology would conduct joint sessions either with his named nurse or with the community care coordinator, utilising them as co-therapists. The purpose of this was to allow Adrian to discuss his concerns and distress in the company of someone he trusted but also nursing staff. He could then evaluate the impact of talking to staff in a controlled way. This would typically help him to approach his named nurse subsequently and then for his named nurse to have joint sessions with other staff members, hence generalising his trust to other members of staff.

Once Adrian was able to trust at least one member of nursing staff he was offered structured activities with them at a separate activity centre attached to the service. This provided distraction from persecutory voices, increased his activity levels (serving additionally as behavioural activation to counter low mood) and gave him some time away from other patients and the presence of large numbers of nursing staff without necessitating him staying in his room all day. Increased visits from his family were included as part of the activity programme.

Component 3: Utilising co-therapists (TBCT)

Staff members were supported and supervised to extend the use of successful CBT strategies devised in individual psychology sessions to re-evaluate the perceived threats from specific individuals in light of his normal relationship with them in regular daily one-to-one sessions, by considering the good things they had done for him in the past. The purpose of this was to address his significant level of 'black and white' thinking about others: that they were either trusted friends or enemies. In addition, he was provided with a dictaphone to record any incidences of the 'mind-machine' or the radio and television speaking to him, to be played back in these individual sessions and evaluate whether these experiences were objectively happening.

Outcome

Through discussing his concerns with nursing staff, Adrian gradually became able to reduce his paranoia about them. Daily CBT sessions typically reduced his distress and conviction temporarily but needed repeating on a frequent basis to maintain the effect. These strategies led to a marked reduction in

Adrian's deliberate self-harm and attempted suicidal behaviour from monthly to three-monthly. This enabled a move on to be considered for Adrian (if other high-risk behavioural excesses could be addressed), albeit to supported (but less-restricted) accommodation where care staff could be supported to continue with these strategies.

Case study 3: Asif

For some individuals, EWS-R can be used for self-monitoring purposes (in a similar way to early warning signs of psychotic relapse) and used to help the individual make changes that reduce the likelihood of engaging in problematic behaviours.

Asif was a 26-year-old man of South Asian origin living in the community under the care of another AOT. Asif had a diagnosis of schizophrenia and a history of deliberate fire setting, threats of fire setting, violence directed at staff and the public using weapons (a curtain pole and a knife), threats to self-harm and attempted overdoses. He also tended to make frequent telephone calls to staff, and made frequent complaints about them not meeting his frequent demands for issues to be sorted out for him immediately. Asif frequently responded to such situations with threats to self-harm or threats to report the AOT staff members to the newspapers. He had a history of delusional beliefs about his involvement with the 2001 September 11th terrorist attacks and also that other people had been using black magic on him.

Asif identified his main recovery goal as being able to live at home with his family, supported by the AOT. However, his multiple problematic behaviours occurring on a regular basis meant that he was often admitted to his local acute psychiatric hospital and his ability to successfully remain in the community living independently with his family was increasingly questioned. His family were under growing strain and were unclear how they would cope with him if there was no improvement.

A CARM formulation (shown in Figure 13.1) highlighted that his mental health problems appeared to act as a disinhibitor to his problematic behaviours rather than being a direct result of acting upon delusions or voices. Asif was, however, consistently unwilling to engage in formal discussion of his psychotic symptoms (past or present) to more reliably establish if this was definitely the case. Moreover, he denied any current symptoms and did not appear overly preoccupied or distressed by psychotic symptoms. Despite average intelligence, Asif's ability to solve everyday problems remained poor and his frustration tolerance was low, reacting badly when his demands were not met immediately or when confronted about his lack of engagement

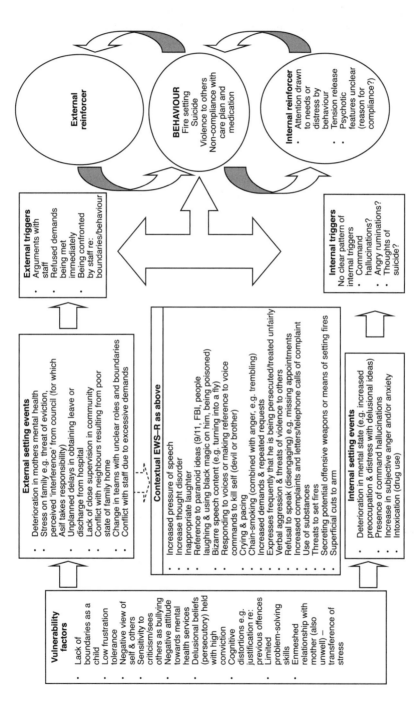

Vulnerability factors

· Lack of boundaries as a child
· Low frustration tolerance
· Negative view of self & others
· Sensitivity to criticism/sees others as bullying
· Negative attitude towards mental health services
· Delusional beliefs (persecutory) held with high conviction
· Cognitive distortions e.g. justification re: previous offences
· Limited problem-solving skills
· Enmeshed relationship with mother (also unwell) – transference of stress

External setting events

· Deterioration in mothers mental health
· Stress on family e.g. threat of eviction, perceived 'interference' from council (for which Asif takes responsibility)
· Unplanned delays in obtaining leave or discharge from hospital
· Lack of close supervision in community
· Conflict with neighbours resulting from poor state of family home
· Change in teams with unclear roles and boundaries
· Conflict with staff due to excessive demands

Contextual EWS–R as above

· Increased pressure of speech
· Increase thought disorder
· Inappropriate laughter
· Reference to paranoid ideas (9/11, FBI, people laughing & using black magic on him, being poisoned)
· Bizarre speech content (e.g. turning into a fly)
· Responding to voices or making reference to voice commands to kill self (devil or brother)
· Crying & pacing
· Chain-smoking (combined with anger, e.g. trembling)
· Increased demands & repeated requests
· Expresses frequently that he is being persecuted/treated unfairly
· Verbal aggression & threats of violence to others
· Refusal to speak (disengaging) e.g. missing appointments
· Increased complaints and letters/telephone calls of complaint
· Use of substances
· Threats to set fires
· Secreting potential offensive weapons or means of setting fires
· Superficial cuts to arm

Internal setting events

· Deterioration in mental state (e.g. increased preoccupation & distress with delusional ideas)
· Presence of command hallucinations
· Increase in subjective anger and/or anxiety
· Intoxication (drug use)

External triggers

· Arguments with staff
· Refused demands being met immediately
· Being confronted by staff re: boundaries/behaviour

Internal triggers

No clear pattern of internal triggers
· Command hallucinations?
· Angry ruminations?
· Thoughts of suicide?

External reinforcer

BEHAVIOUR

Fire setting
Suicide
Violence to others
Non-compliance with care plan and medication

Internal reinforcer

· Attention drawn to needs or distress by behaviour
· Tension release
· Psychotic features unclear (reason for compliance?)

Figure 13.1 CARM formulation of Asif's behaviour.

with the team. All of Asif's behaviours were formulated to be functionally equivalent, being driven by distress and an inability to solve problems coupled with some degree of impulsivity. The key trigger appeared to be the stress associated with having to look after his elderly mentally ill mother and learning disabled brother.

Intervening with Asif's problems consisted of a number of different components.

Component 1: Individual coping strategy enhancement

These sessions focused on coping with frustration and constructive problem solving. Asif was taught a four-stage simple problem-solving technique, which was targeted at solving common daily problems:

1 Define the problem.
2 Identify possible solutions.
3 Weigh up the pros and cons of the solutions.
4 Plan and implement the solution with the most pros.

In addition, he was taught a number of coping skills to help manage his arousal levels. A simplified problematic behaviour formulation was developed containing his EWS-R and problem-solving action plan (see Figure 13.2). Asif could use this to monitor his own EWS-R and engage in more constructive functional behaviours likely to lead to successful community living.

Component 2: Team monitoring of EWS-R

This built upon individual sessions. Team members provided Asif with one-to-one time based on the presence of EWS-R and to help him to think through the problem-solving framework taught to him in individual sessions to solve the current issue distressing him. In other words, they would not solve the problem for him but enable him to do so.

Component 3: Reinforcement of prosocial behaviours

Asif agreed a number of potential rewards that could be provided on a weekly basis:

• being taken by the team to the local supermarket to help with shopping for personal items;
• a trip out each week to a place of interest chosen by Asif (e.g. going to see a film, visiting a cultural centre).

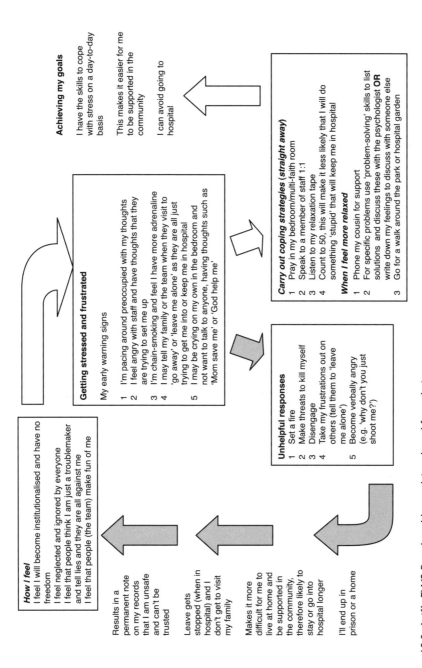

How I feel
I feel I will become institutionalised and have no freedom
I feel neglected and ignored by everyone
I feel that people think I am just a troublemaker and tell lies and they are all against me
I feel that people (the team) make fun of me

Results in a permanent note on my records that I am unsafe and can't be trusted

Leave gets stopped (when in hospital) and I don't get to visit my family

Makes it more difficult for me to live at home and be supported in the community, therefore likely to stay or go into hospital longer

I'll end up in prison or a home

Achieving my goals

I have the skills to cope with stress on a day-to-day basis

This makes it easier for me to be supported in the community

I can avoid going to hospital

Getting stressed and frustrated

My early warning signs

1 I'm pacing around preoccupied with my thoughts
2 I feel angry with staff and have thoughts that they are trying to set me up
3 I'm chain-smoking and feel I have more adrenaline
4 I may tell my family or the team when they visit to 'go away' or 'leave me alone' as they are all just trying to get me into or keep me in hospital
5 I may be crying on my own in the bedroom and not want to talk to anyone, having thoughts such as 'Mom save me' or 'God help me'

Unhelpful responses

1 Set a fire
2 Make threats to kill myself
3 Disengage
4 Take my frustrations out on others (tell them to 'leave me alone')
5 Become verbally angry (e.g. 'why don't you just shoot me?')

Carry out coping strategies (straight away)

1 Pray in my bedroom/multi-faith room
2 Speak to a member of staff 1:1
3 Listen to my relaxation tape
4 Count to 50, this will make it less likely that I will do something 'stupid' that will keep me in hospital

When I feel more relaxed

1 Phone my cousin for support
2 For specific problems use 'problem-solving' skills to list solutions and discuss these with the psychologist **OR** write down my feelings to discuss with someone else
3 Go for a walk around the park or hospital garden

Figure 13.2 Asif's EWS-R and problem-solving shared formulation.

These were provided on the basis of him not displaying any of the high-risk behaviours described above, displaying verbal aggression or threatening staff for at least three days.

Outcome

Using this approach, Asif's problematic behaviours decreased from at times daily incidents to once per week or less. His hospital admissions also decreased from up to three times per year to once during the last year and on this occasion a reduced length of stay compared with previous admissions.

SUMMARY

In this chapter we have provided some examples of working with high-risk behavioural excesses. In addition to fully assessing the risk involved using the shared risk formulation (Chapters 5 and 6), the CARM framework both provides a functional understanding of the problematic behaviour in question and serves as a means of integrating different levels of intervention into a staff-based approach. Monitoring EWS-R allows a titration of the level of supervision required but also signals when staff can intervene to challenge clients' beliefs about specific situations and so reduce distress and the occurrence of problematic behaviours. These techniques can be used alone but where the client can and will engage in individual sessions, such approaches with teams can be used to reinforce belief change from individual sessions or to generalise the use of successful CBT strategies. We have also shown how, in Asif's case, individuals can usefully utilise EWS-R to initiate coping strategies possibly with support from clinicians. Finally, reinforcement techniques such as those discussed in Chapter 12 can be used to reinforce progress and make the intervention more directly meaningful for clients.

Chapter 14

Working with behavioural deficits

INTRODUCTION

Behavioural deficits, as we have termed them, are associated with poor functional outcomes and long-term disability, often with an associated poor quality of life. We propose that the term 'behavioural deficits' avoids the ambiguity present in the term 'negative symptoms' and highlights the frequent co-morbidity of cognitive problems. With a few notable exceptions (e.g. Kingdom and Turkington, 2005), psychological approaches such as cognitive-behavioural therapy (CBT) have not been well developed to adequately address these difficulties. There is some evidence that the newer atypical neuroleptics such as clozapine and resperidone are effective treatments for cognitive deficits, including those in relation to fluency, memory and working memory, and may have greater effects on negative symptoms (Harvey and Sharma, 2002). However, both CBT and medication are less effective in highly treatment-resistant populations where adherence to prescribed medication is poor and engagement in psychological approaches is limited. Our focus here is on the rehabilitation of activity limitations or behavioural deficits that form the barriers to social participation in line with the vast literature in the neurorehabilitation field.

In this chapter we offer an approach to intervening with behavioural deficits that are both high risk (e.g. not eating) and low risk (e.g. staying in bed all day), based on strategies derived from the rehabilitation of people with acquired brain injury as well as from more traditional behavioural interventions. The assessment of behavioural deficits was discussed at length in Chapter 11 along with their association with negative symptoms and cognitive problems. Our seven-stage framework (detailed in Chapter 11) for assessing behavioural deficits and goal setting for care plans is based on the service level formulation, which emphasises working towards increasing social participation:

1 Define long-term goals.
2 Identify required tasks.

3   Identify current behavioural deficits (activity limitations on functional tasks).
4   Identify cognitive impairment, if relevant.
5   Set SMART goals.
6   Devise methods and strategies.
7   Implement, evaluate and revise short-term goals.

This process is used to devise methods and strategies for reducing behavioural deficits, increasing functional skills and improving social participation. We also utilise the Cognitive Approach to Risk Management (CARM) model to identify the most relevant treatment targets. Often these involve working at the level of skills teaching or overcoming cognitive deficits at the level of vulnerability factors. External support may also be needed along with providing motivation at the level of external setting events. Immediate triggers are typically provided via prompting or other methods of helping to initiate actions. Finally, methods of positive reinforcement are used to reinforce progress made.

EVIDENCE FOR COGNITIVE REMEDIATION AND NEUROREHABILITATION INTERVENTIONS

In the general neurorehabilitation literature there is a emerging consensus that attempts to remediate cognitive impairments directly are largely ineffective (Glisky, 2005). Rather, neurorehabilitation is best directed at reducing activity limitations or disabilities arising from the impairments and promoting social participation of those with acquired brain injury. There is therefore more evidence of cognitive rehabilitation as opposed to cognitive remediation. In schizophrenia specifically, repetitive practice on cognitive tasks does not generally improve cognitive performance on other tasks or on everyday tasks (Sartory *et al.*, 2005). There is some evidence for generalisation of learning to different tasks (e.g. learning of lists of words shows some generalisation to recall of story tasks: Hildebrandt *et al.*, 2006), but the evidence for generalisation to everyday memory functioning remains uncertain (Evans 2006). Til Wykes and colleagues (Wykes and Reeder, 2005) have widely investigated the impact of cognitive remediation training. This involves the completion of paper and pencil tasks where the individual is explicitly taught and practises information-processing strategies, for example verbalising out loud, errorless learning (discussed later) or minimising the amount of information to be processed in one go. Such training has shown promise in improving cognitive performance (Jones and Meaden, in press). However, the intervention is lengthy and time consuming, taking up to 40 one-hour sessions three times per week. Furthermore, it remains unclear whether cognitive functions are truly being remediated (e.g. improvement at the impairment level) or the person is acquiring strategies that might generalise across tasks and to everyday tasks (activity limitations level). However, the degree to which such time-intensive training does generalise to everyday improvements in functional skills remains in question and is not supported by the broader neuropsychological literature.

THE TECHNIQUES AND STRATEGIES OF REHABILITATION OF BEHAVIOURAL DEFICITS

Overcoming disorders of drive and motivation

In relation to negative symptoms, Kingdom and Turkington (2005) have noted the importance of ensuring that clients are provided with a chance to succeed and are not overwhelmed by demands they cannot readily meet. For this reason, the focus needs to be on small and achievable goals in the first instance, which can be gradually built upon. In addition, clients with negative symptoms may have problems with initiating action without external aids. Graded task assignment or activity scheduling involves setting small tasks for the client within a specific timeframe (e.g. spend half an hour cleaning the bedroom on Tuesday at 3pm). These necessary life skill tasks should be interspersed with potentially pleasurable activities to increase mood and motivation. The client may need help from staff to plan these out for the coming week and may benefit from a written or pictorial timetable (such timetables are usually arranged in one-hour slots over the duration of each day). Clients may initially be given verbal prompts by staff, which can gradually be faded over time. For some clients, alarms or electronic prompts using a wristwatch, mobile phone or personal digital assistant (PDA) may prove useful. These can act either as specific prompts for an activity or as a general prompt to consult the activity timetable. Preliminary evidence suggests that such electronic prompts can be useful for individuals with executive functioning problems, including problems of initiation (Evans et al., 1998; Manly et al., 2002). Gradually such tasks can be increased in frequency, duration or difficulty. Graded task assignment or activity scheduling is sometimes accompanied by asking the client to give ratings of achievement, mastery and pleasure similar to those used with depressed clients (Padesky and Greenberger, 1995). Here the client is asked to rate activities in which they engage for the degree of achievement, mastery and pleasure they experienced once they have completed the task or activity (on a scale of 0–10), given how they were feeling. This can highlight negative thoughts relating to the downplaying of achievements and self-criticism. Similarly, pleasure ratings may be used to challenge negative predictions that the client is unable to experience any pleasure at all and therefore that there is no point in the activity; they may also highlight the presence of negative thoughts interfering with the enjoyment of the activity.

Overcoming problems with attention/distractibility

It is not uncommon for clients with negative symptoms and behavioural deficits to have problems on tasks because they are easily distracted by stimuli in their environment or drift off after short periods due to problems with sustaining attention. There may also be problems with mental speed of processing information. They may need to be given a lot of extra time to respond, which can be difficult for staff and carers. Furthermore, information may need to be presented more slowly or in smaller, more manageable chunks. Clients may benefit from attempts to minimise distraction by working or studying in quiet environments. For example, when teaching a new task, staff may wish to minimise conversation that is not relevant to the task at hand. Similarly, clients are likely to benefit from engaging in only one task at a time and from avoiding competing demands. Where there are problems with sustaining attention, clients may benefit from a checklist of the different elements of the task to be performed and to tick these off as they go along as a means of keeping track of their progress. Alerting tones provided at regular intervals have shown some promise in improving clients' ability to stay on task even when the prompt itself has no content relevant to the task. This may be because the tone increases arousal and focus (Manly et al., 2002).

Robertson et al. (1995) have also described how clients can be taught to increase their attention to tasks themselves. When performing tasks stroke patients' attention was repeatedly drawn to the tasks by combining a loud noise with an instruction to 'attend'. Patients were then gradually taught to 'take over' this alerting procedure by vocalising and then subvocalising in order to improve their internal, or endogenous, control of attention. Other methods have included teaching clients to verbalise the task at hand (e.g. 'talking themselves through the task') at first out loud and then gradually subvocally in a method described as self-instructional training (Meichenbaum, 1977).

Overcoming problems with memory and skill or task learning

Problems with learning and memory can be common in clients with schizophrenia. In addition, there may be problems with remembering to perform a task at some future point or 'prospective memory' (e.g. remembering to attend an appointment or pay a bill). Reviews of the rehabilitation of memory indicate that external compensation for defective memory is recommended for those with moderate to severe memory deficits but that training in mnemonics may be useful for those with milder impairments (Cappa et al., 2005; Cicerone et al., 2005). Accordingly, those with memory problems should be encouraged to use aids such as notepads, diaries or electronic aids. These can also be useful in providing alarms to remind the client of upcoming events. Of course, for some clients there may not be a complete absence of the ability to learn new information and the client may have a particular strength for the modality of information presented (e.g. visual versus verbal materials) or may be able to learn if the information is simplified and/or repeated to them. The use of dictaphones or notes enables rehearsal of the information at a later date and staff or carers may wish to consider the use of written information.

If staff or carers are helping the client to learn new information or skills then again consideration of which tasks are most important is crucial since generalisation cannot be assumed to occur. One of the problems is that, in learning new skills (e.g. programming a DVD player) or information such as people's names or new routes, people tend to learn by trial and error and may learn their mistakes as much as the correct information. Reviews of rehabilitation methods suggest that methods of teaching and learning that minimise the client's mistakes during the learning process, so-called 'errorless learning' (Wilson et al., 1994), can be more effective than trial-and-error learning (Kessels and de Haan, 2003). In general, this can be thought of as a process of providing enough support or prompting to prevent mistakes in the early stages with increasing success being accompanied by a gradual fading of prompts or support.

One particularly useful approach is 'chaining'. This involves breaking down the behaviour into small steps and then teaching a task one step at a time, and provides clear, concrete goals for the client, maximising their chances of success. Forward chaining involves teaching the first step in the sequence, with the staff member or carer then completing the remaining steps in the sequence or helping the client to do so. In contrast, backward chaining involves teaching the last step in the sequence first, then adding the penultimate step and so on. This is best combined with reinforcement such as verbal praise on completion of the final step. Backward chaining is usually more effective since the client's contribution always leads to task completion (therefore there is an inherent reinforcement: a tidy room, a clean body). One very important point is to be clear and explicit about the stages involved in the task, particularly if different people will be involved in teaching the skill. If different staff are left to help the client to learn how to prepare a simple meal, for example, it is likely that they will have their own methods and ways of doing this, which if applied to the client haphazardly will actually inhibit the client's progress significantly since learning sessions will interfere with each other.

'Shaping' is another useful technique, taken from learning theory. Here a complete behaviour is taught, applying reinforcement to reward a behaviour that is closest to the desired behaviour (e.g. engaging a client who is mute and rewarding them whenever they make eye contact, then rewarding them for nodding or shaking their head and so on). Shaping is less useful for complex behaviours or those requiring a significant length of time to complete (e.g. completing all of the necessary tasks involved in getting up in the morning).

Planning, sequencing and problem solving

Clients with cognitive problems may have issues with the sequencing of steps in a task (e.g. following a recipe in a cookbook). In this case, clients may benefit from written prompts which pre-order the sequence of tasks clearly and explicitly for them. The client can then simply follow the checklist and self-monitor by ticking off each step as it is completed. This can of course be used in conjunction with chaining techniques if required.

Since clients with schizophrenia may have problems with holding information in mind and mentally manipulating that information to perform a task (working memory), they may benefit from writing down elements of the task or problem. This will minimise the load on attention, allowing more resources for thinking through a solution. There have been a number of approaches to teaching clients structured problem-solving approaches as a strategy, which can be used across situations. D'Zurilla and Goldfried (1971) adopted a 'problem-solving' approach to psychological (psychiatric) problems, emphasising the following stages:

- problem orientation;
- problem definition and formulation;
- generating potential alternative solutions;
- decision making concerning the best approach (examining pros and cons);
- solution implementation and evaluation.

Such approaches have also shown some benefit in neurological patients with dysexecutive problems (Rath *et al.*, 2003; Mitto *et al.*, 2008).

A further useful approach has been termed 'goal management training (GMT) (Levine *et al.*, 2000). GMT is based on the notion that patients may fail to generate goal or subgoal lists of how to solve problems (and achieve goals) and/or may fail to monitor themselves in this progression. Clients are taught that their mind is like a "mental blackboard" on which tasks and subtasks are written but are vulnerable to being rubbed off. Clients are taught the stages of: "STOP" (ask: what I am doing? and check the mental blackboard'); DEFINE (the main task or goal to be achieved); LIST (the steps or stages needed to achieve the goal); LEARN (the steps); DO IT (carry out the steps); CHECK (am I doing what I planned?).

Problem-solving training and GMT both rely on the client learning a strategy that can be used across situations, representing a metacognitive strategy. This is in contrast to techniques such as backward chaining, which places less responsibility on the client and are more task specific.

Using positive reinforcement

Progress in reducing behavioural deficits or moving gradually towards the desired goal by meeting subtasks independently can be reinforced on a regular basis. This can be carried out by the provision of positive reinforcement over periods of days or weeks as for high-risk behavioural excesses. Token economies use these principles to reinforce desired behaviour by providing tokens (that may later be exchanged for naturalistic reinforcers) contingent upon the presentation (the patient's performance) of specified target behaviours. Tokens are used to bridge the delay between the expression of the target behaviour and the provision of the contingent reinforcement. These approaches were often used in large psychiatric institutions to help rehabilitate those with chronic psychosis by encouraging the expression of socially desirable behaviours such as ward work and social skills as well as the improvement of self-care. Support for their efficacy was derived from single-case studies. Ayllon and Azrin (1965) carried out a case series of six ABA experimental designs (A, baseline condition → B, treatment condition → A, baseline condition) showing that target behaviours could be increased when reinforcement was provided and decreased when reinforcement was discontinued. Elliot *et al.* (1979) later showed in their series of 18 ABA experimental designs that both personal hygiene and social interaction increased during token reinforcement. In a sequential multiple baseline design involving 13 patients, Nelson and Cone (1979) showed that target behaviours such as personal hygiene, ward work and social skills all showed substantial improvement during token reinforcement; replicating earlier findings by Maley *et al.* (1973). In their randomised controlled trial Shang-Li and Wang (1994) showed that patients receiving token economy showed advantages over matched standard care patients with respect to measures of orientation and general functioning and showed improvement on the scale for the assessment of negative symptoms.

These approaches fell out of favour since they were implemented broadly across settings and did not take into account the function of a behaviour for a given individual. Someone staying in bed, for instance, may do so not due to a lack of motivation or drive but to avoid anticipated persecution.

Special issues regarding working with high-risk behavioural deficits

In addition to the above interventions, clinicians will also need to consider the imminence and seriousness of risk (whether through exploitation or abuse or as a direct consequence of behavioural deficits). In some circumstances, protocols relating to the Safeguarding of Vulnerable Adults (SOVA) procedure, the Mental Capacity Act 2005, DOLS (Deprivation of Liberty Safeguards) procedures or the Mental Health Act 2007 may need to be implemented to ensure the individual's safety. Social services' involvement may be necessitated where there is risk of neglect to dependants or extreme neglect of self. The Challenging Behaviour Checklist for Psychosis (CBC-P) is helpful here in indicating how frequent and severe the behaviour is and can be used to guide such decisions.

In addition to these practical considerations, however, there is the issue of the modification of the approach described in this chapter. Whilst many of the principles and techniques involved will still apply, there will need to be an emphasis on close supervision, which places more of an onus on care staff, and in the case of community-based clients this may necessitate a hospital admission. In practical terms it may be that no or few failures to exhibit the behaviour can be tolerated (e.g. missing doses of essential medication relating to a potentially life-threatening condition). In this case, the care plan will need to be written in a way that allows for improvement by the client (e.g. graded verbal prompts and scaffolding), which is positively reinforced but where, ultimately, the behaviour can be enabled to occur as often as possible. In addition, since the client may be at significant risk in the community (e.g. of diabetic coma or seizures) then punishment procedures such as temporary cessation (negative punishment) of all leave for an inpatient may be justified on ethical grounds.

In the following case studies we illustrate how these approaches derived from the principles of learning theory along with neurorehabilitation strategies can be usefully combined when based on a functional CARM formulation of the problematic behaviour.

Case study 1: Linda

Linda was residing in a slow-stream rehabilitation unit aimed at treatment-resistant clients with high levels of negative symptoms, poor engagement and behavioural deficits. She had a longstanding history of schizophrenia with marked negative symptoms and occasional non-bizarre paranoid delusions. The long-term goal for Linda was to return her to living independently in the community. However, given numerous previous failed attempts at independent living it was felt that a more realistic goal might be supported accommodation with day care staff. In the past Linda had not been able to cope with self-care in terms of eating adequately and maintaining her personal hygiene.

In order to make this transition, a number of tasks were identified that Linda would need to be able to undertake:

- to shop and cook for herself;
- to be independent in self-care in terms of personal hygiene;

- to be able to find her way to the local supermarket and post office where she held an account into which her benefits were paid.

In order to facilitate this it was agreed to undertake a programme with Linda over a six-month period to help her to develop and implement the necessary skills. Linda was assessed as having problems with memory for visual and verbal materials and problems with drive, often struggling to initiate actions without verbal prompts from staff. She had problems writing and following a shopping list, finding her way to the shops and using the washing machine and dryer.

Linda was given sessions with both the occupational therapist (OT) and nursing staff (supervised by the OT). At the beginning of the week, Linda was helped to menu plan for the week and make a shopping list. At the supermarket she was taught to tick off items as she placed them in the trolley and then, before proceeding to the checkout, to check that all items on the list were ticked. She was taught the walking route from the potential supported accommodation (to which she was driven) to the supermarket and post office. This was achieved with a programme of errorless learning, whereby Linda was required to make the final turning towards the supermarket with a verbal prompt and staff facing in the right direction and then without a verbal prompt. This process was gradually backward chained until Linda could successfully negotiate her way to the shops. In addition, whilst learning the route, Linda was encouraged to vocalise to the staff member what landmarks were most noticeable to her and discouraged from engaging too much in casual conversation. Linda was given cue cards for the use of the washing machine and dryer and for cooking basic meals, on which the individual steps were listed. Over time, steps were removed from the cards (the final step first), necessitating Linda internalising the use of the equipment herself. Finally, Linda helped staff to construct an activity timetable for the week that included the above tasks, washing and dressing and attendance at the local day centre, including specific days and times when these tasks would be carried out. Linda was taught how to read her mobile phone diary and whilst unable to set alarms and place appointments herself she agreed that staff at her accommodation would do this at the start of the week for her, having agreed a timetable with them. In this way Linda could be alerted at specific times in advance of activities and this removed the need for self-initiation of activity.

This approach proved successful and Linda was subsequently resettled into the identified supported accommodation. Her Assertive Outreach Team (AOT) monitored her level of self-care with the staff on a twice-weekly basis to ensure that she was keeping to the activity timetable and maintaining her self-care.

Case study 2: Lawrence

Lawrence was a 35-year-old man who had already had experienced repeated admissions to acute psychiatric hospital for attempted suicide. These had been triggered by failures to achieve his life goals by passing his exams to go to university and gaining employment as a computer analyst. Lawrence was eventually unable to continue with his studies as he experienced several relapses and begun hearing voices on a consistent basis. These voices told him to commit suicide and were derogatory in nature towards him. He had become increasingly socially isolated over the previous ten years and his level of self-care had noticeably declined over this period. He was also noted to have poor motivation, depressed mood and negative symptoms including avolition and apathy and behavioural deficits in terms of problems initiating any form of activity, spending much of the day at home doing nothing. Lawrence also developed epilepsy and his seizures appeared to be worsened by high levels of neuroleptic medication. Accordingly, his adherence to such medication was poor. On formal cognitive testing, Lawrence was shown to have a slowing of mental processing speed and mild problems in learning new information (he showed good retention but poor initial encoding of information).

The Community Recovery Team worked with Lawrence to support his goal of attending college to obtain his General Certificates in Secondary Educations (GCSEs) in Maths and English, which would increase his longer-term employ-ability, by attending an access course. They also worked with him to enable him to join a local church-based activity group for young African Caribbean people. Lawrence was given some psychoeducation about his cognitive limitations and a letter of support was written to the college for him to have extra time to complete coursework along with a learning support tutor as required.

Specific strategies were used to help Lawrence engage in these activities. He was taught the use of a dictaphone to record lectures in order to overcome his processing speed issues and to use this to make bullet-pointed notes from lectures for summarising and chunking the information. He was encouraged to review the lecture notes once or twice a week to aid learning but to use short sessions with more frequent repetition. Lawrence was initially provided with telephone prompts to attend college and the activities group but gradually this was faded to him using his mobile phone as a prompt. He was also encouraged to monitor both signs of relapse of his psychotic symptoms and low mood and to use an activity timetable for daily tasks with pleasure and mastery ratings. The purpose of this was to emphasise how much he was managing to achieve in terms of daily tasks and to combat his self-criticism. His learning support tutor was also introduced to these strategies so that they could be consistently applied.

Over time, Lawrence was able to independently attend college and the social activities group, requiring input only to monitor his mental health on an outpatient basis. He became less depressed and there were gradual improvements in his self-care.

Case study 3: Joseph

Joseph was 52 years old and had a long history of negative symptoms and residential care. Like Linda he was residing in a slow-stream rehabilitation unit where he spent much of the day in bed. A CARM formulation, however, revealed that this was not due to poor motivation, loss of pleasure, depressed mood or other negative symptoms. Rather, his behavioural deficit was a result of malevolent voices, which told him that he would be 'chopped up' if he got out of bed. Joseph engaged poorly with the team on the unit and would not discuss his symptoms in any great detail, making individual CBT problematic. In this case the approach was to use team-based cognitive therapy (TBCT), drawing on cognitive therapy for command hallucinations (CTCH) (Byrne et al., 2006). Here TBCT was delivered contingent upon Joseph displaying the behavioural deficit, rather than early warning signs. Team members at these times were able to draw on instances when Joseph had got up and nothing had happened and when other claims made by the voices transpired to be false, and their general fallibility (making them less powerful and the need to comply less pressing).

Using this approach, the team were able to encourage Joseph to spend less time in bed and engage in unit activities (providing further evidence that the voices' threats were false and thus serving as interval reinforcement).

SUMMARY

In this chapter we have described a number of neurobehavioural rehabilitation strategies that can be successfully integrated to address activity limitations and behavioural deficits that form the barriers to social participation. Our service level formulation is the most useful framework here, once the behaviour has been clearly assessed as not having another function that can be addressed through the use of other interventions (as in the case of Joseph). Other approaches may also be needed depending on the serious and imminent risk to the person. The importance of linking these interventions to longer-term goals is also clearly important and requires a bringing together of information from the Recovery Goal Planning Interview (see Appendix 2) and the service level formulation.

Part 4

Implementation issues
Translating SAFE into routine clinical practice

Chapter 15

Translating the SAFE approach into care plans

INTRODUCTION

In this chapter we return to the crucial issues of care planning and goal setting. A formulation and structured evidenced-based intervention is of little use if it is not carried out or if there is no clear way to measure progress, or a lack of progress which might necessitate a reformulation. In this chapter we illustrate how the service level formulation can be usefully translated into effective care plans and goals. As noted in Chapter 2, care plans are often poorly devised and implemented, which can result in interventions being carried out inconsistently or not at all. Consider the following care plan for Claire:

1 Support Claire to improve her personal hygiene.
2 Improve adherence to medication.
3 Encourage contact with the family.
4 Support Claire to engage in social activities.
5 Manage Claire's risk of self-harm.

Such a care plan is not uncommon in Care Programme Approach (CPA) documentation and yet there are several evident problems with it. First, the goals are not clearly (behaviourally) defined: it is not clear, for example, what 'improve personal hygiene' or 'manage risk of self-harm' actually means. Does the former refer to bathing more often or does it refer to brushing one's teeth and hair and wearing clean clothes? Does management of self-harm mean simply monitoring the person or teaching coping strategies? Therefore, the actual target and/or nature of the intervention is by no means clear. Neither is it readily apparent whether or not the care plan is based on Claire's actual needs (the need-adapted treatment principle described in Chapter 2).

Second, the realistic goal of the intervention is lacking. If 'personal hygiene' refers to increased frequency of bathing does this mean one bath per week or one each day? This means that the care plan's success or failure is not measurable. Neither is it clear at what level of functioning the client is currently at in relation to the goal and how any deterioration might be apparent. Additionally, the care plan does not clearly indicate when the goal will be reached and if so in relation to what longer-term goal the care plan goal is set: is the aim to move to independent living, to attend local swimming baths etc? This focus solely on functional skills and behaviour without attending to long-term life goals violates the social participation principle, which we set out in Chapter 2.

Third, the care plan does not appear to describe how these goals will be achieved on a day-to-day basis. They give little guidance for staff on the intervention, meaning that it is likely to be translated into action inconsistently, if at all. It is not clear whether the intervention to be used is evidence based or that it targets the idiosyncratic factors which cause and maintain the problem: the particular specific skill deficits or the impact of psychotic symptoms and phenomenology (the shared phenomenology and need-adapted principles).

EFFECTIVE CARE PLANNING AND GOAL SETTING

In order for a care plan to be effective we believe that it should be embedded within a systematic process of goal setting. The reader will recall from Chapter 11 that an important principle of goal setting is that goals should be SMART (small, measurable, achievable, relevant and time-limited). In order to achieve this we propose a number of stages and components of a care plan. The reader will note some overlap with the principles of assessing behavioural deficits, as outlined in Chapter 11.

Stage 1: Define long-term goals

These should be collaborative if possible but also realistic or at least potentially feasible in the eyes of the care team as well as of the client. The Recovery Goal Planning Interview (see Appendix 2) should be used here to identify the client's goals. A long-term goal might be to:

- live in an independent flat within a core and cluster arrangement (with staff on site but with the client having their own separate self-contained flat and own front door).
- attend college to obtain a plumbing qualification.

The defining of longer-term goals means that the subsequent short- and medium-term goals in the care plan are relevant to the client's social participation goals in line with the service level formulation and World Health Organization (WHO) model described in Chapter 3.

Stage 2: Identify current barriers to participation/ activity limitations

In terms of our adaptation of the WHO model, barriers to participation will be either external or internal to the person. Internal barriers might include skill deficits or activity limitations on relevant functional tasks that would be required to achieve the longer-term goal; this would also include problem behaviours that are likely to limit the person's freedom or access to normal activities. This ensures that again the intervention is relevant and meets the client's unique needs (the need-adapted principle).

Stage 3: Identify a medium-term goal

Agreeing a medium-term goal for the client should be in terms of the barriers to participation identified (e.g. to be able to cook microwave meals safely and without support, to reduce verbal aggression to two occasions per month). Note that the setting of the medium-term goal needs to take into account where the client currently is in their progress and what is likely to be both an achievable and a realistic goal for them in the medium term (for example between CPA review periods). When setting these goals the team will need to be mindful of the person's cultural and social environment. For instance, if the person is living in an area that tolerates a certain amount of verbal hostility and unusual dress then these may not be such important barriers for that person. If on the other hand the person lives in a low-tolerance community then they may easily be stigmatised, excluded or abused.

Stage 4: Identify the approach or method to be used to achieve the goal

There should be a clear description of the intervention to be carried out (ideally evidence based) together with a description of how, when, how often and by whom this would be carried out. This will often necessitate reference to an appended specific guideline for staff to be able to follow without confusion and with consistency. These specific guidelines will often need to be written by staff with expertise in rehabilitation or dealing with problematic behaviours. Such specific guidelines are more likely to be required in considering internal barriers than external barriers since the former necessitate detailed psychologically based interventions such as team-based cognitive therapy (TBCT).

Stage 5: Measurement of progress towards the goal

Change may be slow for many clients with the types of presentations and difficulties that are the focus of this book. Consequently, it is important that any evidence of change is captured as this can be empowering and give hope to the individual client, their carers and the team. We have found that Goal Attainment Scaling developed by Kiresuk *et al.* (1994) particularly helpful in this respect. The Goal Attainment Scaling Tool (GAST) helps to clearly define progress towards achieving a medium-term goal, by measuring change in terms of specific shorter-term subgoals. Levels of goal attainment are clearly defined as realistic individual steps and measurable in terms of progress towards (and away from) the desired goal. The realistic desired outcomes if the behaviour were to improve or deteriorate are clearly specified so that it is clear to all of those involved in the person's care when a step has been achieved or not.

A common method in using GAST is to note where the client is at present – if no change were to occur – and to score this at an anchor point of zero. Small goals towards achieving the medium-term goal are then anchored as +1 and +2. If the client is not far from achieving the medium-term goal then intermediate goals should reflect this and these should be used as the +1 and +2. Alternatively, if the client is far away from achieving the medium-term goal then perhaps two smaller goals should be used as +1 and +2. However, if the client is very unlikely to reach the medium-term goal in the timeframe specified (usually three months in CPA terms) then this may not be realistic and a less ambitious medium-term goal might need to be considered. Deterioration or steps backwards away from the medium-term goal are labelled as −1 and −2, which allows maintenance of the current position to be evaluated in relation to where the client may have been previously.

Marked deterioration:	Daily assaults (−2)
Slight deterioration:	4 assaults per week (−1)
No change:	2 assaults per week (0)
Slight improvement:	1 assault per week (+1)
Marked improvement (desired outcome):	1 assault over the next month (+2)

Ideally, the process of using GAST should involve a collaborative discussion between members of the Case Formulation Team (CFT), the client and, where appropriate, the broader Multidisciplinary Team (MDT). We usually encourage teams to set medium-term goals in relation to a three-month period coinciding with CPA reviews whilst GAST should allow the measurement of smaller goals over this time and should ensure that progress or any lack of progress on smaller goals is readily apparent. This means that the success of the intervention is quite transparent and is not reliant on waiting for CPA reviews before strategies and approaches are altered. We now illustrate the goal planning approach through the case studies of John and Maria, first described in Chapter 3.

Case study 1: SAFE care planning for John

Our service level formulation of John reproduced from Chapter 3 is the starting point for care planning purposes and guides its overall focus. It provides the overarching philosophy of care and ensures that subsequent care planning and goal setting meet the social participation and need-adapted principles of SAFE outlined in Chapter 3.

Level 1: Pathology/diagnosis

- Paranoid schizophrenia.

Level 2: Impairment/symptoms

- A paranoid belief that other residents are trying to kill his mother, coupled with ideas of reference and the belief that other residents can hear his thoughts via sounds (thought broadcast).
- A grandiose belief that he can play guitar just like Jimmy Page.
- Inflexibility and perseveration in his thinking: getting stuck on particular topics.
- Lack of insight into his mental illness.
- Highly distractible, with poor concentration and attention.

Level 3i: Activity limitations/internal barriers to participation

- Inability to pay attention to the context of information without prompting.
- Seemingly bizarre speech and behaviours (e.g. believes that hand driers transmit his guitar music so that he spends time loitering in toilets).
- Assaults other patients (punching them in the face).

Level 3ii: External barriers to participation

- Family and staff lack a detailed understanding of John's delusions and dismiss his seemingly bizarre communication.
- Limited amount of support to leave the unit (e.g. to go to the local shops or visit his mother).

Level 4: Social participation

- Unable to go to the local shops or pub alone.
- Lost contact with friends (lack of social network).
- Other residents avoid him.

- Unable to move home from hospital to live with his mother.

This formulation subsequently helps to set the medium- to longer-term recovery goals and aims for John and the service. We combine this with John's life goals (as identified through the Recovery Goal Planning Interview presented in Appendix 2) and findings from his Cognitive Approach to Risk Management (CARM) and person level formulations to devise a set of broad care plan objectives that aim to address the barriers to participation, including John's assaultative behaviour (framing this in terms of his broader life and recovery goals):

Interventions aimed at reducing external barriers to participation

- The CFT to share the person level and CARM formulation findings with the broader staff team and his family to address their understanding of John's beliefs and behaviour.
- Graded visits home to his mother with visits from the Assertive Outreach Team (AOT) during the visits to monitor risk issues and mental state.
- Escort John once a week to his local pub and once a week to the local shops (addressing delusional speech as outlined below).
- Provide psychology sessions in his mother's home environment to generalise AOT member's ability to challenge his paranoid ideas about staff caring for his mother and to model more empathic interventions with John for his family (in effect extending TBCT from the inpatient setting to the community).
- Support John to join in-group programmes at local community-based day centres.

Interventions aimed at reducing internal barriers to participation

Intervention care plan 1

1   *The target*
    Problem behaviour of violence to others (typically punching other patients and staff in the face).
2   *The goal*
    To reduce John's assaultative behaviour to the level of only one assault per month.
3   *The method and approach*

Staff to monitor John's early warning signs of risk (EWS-R) with reference to specific risk management guidelines.

Nursing staff to approach John when they notice the presence of EWS-R (as detailed in Chapter 13) and enquire about any concerns, employing CBT challenges/dialogue (specified in these guidelines) to encourage him to consider alterative interpretations for his in-situation delusional interpretations.

THE HIERARCHY OF INTERVENTIONS

Step 1: Monitor John by casual observation and interactions with him.

Step 2: Provide one-to-one support. If John expresses ideas or appears distressed then ask him what has been happening and try to give him some one-to-one time to provide reassurance and time to check out his ideas and give him some perspective.

Step 3: If John is concerned about the actions of a member of staff or other resident, try to elicit from him what they did or said that worried him about it. Gently and tentatively challenge (using CBT principles) the meaning of these actions:

(a) Praise John for bringing this to your attention or being open to talking about it.

(b) Support John to look for contradictory evidence about the member of staff.

(c) Remind him of instances when his interpretations where wrong previously.

(d) Get John to talk to the member of staff concerned to check out for himself his interpretation of the incident.

(e) Reassure John about the person (e.g. reinforce the idea that they are there to help; if staff, that they have undergone police checks and they mean him no harm; if fellow residents, that they are also ill and do not have access to the means to harm his mother).

(f) Get John to think about the consequences of his actions and how these work against his longer-term goals).

4   *Measurement of progress*

This to be measured by GAST:

Marked deterioration:	Daily assaults (−2)
Slight deterioration:	2 assaults per week (−1)
No change:	1 assault per week (0)

Slight improvement:	I assault per week (+I)
Marked improvement (desired outcome):	I assault over the next month (+2)

Intervention care plan 2

1 *The target*

Bizzare speech in public regarding delusional ideas.

2 *The goal*

For John to engage in normal topics of conversation in the community with only two verbal prompts by staff being required on each outing (to discuss delusions in structured sessions and with staff in private).

3 *The method and approach*

Staff to actively engage John in normal topics of conversation, when out in the community:

- If John begins to discuss topics regarding the demon of darkness, Killer Queen, or attempts to play his imaginary guitar by banging on objects, staff to remind him that others may not understand his experiences as well as staff do.
- Staff should prompt him to save any discussion of the topic until they are in private.
- If John appears distressed and there is a theme of threat as detailed in his EWS-R then staff should use the techniques listed in his EWS-R plan.
- If necessary use distraction by asking him normal everyday questions or engaging him in activities such as playing on the fruit machine in the pub or looking at the menu.

4 *Measurement of progress*

This to be measured by GAST:

Marked deterioration:	8+ verbal prompts required (−2)
Slight deterioration:	7–8 verbal prompts required (−I)
No change:	6 verbal prompts (average) on each visit (0)
Slight improvement:	4 verbal prompts required (+I)
Marked improvement (desired outcome):	2 or less verbal prompts required (+2)

SAFE care planning for Maria

Our service level formulation of Maria is used in the same way as that for John and provides a further example of the process, but in this case for someone with marked behavioural deficits. Again the aim is the same: to reduce barriers and enable social participation and recovery goals to be realised.

Our service level formulation of Maria is reproduced from Chapter 3 below.

Level 1: Pathology/diagnosis

- Schizophrenia.

Level 2: Impairment/symptoms

- Cognitive difficulties with planning and sequencing activities.
- Poor concentration and working memory.
- Low motivation and loss of pleasure in previously enjoyed activities.

Level 3i: Activity limitations/internal barriers to participation

- Unable to follow conversations.
- Unable to set goals and work towards them without heavy prompting.
- Difficulty with complex instructions or several step actions (e.g. tidying her bedroom).
- Gives up easily on tasks.
- Personal hygiene and grooming is poor.
- Spends most of the day in bed and complains of constant tiredness, lack of energy and fatigue.

Level 3ii: External barriers to participation

- Belief of her partner that Maria is lazy.
- Lack of knowledge by her partner and divided opinion amongst the care team about how to best help with negative symptoms and behavioural deficits.

Level 4: Social participation

- Spends long periods smoking/staring at the television.
- Personal hygiene limits friends and access to the local shops, swimming and cinema, which she used to enjoy.

Interventions aimed at reducing external barriers to participation

- Share person level and CARM formulations with the whole team and relevant elements with her partner Tony to address team beliefs (that she 'cannot be helped' or 'just needs to be in supported accommodation') and carer beliefs that Maria is just being 'lazy'.
- Provide carer education about negative symptoms and behavioural deficits.
- Provide training and supervision for the team in the use of agreed behavioural strategies.
- The team to provide at least two trips into the community per week for Maria to help increase her motivation. This should involve pleasurable activities that she used to enjoy, including shopping at the local market, swimming, going to the cinema and going out for a pub meal.

Interventions aimed at reducing internal barriers to participation

Intervention care plan 1

1   *The target*
    Problem behaviour – Maria not washing more than once every two weeks.
2   *The goal*
    For Maria to bathe twice per week prior to her supported trips into the community from her home.
3   *The method and approach*
    The team to call Maria the previous day, again first thing in the morning and again an hour before going out on a community trip to prompt her to bathe.
    Maria to be provided with a written prompt sheet regarding bathing to remove the planning and sequencing elements of the task:

(a) Turn on the hot water tap.
(b) Get a clean towel and place it in a convenient place.
(c) Wait until the bath is two-thirds full – turn off the hot water tap.
(d) Check temperature and add cold water if necessary (Maria has badly scalded herself in the past by not paying attention to the water temperature – reinforcing her not bathing).
(e) Wash body using shower gel and a sponge (staff to also help Maria shop for special toiletries she likes to increase her pleasure in the activity).
(f) Wash hair with shampoo and conditioner.

(g) Empty the bath.

(h) Dry self with the clean towel.

(i) Put on deodorant.

(j) Brush hair.

(k) Brush teeth.

(l) Get out clean clothes and get dressed.

4   *Measurement*

This to be measured by GAST:

Marked deterioration:	Bathes less than once per month (−2)
Slight deterioration:	Bathes only once per month (−1)
No change:	Bathes once every two weeks (0)
Slight improvement:	Bathes 3 times every two weeks (+1)
Marked improvement (desired outcome):	Bathes twice per week (+2)

Intervention care plan 2

1   *The target*

Problem behaviour – does not tidy her bedroom or clear away used food dishes (she often eats in bed).

2   *The goal*

Maria to tidy her bedroom once per week with assistance from AOT staff on their visit with a maximum of four prompts during the task.

3   *The method and approach*

Maria to be provided with a wall chart for her bedroom with an exact sequence of tasks as to how to tidy it (e.g. look for dirty dishes and place in sink, pick up clothes and put away etc.). The same sequence to be used on every occasion as per the chart provided.

AOT staff to help with each task, in order, and prompt Maria towards the chart before beginning each step. Staff to initially help with all tasks except the last one until Maria does the last step without prompting being required. Staff to then move to helping and prompting on all steps with the exception of the last two steps (there are eight steps in total on the chart).

Staff to sit with Maria afterwards and complete ratings of mastery or achievement and pleasure and compliment Maria on her appearance.

Staff to introduce natural reinforcement: buying nice or favourite bath products to use, buying a perfume to wear once hygiene has been attended to.

4   *Measurement*

This to be measured by GAST:

Marked deterioration:	Not applicable (−2)
Slight deterioration:	Completes none of 8 steps independently (−1)
No change:	Completes 1 of 8 steps without prompt (0)
Slight improvement:	Completes 4 of 8 steps independently (+1)
Marked improvement (desired outcome):	Completes 8 out of 8 steps independently (+2)

SUMMARY

In this chapter we have illustrated how our service level formulation and subsequent SAFE formulations combined with our integrative need-adapted MDT-based interventions described in Part 3 can be used to enable the team to devise an effective care plan. SAFE care plans as presented here may appear deceptively simple, but in our experience require a great deal of effort to develop. In John's case, standard approaches were not working and a significant amount of resources had previously been used in unproductive attempts to address his problematic behaviours. Care planning and its implementation is the culmination of the SAFE process, although as the need-adapted principle implies, the process may need to be repeated as needs change, at least until service and recovery goals have been (as far as possible) met. In the next chapter we focus on issues in applying the process in different settings.

Chapter 16

Applying SAFE and CARM in specialist settings

INTRODUCTION

In keeping with the need-adapted principle described in Chapter 2, separate elements of the Shared Assessment, Formulation and Education (SAFE) approach can be adopted for use in different settings. In this chapter we suggest where these can be most appropriately applied. In Chapter 17 we discuss in more detail some of the issues in implementing SAFE and describe our own experience of doing so. For the purposes of the present chapter, however, it is useful to consider the following:

- the amount of time available;
- the level of resources available;
- the level of expertise and appropriate skills available;
- existing service priorities;
- which clients currently raise the most concern;
- current service approaches and models that might adapt themselves most readily to SAFE processes.

SAFE is a flexible process and contains a number of useful tools and templates applicable to most service settings where clients present with treatment-resistant psychosis and problematic behaviours. Our focus here, however, is on specialist community and inpatient settings where such presentations are more common and where an intensive team approach and greater resources are available to support the implementation of SAFE.

USING SAFE IN INPATIENT AND RESIDENTIAL SETTINGS

Inpatient care has traditionally provided a solution to managing those with problematic or risk behaviours. These behaviours continue to be a factor in the low rates of discharge from such settings (Cowan *et al.*, in preparation).

As Morgan (1998) has noted, there has often been an underlying assumption that risk can be managed or eliminated through detainment and restrictive schedules of daily functioning (Goffman, 1961; Lloyd, 1995). In line with our principle of social participation as detailed in Chapter 2, assessment and intervention in these environments should have the aim not merely of reducing or eliminating problematic behaviours but also of promoting therapeutic risk taking and reducing barriers to community involvement.

Assessment issues

In general, inpatient and other residential settings usually afford the opportunity to carry out the full range of assessments and formulation processes linked to the SAFE process, over an extended period of time. However, staff in some of these settings (e.g. residential rehabilitation units, continuing care facilities), especially those in the voluntary and independent sectors, may have little training in observation skills and assessment methods. Staff here may require additional support and training (see Chapters 17 and 18) and this should be borne in mind before embarking on the SAFE approach. The Challenging Behaviour Checklist for Psychosis (CBC-P), presented in Appendix 1, is often helpful here since it offers clear operationally defined descriptions and can serve as a useful starting point. This can be subsequently combined with the Challenging Behaviour Record Sheet for Psychosis (CBRS) provided in Appendix 4, along with other behavioural assessment methodologies (described in Chapter 9). This is particularly applicable to inpatient settings since staff are well placed to make frequent behavioural observations, which may be more difficult to conduct in community settings. Using the CBRS the client's own view of their behaviours can also be sought. More complex assessments such as those designed to assess the phenomenological aspects of a client's psychosis and potential cognitive problems are likely to require access to more specialist resources such as input from a clinical psychologist or other team members trained in psychological and psychosocial assessments (see Chapter 4 for a discussion of these tools and methods).

SAFE formulations

Service level formulations are often helpful for these services since they tend to lack a clear service model or specification in the absence of national guidelines or service plans for them. Service level formulations can thus help the team to establish clear service goals alongside participation and recovery goals for the individuals that use the service. The four principles of SAFE (described in Chapter 2) may also be adopted to support the philosophy of care and inform its procedures for referral, selection and admission: programme planning and review, case coordination and recording. Chapter 15 provides a structure that can be translated into most service settings for care planning purposes.

Staff attributions along with patterns of expressed emotion as noted in Chapter 8 are of particular concern in residential and inpatient settings. This is especially true in those providing long-term care where staff may take on the role of family members (particularly if the person has lost all contact with relatives and friends) and may act out previous family dynamics (as discussed in Chapters 2, 3 and 8). These patterns can be identified through the service level assessment process described in Chapter 18. More readily they can be assessed through the use of ABC formulations of staff beliefs in the context of Cognitive Approach to Risk Management (CARM) and other SAFE formulations (described in Chapter 8). These can serve as the basis for developing more positive views of the person and their behaviour and fostering a more therapeutic approach.

Our CARM model (outlined in Chapter 7) is particularly suited to inpatient or residential settings since team members will have the opportunity to observe (and subsequently intervene with) the person's behaviour in some detail. The model itself promotes understanding of the person's physical and social environment (in terms of setting events and triggers), which may not be possible in community contexts. Reinforcers can also be assessed and contingencies subsequently altered to a far greater extent and over a more immediate timeframe than is often feasible in the community.

SAFE interventions

Our early warning signs of risk (EWS-R) methodology (described in Chapter 10), designed for working with high-risk behavioural excesses, is particularly suited to inpatient settings since high levels of observation are possible, enabling close monitoring and timely intervention. We frequently link this to daily team-based cognitive therapy (TBCT) to help address the client's specific in-situation inferences. Most staff can learn to use the EWS-R methodology but may require more expert involvement in order to elicit and draw up the initial signs along with additional guidelines for how to intervene with clients' in-situation beliefs using cognitive-behavioural therapy (CBT) principles.

Historically, behavioural management approaches have been applied in these types of settings, and have been most associated with the traditional institutions. However, these interventions should always be individually tailored and based on an understanding of the function of the behaviour using a CARM formulation rather than more blanket approaches such as token economies, referred to in Chapter 14. Addressing behavioural deficits through the application of neurorehabilitation and behavioural management strategies will be most suited to these settings, which enable their systematic and frequent application; supporting the notion of rehabilitation. The SAFE care planning framework illustrated in Chapters 11 and 15 makes clear the way in which staff should intervene on a day-to-day level in carrying out such behaviourally based care plans. This is equivalent to the explicit guidance given for EWS-R for behavioural excesses. The advantage of the SAFE goal and care planning approach is that care plans are unambiguous and specific and can thus more readily be followed and are more consistently implemented. In our experience even the best social participation oriented care plans can fail if they remain general and do not give specific guidance to staff, many of whom will be untrained.

Ideally, the person should be involved in collaboratively agreeing any behavioural management strategies with the aim of establishing more appropriate ways of meeting the function that the behaviour serves. However, reinforcement principles may be applied when engagement cannot be achieved (in a way that is not possible in the community) since contingencies can be altered by staff and factors in the environment changed (e.g. using only female or male members of staff, giving praise to shape desirable behaviours as they naturally occur).

SAFE IN ASSERTIVE OUTREACH AND EARLY INTERVENTION TEAMS

Risk management presents greater challenges in the community compared with inpatient or specialist residential settings. Despite the intensive nature of community-based Multidisciplinary Teams (MDTs), which offer lower caseloads and greater resources, subgroups remain who are persistently difficult to engage (Gillespie and Meaden, 2009; Paget et al., 2009) and are resistive to both standard care and the newer psychosocial treatments (Holloway, 2005). As noted by Shepherd (1995), whilst care is possible in the community, the practical and legal freedoms enjoyed by our clients make control impossible. The recent development of Compulsory Treatment Orders (CTOs) has not improved outcomes further (Kisely and Campbell, 2007) for this group of clients. Yet a broader group of clients exist in the community who continue to experience high levels of unmet need and disability, sometimes described as the 'forgotten generation' (ReThink, 2004). This population may be described as being institutionalised in the community. They often have behavioural deficits and may be at significant risk of self-neglect, social exclusion as well as being vulnerable to abuse and exploitation by others. SAFE does not provide a complete solution to the needs of these client groups but does offer a process for improving care and the quality of risk assessment and management processes.

Assessment issues

Less frequent but high-risk (excess) behaviours will be easier to track and therefore assess since they are likely to attract attention and concern from others. Low-risk behavioural excesses may less frequently come to the attention of the MDT in the community and may be more easily hidden. Similarly, high-risk behavioural deficits may be harder to recognise, especially if the person is seen routinely outside the home or where carers perform these functions, thus camouflaging any deficits. Where this is the case and behavioural deficits are suspected then opportunities for observing the client in other social, recreational, educational or work settings should be sought. They may also be apparent on home visits (where access is possible), through physical appearance (e.g. being unkempt) or by marked levels of social avoidance.

SAFE formulations

Service level formulations may be less useful in community settings as many forms of intensive community services have well-developed philosophies and models (e.g. Early Intervention Services [EIS], Assertive Outreach Teams [AOTs]) but can still be helpful with clients who do not respond to these approaches. In these cases a reconsideration of the way forward and setting realistic service goals can be helped by adopting the World Health Organization (WHO) model described in Chapter 3. Other forms of specialist community teams, community rehabilitation and recovery teams and community mental health teams may lack such a clear focus; Service level formulations can be particularly useful here.

AOTs and EISs are both arguably underpinned by a team approach and so arriving at a consensus of the way forward is particularly important. The fact that the team will be working apart for much of the time makes developing a shared consistent approach essential. Team splitting and negative staff attributions occur in community teams. Person level formulations provide the opportunity to collate and integrate information pertinent to understanding the person's problems. They can also provide a useful focus for the team getting together. Using our template in a case-busting session where the care coordinator presents a summary of the person and the team completes the template can be useful and engaging for team members. Further work will, however, need to be done outside of the meeting in order to better refine the formulation and improve its reliability and validity. The person level formulation also offers a means of engaging with the person since many will reject psychiatric labelling, finding it stigmatising, and may find an approach that looks at them as a whole person more acceptable.

Shared risk formulations (described in Chapter 6) are perhaps more relevant than CARM formulations in the community. These offer a clear framework for organising the information already available and (drawing on other known risk factors) identifying gaps that can be filled through skilled observation, interviews and other assessment measures. For EIS clients this may be more difficult as they will tend to have shorter risk histories. Shared risk formulations provide a framework for sharing information and improving communication alongside setting treatment or management and supervision targets. Our EWS-R methodology can be also applied in community settings but will need to take account of potentially more limited opportunities to accurately observe the emergence of signs. More minor changes in behaviour will be more difficult to monitor in the community and larger changes may occur too late to prevent the risk behaviour occurring. Where changes are more difficult to notice, more frequent visits and opportunities to interact with the person (e.g. through social activities) should be considered. Getting carers and others who may be supporting the person on board may be possible and should be considered as a useful adjunct.

In cases where there is a clear link between risk or problematic behaviours and psychotic relapse, both can monitored. When admission does occur a post-admission debrief process is often helpful, focusing on the following areas.

- A description of changes in mental state or behaviour leading up to the admission.
- Presence of specific stressors or other potential triggers (e.g. housing problems, family crisis, changes in substance misuse, symptom severity/frequency and related distress, medication compliance, lack of staff resources, visits by less familiar staff, engagement).
- Were the signs of relapse missed, if so what were they?
- How could the team respond differently next time?

Multi-agency work is also common in these teams. Both person level and shared risk formulations provide a useful means of involving others outside of the team, promoting understanding and managing risk more effectively.

SAFE interventions

Daily TBCT may not be possible in community settings. Team members, however, may still be co-opted as co-therapists and indeed joint visits are more usual in AOT and EIS settings (although shift patterns may make this difficult to maintain). Specific cognitive strategies and dialogues can be usefully agreed following SAFE formulations and incorporated into a consistent approach to be adopted by the team in their ongoing contact with the person. This may focus on the presence of EWS-R to manage acute dynamic risk or more general distress reduction in the presence of specific stressors or activating events.

Behavioural approaches may be less easy to apply but team members should be familiar with the principles. Understanding the function of a behaviour in CARM terms can be helpful both to address unhelpful team beliefs but also to promote therapeutic interactions with clients: those who make frequent demands on the service or team members or make threats of violence and suicide.

SUMMARY

In this chapter we have outlined where aspects of SAFE can be most usefully applied in different service settings. The daily use of TBCT and behavioural management approaches are most easily adopted in inpatient or residential settings, whilst SAFE risk frameworks can be applied more broadly. Our formulation processes are useful in both types of settings and can help to address unhelpful team beliefs and dynamics and promote a more consistent approach to working with those with problematic behaviour and psychosis.

Chapter 17

Implementing SAFE

The dynamics of change

INTRODUCTION

Getting innovations adopted by complex organisations is often a slow process and one that requires careful persistent efforts. An understanding of the dynamics within which one is working (e.g. those operating within the care team, unit, programme or wider organisation) and what the barriers are to change might be (e.g. resources, performance targets etc.) is required. Potential champions and allies of the approach to be adopted will also need to be identified. In this chapter we describe the implementation issues of getting our Shared Assessment, Formulation and Education (SAFE) approach adopted into routine practice in the various settings we have highlighted as suitable. We reference the good practice literature and identify what lessons can be learned from it, as well as what we have learned ourselves from both our successes and mistakes to date.

Research has identified many strategies that improve the chances of successful adoption of innovations. Greenhalgh *et al.* (2004) reviewed more than 1000 documents concerning innovation and change management. They concluded that innovations are more easily adopted if they:

- have a clear, observable, unambiguous advantage, such as greater effectiveness;
- are compatible with the values, norms and perceived needs of the intended adopters;
- are perceived by key players as simple to use;
- allow intended users to experiment with them;
- can be adapted, refined or otherwise modified to suit their users' needs.

THE BENEFITS OF ADOPTING SAFE

We have found SAFE and our Cognitive Approach to Risk Management (CARM) model to be effective in working with those with problematic behaviours and they have proven their benefit where no other approaches have previously been successful, as illustrated through the case studies described in this book. Importantly, our methods and approaches fit well with the increased priorities given to both risk assessment and management. The many advantages of adopting SAFE and our CARM model can be clearly identified:

1   They provide a useful and clear role for all of the professionals involved in a client's care and illustrate how these roles may be different yet complimentary. The SAFE approach therefore underpins a coherent Multidisciplinary Team (MDT) approach.
2   They support the development of the whole team's skills in adopting a cognitive-behavioural therapy (CBT) approach and importantly facilitate access to psychological care for those who are hardest to reach with such psychological interventions.
3   They provide a framework for high-quality shared risk assessment.
4   They further support MDT assessment and care planning processes: they provide a means of improving team communication, the setting of clear goals and how these can be most usefully translated into day-to-day interventions and care-plan implementation.
5   They emphasise an understanding of the person's goals and reducing barriers to participation in ordinary community living (matching to the increased focus on recovery and social inclusion).
6   SAFE and CARM can potentially reduce lengths of stay in inpatient services (enabling the move away from continuing care [see Chapter 18 on outcomes]).

Services and clinicians can also adopt particular aspects of SAFE to suit their own needs by using the different templates and adapting the way in which they are completed or shared (e.g. using them for case busts, using the shared risk formulation alone). SAFE and CARM, however, are not simple and team members are likely to require support, supervision and training to fully implement them, a topic we address in Chapter 18.

When embarking on the process of innovation, especially to what are often well-established clinical practices, it is key to identify at an early stage who the most likely adopters will be. These are likely to be those who can be readily persuaded of its benefits and have the necessary skills to implement it. These so-called early adopters will be more likely to adopt SAFE and CARM if they meet a need that they have already identified, especially one that is a service priority. If this priority is also shared by higher management, service users and other key stakeholders then they are more likely to be adopted. As we have already stated, we believe that the current focus of healthcare is ripe for such an innovation. Some of these benefits will be more readily apparent to clinicians and some will fit better with managers and other stakeholders.

As Greenhalgh *et al.* (2004) note, within organisations, other influences operate regarding whether an individual adopts a particular innovation. Of particular importance is the decision-making process: who decides if an innovation is acceptable and whether they have the power to block it or facilitate its acceptance. Understanding the types of communication and influence operating within different professional groups is helpful. These can be described as lying on a continuum between pure diffusion in which the spread of innovations is unplanned, informal and decentralised and active dissemination in which the spread of innovation is planned, formal and centralised. The main factor, however, in promoting the adoption of innovations has been identified as the influence of social networks. Greenhalgh *et al.* (2004) note that doctors (and we would add psychologists and occupational therapists) tend to operate in informal, horizontal networks, while nurses often have formal, vertical networks. These social networks work in different ways. Horizontal ones are said to be more effective for spreading peer influence and supporting people to understand the personal relevance of an innovation, whilst vertical networks are seen as more effective for cascading information and for passing on authoritative decisions.

ASSESSING READINESS AND THE NEED FOR CHANGE

An innovation is most likely to be successfully adopted when an organisation is ready for change (Greenhalgh *et al.*, 2004). Several key features indicate when this point has been reached:

- when staff perceive that the current situation is intolerable;
- when the innovation fits with the existing values norms, strategies, goals and the ways of working of the organisation;
- when the organisation has made a full assessment of the implications of the innovation;
- when supporters of the innovation outnumber opponents, and are more strategically placed than them;
- when the innovation has been allocated adequate resources;
- when the organisation has systems in place to monitor and evaluate the impact of the innovation and can therefore respond rapidly to its consequences both predicted and unpredicted and intended and unintended.

We have found that SAFE has been most valued when staff become stuck with clients and feel frustrated and deskilled by working with them. Over time more staff have perceived the benefits of our approach. Allocating sufficient resources to this process has always been difficult and it is often helpful to let the team decide the most appropriate use of what is often a scarce resource.

For example, the first author (AM) continues to work as a clinician in an Assertive Outreach Team (AOT) where the team have clearly identified that high-risk clients are a priority for shared risk assessment and formulations. Utilising single case studies has been a useful tool in demonstrating to the team the benefits of SAFE in residential settings. This is most clearly demonstrated in John's case, where reducing barriers to community living and successful discharge have provided powerful and tangible evidence of the approach's impact.

The Northfield experiments show that if services become too internally focused then they may lose sight of the external world, they often create anxieties in others (e.g. service managers) and become a source of concern (Farquharson, 2004). Using more formal measures and service evaluation tools can be helpful in identifying the need for changes in practices. We use the QUARTZ system (Clifford *et al.*, 1989) as a problem-solving tool that avoids attributing blame for service failiures or difficulties. A QUARTZ review assesses the quality of care across a range of mental health settings. The review addresses five key areas: service aims; referral, selection and admission; programme planning and review; case coordination and recording; and service review. The QUARTZ is in the form of a semi-structured interview carried out potentially with the whole service team. Following the interview, initial findings are fed back and any amendments made to the review findings. The final set of recommendations and findings are then fed back to the whole staff group in a problem-solving format which may take the form of an away day aimed at generating possible solutions to any difficulties highlighted by the review and to plan the way forward. SAFE can be offered as one possible solution to some of the problems identified if appropriate. Other potentially useful tools are measures of expressed emotion (applied to staff) and the Ward Atmosphere Scale (Moos, 1996).

WHERE TO START

We have adopted a gradual process of implementing, testing out and developing SAFE and CARM, often targeting the most problematic-to-manage cases that result in the highest team anxiety and frustration. We began with one residential rehabilitation unit and one AOT using shared person level formulations. Clinicians readily found this process helpful in better understanding the problems they and the client faced and often wished to adopt them as case busts in the community team. Sharing this approach with other psychologists through a horizontal process (e.g. via special interest groups and workshops) has led to wider adoption. We found psychiatry colleagues to be particularly influenced by the benefits of a shared risk assessment and our CARM formulation framework. These have of course fitted well with priorities surrounding improving risk assessment and management.

Persuading other residential units of the benefits of adopting the assessment elements of SAFE and CARM has proved more difficult. A vertical network approach whereby information and practice are disseminated and supported by senior nursing colleagues has helped to mitigate resistance to adopting this aspect of SAFE. Concerns about the effectiveness of these residential rehabilitation units has also ironically been helpful in persuading teams of the benefits of evaluating their work more routinely using measures such as the Challenging Behaviour Checklist for Psychosis (CBC-P), which have now been integrated into the care record system. However, the main key to successfully adopting them has been to evolve a clear process whereby assessment findings can be routinely translated into care plans by the MDT. One clear advantage of the CBC-P is that the items can be directly used as care plan items (unlike other tools, which provide only broad treatment targets). More specialised assessments such as those undertaken by psychologists or occupational therapists will first require interpretation of their often complex findings and translation into achievable strategies.

SAFE formulations will also require some translation if their findings are to be made relevant to care plans. The role of the psychologist can be most helpful here since formulations are a common feature of their practice. However, this also needs to be a multidisciplinary process. A pre Care Programme Approach (CPA) meeting is one method we have developed whereby the different professionals involved (usually the Case Formulation Team [CFT]) can bring together assessment and formulation findings and agree intervention targets, which can then be translated into care plan goals, as described in Chapter 15. Service level formulations may be less easy to implement since adopting them implicitly requires a change in service philosophy, aims and values.

Some staff will inevitably not be persuaded by a new approach and may even actively sabotage efforts to promote it. Having senior managers on board is vital in this respect as such staff may require active management to bring them on board or enable them to move on to other services that may better suit them. Burnout and what may be termed 'change fatigue' are also important to consider. Staff, particularly those working in residential rehabilitation services and some community mental health teams, tend to be a neglected group and will often not have been supported to adopt new practices; these are topics addressed in Chapter 18. Staff may also need time to see the benefits accrue and that in actual fact people become easier to manage once initial efforts have been made to successfully implement new practice. Staff will also bring to their jobs not only their formal role prescriptions but also their personal histories and professional experiences, which are not always benign (Farquharson, 2004). Training and supervision are important here if staff are to be helped to develop more compassionate ways of working. Our approach to formulating staff beliefs alongside clients' difficulties (described in Chapter 8) is also useful here.

We have faced many of these difficulties when working with staff groups. We have found that it has been important to accept that change may be slow, formulate the reasons why new practices are rejected, have our own supervision, be persistent and maintain a belief that what we are offering is something that is better. If others can persuade us of the benefits of a different approach then this is welcomed. Indeed, we would not wish to suggest that all of the ideas in this book have grown in isolation. Rather, we have developed our work through an ongoing interaction with colleagues from all disciplines and in sharing, discussing and problem solving with them and subsequently modifying our work in response.

SUMMARY

In this chapter we have described something of our own approach to innovation and highlighted some of the main factors we have considered in implementing our work and getting it adopted by others. Of course, to sustain an innovation and spread its implementation throughout an entire organisation, or even wider, requires consideration of a broader range of factors (see Greenhalgh *et al.*, 2004). However, we feel that we have made a useful start within certain areas of specialist services within one trust. The second author (DH) is currently extending SAFE to neurorehabilitation settings in the independent sector. This book is an attempt to make our work available to a wider audience. In our next and final chapter we offer some guidance on the role of training in supporting the adoption of SAFE and CARM and discuss how supervision and reflective practice may usefully compliment this.

Chapter 18

Training, supervision, reflective practice and staff support groups

INTRODUCTION

The potential for teams to re-enact clients' early patterns of interaction with other care givers is high when working with treatment-resistant clients. Dysfunctional staff–client interactions can reflect dynamics such as splitting (Davenport, 2006) and malignant alienation syndrome (Holmes, 2004) or in behavioural terms mutual reinforcement of avoidance and the use of punishment behaviours. Staff can also develop unhealthy dependency issues and may assume complete responsibility for those whom they care for (Hinshelwood, 2004). Although aspects of the Shared Assessment, Formulation and Education (SAFE) process are designed to help address these patterns of care giving we recognise that other processes will be required to ensure that staff can engage in a more therapeutic way with their clients and maintain appropriate boundaries with them. Ongoing training, detailed supervision of clinical work and the provision of staff support are integral to psychologically informed practice (Holmes, 2004). These form part of a package we have developed in order to successfully implement SAFE-informed practice. In this chapter we highlight the need for training, supervision, reflective practice and staff support groups and provide an overview of how we have undertaken this process.

STAFF STRESS AND BURNOUT

The Department of Health recognises work-related stress and low morale as widespread problems in health services (DH, 2000, 2003). The prolonged effects of stress brought about through continuous high levels of demand, such as that experienced in care giving, has implications for the physical and emotional wellbeing of staff. Such stress can be serious, leading to a state of exhaustion often described colloquially as 'burnout' (Payne, 1999). Burnout can include emotional exhaustion (Maslach, 1982) and in our experience can increase the tendency of staff and carers to make negative attributions (sometimes called 'depersonalisation' in this context), to jump to conclusions and to perceive threat more readily (just as it does in our clients). Ultimately, this reduces the capacity to care for others and deliver that care effectively. This can subsequently impact upon outcomes such as increased hospitalisation (Priebe *et al.*, 2004).

One factor often linked to burnout is that of reciprocity (Schaufeli, 1999). Lack of reciprocity (seeing improvement or receiving gratitude) is often inherent in relationships with patients but can be especially marked in those clients with psychosis who are hardest to engage and treat. Frequently, recovery is only partial and any gratitude may be numbed by clients' maladaptive relationships (Hinshelwood, 2004). They will often resent services and treatment being imposed on them. In addition, such clients may have very little if any insight, may not be distressed (a basis often for help seeking) and may see their behaviours as non-problematic and indeed quite justified. As Gray and Mulligan (2009) note, the attitude and behaviour of the wider organisation can also lack reciprocity.

High levels of contact with those with severe mental illness lowers satisfaction in workers (Oberlander, 1990). The seriousness of the illness, degree of dependency and aggressive hostility have all been associated with burnout (Maslach, 1978). Similarly, threats of violence and suicide in community patients are experienced as stressful by staff (Prosser *et al.*, 1996). Workers themselves come into care work for a variety of reasons (e.g. social status, the need to be needed) and it is important to understand when these are present and particularly when they are thwarted since staff may then react in unhelpful ways (see Hinshelwood, 2004 and Gray and Mulligan, 2009 for a fuller discussion of these issues).

USING SUPERVISION, REFLECTIVE PRACTICE AND STAFF SUPPORT GROUPS TO REDRESS THE BALANCE

In their recent book on staff support groups, Hartley and Kennard (2009) note that the need to both care for staff and provide a staff support mechanism, whilst widely recognised, is all too often neglected. Importantly, groups such as staff support groups may reduce violent episodes on wards (Kho *et al.*, 1998) and are valued by at least 50 per cent of staff who use them (Hartley and Kennard, 2009). Different types of groups may be needed for different purposes. We have employed supervision, reflective practice and staff support groups at different times (facilitated by either our colleagues or ourselves) to directly support SAFE-based approaches or to meet other needs identified by the teams and services we have worked with. Each has different merits. In their overview of the different types of groups, Hartley and Kennard (2009) provide a useful set of considerations. Staff support groups are noted as being useful for staff groups who work closely together under some stress. These aim to help members talk about the emotional impact of their work and support each other in coping with stressful situations. They can promote wellbeing and enable staff to avoid shutting down emotionally in order to protect themselves. Support groups can therefore help the team to better communicate and work through obstacles to team working practices arising from problems either between team members or between the team and the wider organisation. These groups offer a protected time in which staff can obtain support and learn from each other. Ultimately, these benefits should accrue to produce better care and smoother team functioning.

Reflective practice groups tend to focus more on analysing decision-making processes. They have been defined by Hartley and Kennard (2009) as the process whereby practioners stop and think about their practice, consciously analyse their decision-making processes and relate theory to what they do in their practice. Such groups have tended to take the place of more traditional staff support groups but may be more structured, with timed endings and action points. The facilitator may take a tutorial role as well as helping members to reflect on what was done and the feelings it aroused and encourage the sharing of feelings and experiences. These groups provide the opportunity to share with and learn from others who will often have had similar experiences.

In keeping with Ross (1990), we have used reflective practice groups to generate hypotheses about what things are done and how and why they are done, explore the consequences of practice and generate alternatives. This can be particularly helpful in enabling staff to look at the way they respond to clients and identify unhelpful reinforcement patterns. We have also used these groups in a similar way to Cowdrill and Dannahy (2009) who describe their use on acute wards. They can be used to reflect on the everyday practices of the unit or team and to share feelings and experiences of the work. These can be useful in building on our training programme, which we discuss below.

Supervision groups aim to help practioners monitor and improve the quality of their work as well as having a more supportive function. Three broad types of supervision group have been identified by Hawkins and Sholet (2000): those that meet only for supervision; those that work as a team but with different clients; and those that work as a team with the same client group. These groups are typically small, focused on individual learning (often with reference to theory–practice links) and may have defined roles and responsibilities. Case discussion groups are similar but are more focused on the particular issues of a single case rather than the wider aspects of learning and practice (Hartley and Kennard, 2009).

We have favoured the third type of supervision group outlined by Hawkins and Sholet (2000) but include elements of a case discussion group (as it readily links to the Case Formulation Team [CFT]. The CFT comprises a core group of staff who work closely with the person and following on from initial assessment and formulation tasks go on to deliver or facilitate the core interventions agreed in their care plan. The CFT also affords the opportunity to consider whether what they are doing is effective, whether or not needs have changed (the need-adapted principle[1]) and whether the interventions confirm or support working hypotheses (the evidence-based principle). The CFT may also reflect on the need for more assessment and whether a shared reformulation is needed in the light of this learning process.

Establishing a CFT is more difficult in services such as Assertive Outreach Teams (AOTs) that operate a whole team approach where we have favoured a more reflective practice format. Staff support groups are also helpful. These require time and consistency focused on establishing trust between members and with the facilitator in order that emotional issues can be more fully explored and addressed.

Barriers to establishing support and learning mechanisms

Although the various types of support and development mechanisms we have discussed so far are accepted as important and useful, they are not always readily taken up. We have found that they can sometimes be viewed with suspicion by teams and care staff and as ready-made solutions by managers to staffing or service problems. They are of course not such panaceas. Consideration needs to be given first to planning and establishing any group or supervision process if both facilitator and participants are to find them rewarding and productive (see Hartley and Kennard, 2009 and Hawkins and Shohet, 2000 for more detailed guidance). As Hartley and Kennard (2009) note, those in the caring professions often see themselves as providing rather than receiving care; they also may see work-related stress as normal or have sufficiently difficult relationships with team members to warrant not feeling comfortable sharing their concerns or feelings with them in a group. Individual supervision may be preferable for some people in this latter category, but the benefits of a group approach for dealing with such issues should not be overlooked (Thomas, 2003; Punter, 2007). Recognising that others may feel the same and that work-related stress is normal can be one of the main benefits of staff support groups (Hartley and Kennard, 2009). We incorporate a discussion of these issues into our training programme outlined below. Our supervision groups follow on from this training and so help to set the scene by normalising these issues in advance. An organisational culture that proactively encourages the development of mechanisms such as staff support groups, Hartley and Kennard (2009), argue is more likely to make it easier for employees to ask for or offer support.

1 See Chapter 2 for a discussion of SAFE principles.

TRAINING ISSUES

Holmes (2004) has noted (in relation to ward-based staff in particular) that equipping staff with psychological interventions can help them build better therapeutic alliances with clients. It can also help staff to develop self-awareness and reflective practice to reduce projection and lower expressed emotion and the likelihood of malignant alienation syndrome. Skills often atrophy in the traditional ward setting and not enough attention is paid to providing training that is appropriate to the setting and to the management structures needed to support it (Holmes, 2004). Even when training is more routinely available and taken up it is often not utilised, as in the case of behavioural family therapy (e.g. Fadden, 2006). There are a variety of explanations for this (Fadden et al., 2004), including caseload demands, engagement difficulties and clients meeting the appropriate criteria. We have also observed that training is often not tailored to the complex needs of those with the most treatment-resistant and challenging presentations and hence is perceived as less relevant by staff. Consequently, these clients are even less likely to receive good-quality psychological care.

Training itself can be used as an opportunity for understanding staff pan-situational care beliefs and eliciting unhealthy team dynamics. We often ask teams to choose a difficult case that they are struggling with. This quickly reveals team disagreements and conflicts as well as staffs' beliefs about their roles and their personal values. If tackled sensitively, this can be an opportunity for group cognitive behavioural therapy (CBT) with the whole treatment team.

In considering what to focus our training efforts on we have observed how behavioural approaches have fallen out of favour in recent years whilst the current push towards manualised CBT is often unrealistic for the clients whom we have presented in this book. Nevertheless, in our experience, staff continue to undertake training (often in general CBT principles but sometimes those specific to psychotic populations) but then often find it hard to translate this into working with more complex treatment-resistant individuals. In contrast, the valuable skills of correctly applying behavioural interventions have often been lost and may be seen as lacking a recovery focus. Training in the use of the World Health Organization's (1999) *International classification of functioning and disability* (ICIDH-2) model (described in Chapter 3) is useful here in helping staff to recognise the value of behavioural principles. By relocating clients' difficulties at the behavioural level and illustrating how these create barriers to social participation and recovery, clinicians can more readily see the value of a behavioural perspective. The Cognitive Approach to Risk Management (CARM) model (described in Chapter 7) further illustrates how these principles can be utilised successfully alongside more contemporary cognitive approaches. For those team members who may have undertaken some CBT training we have found that their training may also be at odds with the more rational emotive behaviour therapy derived approach we draw on in this book. Consequently, some training in an ABC-informed model is necessary, especially since it is the model we encourage them to apply to themselves. In addition to this we provide training covering the following areas:

1 Understanding and using the CARM model.
2 Understanding and using the components of each aspect of the personal level formulation.
3 Applying the WHO ICIDH-2 model.
4 Understanding the key aspects of the shared risk formulation model.
5 Learning theory and the principles of behavioural management.
6 An understanding of the nature and impact of negative symptoms. This is essential when working with behavioural deficits.
7 Engagement skills: how to talk to people experiencing psychosis in order to elicit and understand the phenomenology of their psychosis and their view of their behaviour.
8 Specific CBT intervention strategies: how and when to apply them.
9 Using early warning signs of risk and psychotic relapse.
10 Goal planning and writing care plans (SMART goals and Goal Attainment Scaling).

We provide training over six days with time in between to practice skills and reflect on each module. Ideas and skills taught in the initial module are integrated into later days, thus gradually building a more complex understanding of the various SAFE components. We have found that this training has been consistently taken up and positively evaluated and has the support of senior colleagues and managers. This has been key to successfully implementing SAFE and using our CARM model and other shared formulation templates in routine clinical practice.

TRAINING AND SERVICE OUTCOMES

Over the past two years we have trained approximately 60 per cent of staff locally in Birmingham and Solihull who work in non-acute inpatient services, supported by the supervision processes we have described in this chapter. SAFE formulation frameworks and templates are used as standard in these services and we have incorporated many of the assessment tools (e.g. the Challenging Behaviours Checklist for Psychosis [CBC-P]) as part of a standard assessment suite, which commissioners have adopted as service outcome measures.

It is difficult to disentangle how these developments have improved outcomes in a time of great change within the National Health Service in the

United Kingdom. However, over the last two years we have gathered length-of-stay data, which show that those staying over seven years have reduced from 67 per cent to 40 per cent and those staying over five years have decreased from 47 per cent to 26 per cent.

The second author (DH) has delivered training on risk assessment and the shared risk formulation to all eight AOTs in the Birmingham area. Sixty-eight per cent of the AOT staff felt that the risk training was 'extremely helpful' and 32 per cent felt that it was 'helpful', with no one rating it as 'unhelpful'. Prior to the training, 15 per cent of staff felt that they had *no* success in implementing risk assessment, management and formulation, 42 per cent felt that they had *little* success and a further 42 per cent felt that they had been *reasonably* successful. Only 1 per cent felt that they had been *fully* successful in implementing risk assessment, management and formulation. In terms of knowledge before training, 4 per cent of AOT staff felt that they had *no* knowledge about risk assessment, management and formulation, whilst 51 per cent of staff felt that their knowledge regarding risk assessment, management and formulation before training was *little*. Forty-five per cent felt that their knowledge was *reasonable* and none of them felt *completely* knowledgeable before training. After training, 37 per cent of staff felt *completely* knowledgeable about risk assessment, management and formulation. Sixty-two per cent of staff now considered that they had a *reasonable* knowledge of risk assessment, management and formulation. Only 1 per cent of staff felt that they now had *little* knowledge and 0 per cent felt that they had *no* knowledge. In regards to confidence conducting risk assessment, management and formulation, before training 10 per cent judged themselves as having *no* confidence, 49 per cent rated their confidence as *little*, 39 per cent rated their confidence as *reasonable* and only 2 per cent felt that they were *completely* confident in conducting risk assessment, management and formulation. After training, 39 per cent of staff now felt that they were *completely* confident in conducting risk assessment, management and formulation, 56 per cent of staff rated their confidence as *moderate*, 6 per cent rated their confidence as *little* and 0 per cent thought they had *no* confidence after training.

The training and formulation framework provided were clearly viewed as useful by staff. Notably, the three areas most highly rated by staff as crucial to the success of implementing the framework were a team approach to assessment and formulation, ongoing training and time allocated to completing risk assessment. The risk assessment frameworks presented in this book are now used routinely across the teams are the focus of regular case-busting sessions.

The first author (AM) has also delivered training to early intervention services locally in the principles of person level and service level formulations. Again it is difficult to evaluate the individual impact of this, but informal feedback suggests that shared formulation has become an increasingly standard part of care planning processes.

SUMMARY

Understanding the ever-increasing multiple demands now placed on clinical staff and the emotional impact of working with highly treatment-resistant clients with problematic behaviours is key in engaging the staff team and in changing practice. Staff support, reflective practice and supervision groups can help address these difficulties and reduce staff stress and burnout. We support this through the routine use of personal level and CARM formulations, cognitive and behavioural measures, psychologically informed care plans (see Chapter 15), co-working (modelling skills) and individual supervision. Supervision and reflective practice groups can be used to support the transfer of skills and knowledge from SAFE-based training programmes and ensure that they are integrated firmly into routine clinical practice.

Challenging Behaviour Checklist for Psychosis (CBC-P)

Date rated: **Service/unit:**
Client's name: **Rater's name:**

To be completed with reference to clinical and psychiatric notes.

- For each item, please rate '*recency/frequency*' on a scale of 0–8 (refer to the Rating Scale).
- For all items rated greater than '0' on '*recency/frequency*', also rate the item for this client on a scale of '*severity/risk*', ranging from 0 to 4 (refer to the Rating Scale).
- **DO NOT** complete severity/risk ratings for items rated as zero on the '*recency/frequency*' scale (if they have never occurred then they are not relevant to the client concerned).

Please use the Rating Scale below to rate each individual item.

Stage 1: Rate each item for recency/frequency (0–8)

RECENCY/FREQUENCY

The behaviour HAS occurred in the last month:

8   In the LAST WEEK the behaviour has occurred:
(i) daily or almost daily or (ii) 3 times or more per day for at least 3 days
7   Has occurred on at least 3 occasions in the last week
6   Has occurred 1–2 times in the last week
5   Has occurred in the last month but not the last week

The behaviour HAS NOT occurred in the last month:

4   Present in the last 3 months (but not the last month)

3 Present in the last 6 months (but not the last month)
2 Present in the last 12 months (but not the last 6 months)
1 Present in client's history but not in last 12 months
0 Never present

Stage 2: Only rate 'severity/risk' for items with recency/frequency scores >0

SEVERITY/RISK

When the behaviour is present how problematic is it?

4 Direct and imminent physical harm, potentially life threatening to self or others
3 Imminent physical harm to self or others (non-life threatening)
2 Emotional distress to others or long-term threat to physical health or safety of self or others
1 Social exclusion or barrier to person participating in daily living
0 No challenge (none of the above)

Intentional / deliberate harm to self	Recency/ frequency	Severity/ risk
1. Intentionally scratching self without drawing blood		
2. Intentionally scratching self – drawing blood		
3. Picking persistently at wounds		
4. Pulling out hair		
5. Cutting self superficially (not requiring the use of medical intervention)		
6. Cutting self – serious attempts to sever blood vessel		
7. Biting superficially (not requiring the use of medical intervention)		
8. Biting – serious attempts to sever a blood vessel		
9. Attempt to amputate limb or body part		
10. Attempt to remove sense organ e.g. eye		
11. Stubbing out cigarettes on self		
12. Setting self alight (body or clothing whilst worn)		
13. Self-suffocation/strangulation (non-hanging)		
14. Self-suffocation/strangulation (by hanging)		
15. Starving self		
16. Banging head off objects		
17. Hitting self		
18. Swallowing inedible objects		
19. Hoarding prescription medication for suspected overdose		
20. Attempted overdose of prescribed medication		
21. Ingestion of noxious or poisonous substances		

Verbal aggression	Recency/ frequency	Severity/ risk
22. Non-directed shouting, swearing		
23. Shouting, swearing or abusive comments to others (non-threatening) – staff		
24. Shouting, swearing or abusive comments to others (non-threatening) – patients		
25. Threats of physical harm to patients		
26. Threats of physical harm to staff		
27. Threats to kill staff		
28. Threats to kill patients		
29. Threats to kill others important to staff or patients		

Physical aggression against objects	Recency/ frequency	Severity/ risk
30. Hitting doors/walls		
31. Smashing windows		
32. Throwing objects (not directed at others)		
33. Breaking possessions of others		
34. Breaking own possessions		

Physical aggression towards others	Recency/ frequency	Severity/ risk
35. Bumping into others		
36. Blocking path of others deliberately		
37. Threatening gestures to others		
38. Pushing others		
39. Hitting/kicking others		
40. Pulling hair of others		
41. Grabbing others by limbs in forceful manner		
42. Grabbing others by throat		
43. Tripping others up		
44. Spitting directed at others		
45. Throwing objects at others (not weapon)		
46. Use of weapons against others		

Sexually inappropriate behaviours	Recency/ frequency	Severity/ risk
47. Sexually inappropriate speech (non-directed)		
48. Asking overly personal questions of others (non-sexual)		
49. Asking personal sexualised questions (non-suggestive)		
50. Making sexual requests or demands of others		
51. Non-sexual touching of others (inappropriate)		
52. Exposing self (inadvertent)		
53. Exposing self (directed)		
54. Public touching of own genitals		
55. Public masturbation		
56. Attempts to touch private parts of others		
57. Attempts to rub against others		
58. Attempts to force sex on others		

Fire risk behaviours	Recency/ frequency	Severity/ risk
59. Leaving lit cigarettes in inappropriate places		
60. Leaving on appliances which have a high likelihood of causing fire		
61. Hoarding of potentially flammable materials		
62. Attempts to gain access to means to start fire (e.g. matches, lighter)		
63. Deliberate fire setting with low chance of collateral damage		
64. Deliberate fire setting with raised risk of collateral damage		

Compulsive behaviours	Recency/ frequency	Severity/ risk
65. Excessive checking of environment (e.g. appliances)/ own appearance (delete as appropriate)		
66. Excessive cleaning of self/environment (delete as appropriate)		
67. Ritualised behaviours (e.g. behaviours which subjectively need to be carried out in exact sequence or manner)		
68. Hoarding of objects for no apparent purpose		
69. Excessive eating of appropriate food		
70. Excessive consumption of unhealthy food		

Acquisitive behaviours	Recency/ frequency	Severity/ risk
71. Excessive borrowing from others without reciprocity		
72. Extortion of property from others by threat		
73. Theft of property of others		

Absconding	Recency/ frequency	Severity/ risk
74. Loitering without reason near to potential exits or escape routes		
75. Failure to return from leave on time		
76. Failure to attend approved leave destination		
77. Leaving ward without permission		
78. Tampering with locks or secreting devices which might be used to do so		

Socially inappropriate behaviours	Recency/ frequency	Severity/ risk
79. Shouting or talking loudly to self in public		
80. Wearing excessive clothing		
81. Wearing clothing which is too revealing		
82. Wearing items which would appear strange to others		
83. Invading personal space of others		
84. Spitting (non-directed)		
85. Urinating in inappropriate places		
86. Defecating in inappropriate places		
87. Bizarre speech content		
88. Making requests without appropriate politeness		
89. Making frequent and excessive demands of others (too often or too impatient)		
90. Assuming odd postures for extended periods		
91. Excessive and unfounded complaints about staff and patients		
92. Inappropriate phone calls to others e.g. family		
93. Inappropriate phone calls to emergency services		
94. Consumption or ingestion of illegal or non-permitted substances (must be evidenced by being caught in possession or positive drug/alcohol screen)		
95. Attempts to sell illegal or non-permitted substances		
96. Attempts to pass illegal or non-permitted substances to others		
97. Accidental overdose of illegal substances		

Behavioural deficits	Recency/ frequency	Severity/ risk
98. Wearing too little clothing to maintain appropriate body temperature		
99. Crossing roads without awareness of personal safety		
100. Failure to consume adequate food or fluids		
101. Failure to make provision to safeguard against monetary exploitation by others		
102. Failure to make provision to safeguard against sexual exploitation by others		
103. Failure to make provision to safeguard against physical violence from others		
104. Refusal to speak to others for several hours at a time		
105. Refusal to wash		
106. Refusal to change clothes		
107. Refusal to use sanitary items		
108. Refusal to maintain oral hygiene		
109. Refusal to get out of bed at appropriate times		
110. Refusal of oral medication		
111. Refusal of depot medication		
112. Refusal of appropriate medical examinations		
113. Sleeping excessively during the day		
114. Lack of participation in activities		
115. Avoidance of leaving room		
116. Avoidance of leaving ward		

Please use the space below to include any further challenging behaviours not listed above that are presented by the named client, detailing the behaviour and indicating the recency/frequency and severity/risk for each behaviour.

Challenging behaviour	Recency/ frequency	Severity/ risk

Recovery Goal Planning Interview

SECTION 1: LONG-TERM LIFE GOALS

As part of planning your care I'd like to talk to you about long-term goals you might have for your future and how we might work towards them together. Sometimes people have clear goals in mind and sometimes they don't; if you don't that's okay, we can think about them together. You might want to think about things you used to do or things other people do which you might like to try. In order to help you, I'll ask you about some common areas people think about in their lives but if there are any other areas, we can cover those too.

Accommodation: Where would you like to be living in the future? What sort of accommodation do you see yourself living in (e.g. supported living, own flat, still in hospital, with friends or family etc.)?

Employment: Would you like to work in the future (either paid or voluntary)? What sort of work would you enjoy/like to be able to do? What sort of work have you done in the past that you were good at or enjoyed?

Education: Do you have any qualifications already? Are you interested in pursuing further education or training (e.g. job coaching, college, literacy, practical skills such as DIY, car maintenance or cooking)?

Intimate relationships: Are you in a relationship at the moment? If yes . . . do you see yourself continuing with this relationship? Would there be things you'd like to change or things you might need support with? If no, do you see yourself having a relationship in the future? How did you go about meeting people before and do you have any plans?

Relationship with family and friends: Do you have friends or family around at the moment? Would you like to change these relationships in any way (if so how) Would you like to re-establish contact with people you used to see? Would you like to make new friends? If so, how did you used to do this?

SECTION 2: HOBBIES AND LEISURE INTERESTS:

In this next section I would like to ask you to list any hobbies or interest (past or present) that you enjoy or would like to think about in the future

Home and garden (e.g. cooking, DIY, listening to music, watching films, gardening, having pets)

Arts and crafts (e.g. photography, painting/drawing, collecting)

Sports and physical activities (e.g. watching live sports, going to the gym, cycling, dancing, playing pool, country walks etc.)

Getting out and about (e.g. holidays or day trips, going to the cinema, clubs, bowling, visiting museums or art galleries, shopping, pubs and eating out, joining local interest groups)

SECTION 3: CHOICES AND NEEDS

In this final section I would like to ask you about what choices you would like to make that might form longer-term goals for us to work towards helping you meeting.

Choice of mental healthcare: What sort of service would you like in the future (e.g. hospital-based care, community team, crisis support, respite care, GP)? What level of contact would you ideally like in the future? What professional input do you think would be useful to you (e.g. psychiatrist, psychologist, social worker, nurse etc.)?

Spiritual needs: Are you religious or do you have any spiritual beliefs? Are these being met at the moment? Would you like to develop more opportunities in this area (e.g. attending mosque, church groups etc.)?

Physical health: Do you have any goals to improve or maintain your physical health? (Are you being regularly checked out by your GP; do have any concerns about your physical health; are there things you'd like to change such as diet, exercise, giving up smoking?)

Financial security/independence: Do you have any goals about your future financial situation? (e.g. do you have debts you need to clear or which you need advice about; are you getting the full range of benefits you are entitled *to; do you need to set up a bank or post office account or start saving for things?)*

Based on what we've discussed so far, what specific goals would you like to achieve in the future?

1   ....
2   ....
3   ....
4   ....
5   ....
6   ....
7   ....
8   ....

SECTION 4: ESTABLISHING COLLABORATIVE AND REALISTIC GOALS

If we now look at the goals we've written down, do you see them as being realistic goals for you to achieve in the longer term? If not realistic, can a compromise be reached? Ask questions such as (1) What is the most important aspect of this goal for you? (2) Are there any other ways of achieving this aspect of the goal?

If the client feels that some goals are not achievable then the interviewer should explore why this is (consider lack of confidence as an issue if it seems achievable from your knowledge of the client).

If the client feels that the goals are achievable and realistic but the interviewer and others do not, then ask the client:

1   *How realistic and achievable would other people say this goal is for you (e.g. carers, friends, staff etc.)?*
2   *Have you tried to attain this goal before?*
3   *What caused you not to succeed in achieving this goal before?*

What would be some goals for us to aim at that we could both agree are achievable and realistic for you?

1   ....
2   ....
3   ....
4   ....
5   ....
6   ....
7   ....
8   ....
9   ....
10 ....

SECTION 5: IDENTIFYING ACTIVITY LIMITATIONS/ BARRIERS TO PARTICIPATION

In this section I would like to explore with you what some of the potential obstacles or barriers might be.

1   *What support might you require to achieve these goals?*
2   *What things outside of yourself are getting in the way?*

Do you do anything that might contribute to you not achieving these goals in the future? [The interviewer should raise any objective barriers e.g. risk or behavioural excesses gently here as potential barriers if the client does not do so.]

What things would you need to be doing/be able to do that you are not doing/not able to do at the moment, in order to achieve these goals?

Spontaneous answer ....
....
....
....
....
....
....

Consider the following areas to prompt the client:

- personal care and mobility (e.g. hygiene, dressing, toileting etc.);
- domestic tasks (e.g. cooking, housework, paying bills);
- community access (e.g. use of public transport, shopping, menu planning, use of money);
- social interactions (e.g. communication ability, bizarre speech, invasion of personal space);
- awareness and safety (e.g. crossing roads, poor concentration);
- cognitive problems (e.g. poor memory, easily distracted).

SECTION 6: SHARED TREATMENT TARGETS

In order for us to work together to help you achieve the goals we've discussed, what areas would we need to work on with you as a team? [The interviewer should attempt to establish clearly defined areas for treatment and intervention.]

1 ....
2 ....
3 ....

4   ....
5   ....
6   ....
7   ....
8   ....
9   ....
10 ....

Personal, Social, Developmental and Psychiatric History Assessment

Used as part of a semi-structured interview to assess for capacities, developmental influences, attitudes, values and beliefs.

EARLY DEVELOPMENT

Include here any factors known to have implications for development: organic, social, familial and how these were dealt with by others.

1 Indications of complications during conception, pregnancy or birth (e.g. mother significantly ill or involved in accidents during pregnancy, alcohol or drug misuse during pregnancy, pre-term birth, low birth weight, anoxia at birth, etc.).
2 Indications of temperament (e.g. profiles of action and mood such as extroversion–introversion, shyness, anxiousness, hyperactivity). Information on ease or difficulty to care for as a baby, feeding, sleeping, crying patterns, etc. How temperamental patterns were subsequently dealt with (e.g. goodness of fit with care giver).
3 Information about developmental milestones and any indication of any abnormal delay in achieving them: crawling (average 7 months; consider 12–18 months or later a delay); standing alone (average 11 months; consider 17–24 months or later a delay); walking alone (average 11–12 months; consider 18–24 months or later a delay); first words (average 11–12 months; consider 19–26 months or later a delay).
4 Infancy illnesses, injuries, malnutrition, neglect impacting on brain development (e.g. encephalitis, meningitis, epilepsy).
5 Note conditions of worth (in order to feel worthwhile in the eyes of significant others). Consider personal codes, moral values learned from parents and important others' rules for living. Consider interpersonal schemas (beliefs about how to relate to others). Note psychotic and non-psychotic pan-situational and in-situation beliefs.

FAMILY HOME

Consider relevant features of home and family life throughout childhood and adolescence, including the physical and social environment and emotional characteristics.

1   What was their home life like: chaotic, transitory lifestyle, financial deprivation? Who was present at home?
2   Have they ever been in local authority care, in a foster home or children's home? If so, at what age, for how long, why, and what was their reaction to this care?
3   Any indications of any material, emotional, physical or sexual abuse or neglect?
4   Any significant breakdown of the family structure during childhood or adolescence (e.g. divorce, death of parent or sibling, absent parent, brought up by grandparents or relatives as main carers)?
5   Approach to discipline within the family: presence of appropriate rules and boundaries. How was any rule breaking dealt with? Who did most of the discipline? Was the discipline fair and consistent etc.? Was physical or extreme discipline used?

FAMILY HISTORY

Information should be gathered in relation to all significant carers throughout childhood (e.g. parents, step-parents, other substitute carers). For each significant carer, information should be gathered about the following areas.

1   Their description of the person and their relationship with them.
2   Family patterns pre-morbid and post onset: emotional over-involvement, overprotection, hostility and criticism.
3   History of substance use, criminal or psychiatric history of the significant carer.
4   How did the significant carer deal with problems and stress, including any indications of temper dyscontrol, violence, or over-control of emotions?
5   Current relationship and contact between the client and the significant carer.
6   Similar information should also be gathered about the individual's siblings.

OTHER IMPORTANT RELATIONSHIPS

Information should be gathered regarding the pattern of significant relationships (other than the family) that the individual has been involved in: age of onset, age and gender of partner, durations, seriousness, and problems encountered.

1   Ability to sustain close friendships (male and female).
2   Any work relationships including problems maintaining appropriate boundaries.
3   How problems within the relationship were dealt with.
4   Whether it was a sexual relationship.
5   Presence of any sexual problems within the relationship.
6   Reason for relationship breakdown.
7   How the individual coped with and accepted the breakdown of the relationship.
8   How long was it before the next relationship began?

EDUCATIONAL HISTORY

Information should be gathered about the individual's progression through the education system.

1   How old when first attended school?
2   How many schools attended? What was the reason behind any change of schools? Was there a normal progression through school? Was there any evidence of behaviour problems, learning problems?
3   Were the schools attended all mainstream schools? Did they attend any remedial classes, special schools, or receive any individual tutoring?
4   Were they ever 'statemented' as having special educational needs? If so, under what category and at what age? Any evidence of specific learning difficulties (e.g. dyslexia)?
5   When did they first go to school? Any indications of school refusal?
6   What was their overall view of school? What was good/bad about it?
7   Information should be gathered about the individual's ability to form friendships at school. How did they relate to and get on with other pupils; were they ever the victim of or the perpetrator of bullying?
8   Information on how the individual got on academically at school.
9   Any problems learning to read or write.
10   Any problems keeping up with the pace of the lessons.
11   Any difficulties concentrating or attending for periods of time.
12   Indications of hyperactivity and level of interest in school and in learning.
13   Information on how the individual related to teachers, any indication of hostility towards authority figures.

14 Any difficult behaviour at school: disruptiveness, rudeness to teachers, truancy, fighting, vandalism, lying, stealing and cheating (include age of onset, frequency, severity, punishment received, effect of punishment).
15 Has the individual ever been suspended or expelled from any schools?
16 What age did they leave school?
17 What exams were taken and/or passed? How did this match their and others' expectations? Do exam results reflect their abilities?
18 Any higher education courses or training courses attended (state if completed and level attained).

EMPLOYMENT HISTORY

Information should be gathered on the individual's record of employment since leaving school.

1 What kind of employment have they been in?
2 What are the relative time periods that they have been in work and out of work?
3 Have they ever been sacked, when and why?
4 What has been their relationship with employers and work colleagues?
5 What is their current employment situation?
6 Is there any pattern to periods of employment? A few jobs, held for long periods? Many jobs of short duration?

COPING STRATEGY HISTORY

Consider here the use of both functional (e.g. going for a walk, talking with others) and dysfunctional strategies (e.g. substance misuse, shouting out loud to the voices when in public), past and present strategies for both general problems and psychotic-related distress and behaviour.

1 How are problems dealt with/reacted to?
2 Information about any use of illegal substances, misuse of prescribed medication, pattern of use, periods of misuse and indication of dependency.
3 History of use of alcohol, pattern of use, periods of misuse and indication of dependency.
4 Information regarding any efforts to deal with any substance misuse problems.
5 Any indication of ruminating over problems, sleep problems.

NEUROLOGICAL ACCIDENTS OR ILLNESSES

Information should be gathered regarding whether the individual has a history of any serious illness or accidents resulting in head injury, concussion or especially unconsciousness, including self-inflicted injuries.

1   Record any event and injuries sustained.
2   Severity of the trauma: did it lead to concussion, hospitalisation (for how long, type of hospital, any follow-up appointments), unconsciousness (for how long)?
3   Did it result in amnesia (for how long)?
4   Problems/differences noticed after the event, what problems continue today, what specialist input is ongoing.

PSYCHIATRIC HISTORY

Include here details of all mental health problems and diagnoses as well as history of treatment and service use and their response to these.

1   Formal history of psychiatric illness, including diagnoses (primary and secondary) and any changes in diagnosis.
2   First contact with psychiatric or psychological services.
3   Number and length of inpatient or home treatment episodes (state if under Mental Health Act or other section, use of Compulsory Treatment Orders and if force was used)
4   Engagement history, including history of compliance with medication, engagement with services and treatments.
5   Any family history of mental illness.

RISK AND PROBLEMATIC BEHAVIOUR HISTORY

Record a description of the behaviour, when it occurred, under what circumstances and what were the short- (was rescued, rebuked, hit back) and longerterm consequences (excluded from school, anti-social behaviour orders [ASBOs] etc). Consider triggers for, frequency, intensity, duration of the behaviour. Information should be gathered regarding any instrumental use of violence, and age of onset.

1   Indications of early emotional or behavioural problems.
2   Any history of self-injurious behaviour.
3   Any history of past or present suicide thoughts or plans, statement of these plans or suicide attempts. Information should be gathered regarding

the nature of these thoughts/attempts and the severity of current suicidal plans.

4 Use of instruments/weapons (including hoarding or collecting and type of weapon).

6 Where violence appears to have been instrumental in nature, try to establish what the end goals were.

5 Injuries sustained (to self and others), including specification of the body area affected.

6 Details of any victims (e.g. age, gender, relationship to offender).

7 Presence of any relationship violence.

8 History of anger problems.

9 History of harbouring grudges, revenge fantasies, making threats (verbally or in writing).

10 Criminal history: age at first arrest, caution, conviction, number of convictions, type of offences, indication of escalation in offending.

11 Acts of arson: age at offence, number of offences, details type of property, threat to life, accelerant used, intent to cause damage or serious harm to property or people.

12 History of stalking, details of the incident/s and circumstances, victim characteristics.

13 Kidnapping, details of the incident/s and circumstances, victim characteristics.

14 The individual's current explanation for their past behaviour, acceptance of responsibility, attitude towards it, acknowledgment of behaviours as a problem, view of the victim/s.

SEXUAL HISTORY

Where relevant (e.g. if there is any offence with a sexual element, or where concern has been raised currently or previously about deviant sexual behaviour) information should be gathered about the individual's sexual development. Information should also be gathered about the nature of the index offence or behaviour of concern.

1 Nature of education in sexual matters (e.g. peers, sex education programmes, parents, television, books and magazines, the internet).

2 How they felt about sexual matters, age of onset of sexual interests, masturbation and sexual intercourse history.

3 Sexual partners, number, age range, gender, other relevant characteristics.

4 Sexual interests, appetites and activities. Any fetishistic, atypical or deviant sexual interests or appetites. Use and nature of pornography.

5 Nature of current sexual fantasies. Frequency and intensity of sexual fantasies, masturbation and sexual activity in relation to fantasies.

6   Presence of any sexual dysfunction (including side effects of medication).
7   Description of any sexual offences: what happened, in what circumstances, with whom, to whom.
8   The individual's current explanation for their past behaviour, acceptance of responsibility, attitude towards it, acknowledgment of behaviours as a problem; view of the victim/s.

Challenging Behaviour Record Sheet for Psychosis (CBRS-P)

You should complete the CBRS for a specifically defined behaviour; see notes overleaf. Fill this sheet in each time the behaviour occurs even if the behaviour is dealt with successfully and quickly. If a specific recording system already exists for the behaviour, complete the CBRS as well.

Service user name: **Date of incident:**
Time of incident: **Filled in by:**

What was the behaviour? Please describe the behaviour as accurately as possible. (overleaf note 1)

Client's early warning signs? What were the service user's presentation and behaviour like leading up to the event in the few hours or minutes before? (overleaf note 2)

Distant triggers? What events had occurred prior to the incident, which were not the immediate trigger but may have contributed to making the behaviour more likely later on? (overleaf note 3)

Immediate trigger? What happened to make the behaviour occur at the particular moment that it did? (overleaf note 4)

Intervention and effect? Reactions of others? What did staff do? What effect did this have? (overleaf note 5)

Client's view (interview when calm!) What was [X]'s view of what happened? (overleaf note 6)

(1) Behaviour

Behaviours that are both excessive (e.g. shouting, making frequent demands) or represent a deficit in what the person may normally be expected to do (e.g. not washing) can be recorded using the CBRS. They may also pose a significant risk to the client or other people (e.g. inappropriate sexual behaviour, suicide or deliberate self-harm attempt or threat, physical aggression, absconding).

Remember to only clearly describe what would be observable to others – describe what you saw, not explanations or judgements – WHAT, NOT WHY! If there is a series of behaviours that occurred together, describe the sequence.

(2) Early warning signs

Try to describe how the client appeared in the minutes or hours before the behaviour (the actual length of time to consider will vary from client to client – some will show a build-up for hours before, some only minutes before; you will need to use your judgement).

Stick to what you can see, rather than judgements about it. Rather than say 'agitated' for example, say 'pacing up and down, chewing finger nails and chain smoking'.

(3) Distant triggers

Consider things about the person themselves (e.g. having had a poor night's sleep, pain). Consider things about their interactions with others (e.g. family didn't turn up to visit, had an argument with another client, had been refused a trip out by staff). Consider also environmental factors (e.g. disruption of the unit).

(4) Immediate triggers

This should occur very close in time to the behaviour actually happening. Typical triggers include being asked to do something, being refused something or asked to wait, change of environment, presence of a particular staff member or type of person (e.g. female versus male).

(5) Staff intervention and reactions of others

What did you or other staff do when the behaviour occurred and in the short while afterwards? Please be honest even if you think you didn't do the right thing when you look back. This isn't to judge staff but to consider what might be maintaining the behaviour.

Consider also how others reacted. Did other clients back away or start to get aggressive, etc.

(6) View of the client

Wait until the client is calm (at least half an hour or longer after the event) and is unlikely to be agitated by being asked about the incident. If possible try to record their view on why they exhibited the behaviour and what set it off. Record what the client says objectively even if it makes no sense to you, rather than making a judgement or giving your own opinion.

Appendix 5

Idiosyncratic Behaviour Monitoring Checklist for Psychosis (IBMC-P)

Time	EWS-R code	Trigger code	Behaviour code	Reaction/response code
10.15				
10.30				
10.45				
11.00				
11.15				
11.30				
11.45				
12.00				

Behaviour code examples:
B1: verbal threats to other patient; B2: threats to staff; B3: hits patient; B4: hits staff; B5: hits doors or walls; B6: throws or smashes own possessions; B7: throws or smashes possessions of others

Trigger codes:
T1: asked to clean room; T2: asked to attend to own hygiene; T3: asked if wishes to go on leave to shops; T4: refused cigarette; T5: phone call from parents; T6: appears to be responding to voices

Staff reaction/response codes:
R1: ignore; R2: remove other patient(s); R3: remove client from situation; R4: attempt to distract with talk or activity

Early warning signs of risk code:
EW1: pacing; EW2: wearing dark glasses; EW3: staring at other residents; EW4: talking to themselves; EW5: holding hands, thumb and middle finger together

Early Warning Signs of Risk (EWS-R) Checklist

CONTEXTUAL EARLY WARNING SIGNS

- ☐ Contact with family
- ☐ Arguments with family
- ☐ Being bullied by others
- ☐ Presence of particular staff
- ☐ Busy, noisy environments

- ☐ Boredom/lack of activity
- ☐ Change in staff
- ☐ Change in patients
- ☐ Disruption from other patients
- ☐ Lack of finance
- ☐ Reduction in social network
- ☐ Time of year/ season
- ☐ Significant anniversaries

- ☐ Holidays/festive seasons
- ☐ Time of day
- ☐ Lack of access to cigarettes
- ☐ Refusal of requested leave
- ☐ Other (please specify)

....
....

VISUAL EARLY WARING SIGNS

- ☐ Pacing
- ☐ Vocalising out loud
- ☐ Social withdrawal
- ☐ Quiet
- ☐ Increase in demands
- ☐ Increase in insults/ threats
- ☐ Staring
- ☐ Refusal to take medication
- ☐ Invading personal space

- ☐ Agitation
- ☐ Erratic sleep patterns
- ☐ Refusal to eat
- ☐ Wearing inappropriate clothing
- ☐ Argumentative with staff
- ☐ Argumentative with other clients
- ☐ Increased smoking
- ☐ Decreased smoking
- ☐ Punching objects/ walls

- ☐ Kicking objects/ walls
- ☐ Secreting objects (weapons?)
- ☐ Increased bad language/swearing
- ☐ Increased alcohol use
- ☐ Requests for lighters/paper
- ☐ Increased masturbation
- ☐ Buying pornography
- ☐ Exposing
- ☐ Increased letter writing

- ☐ Increased telephone calls
- ☐ Loss of engagement in activities
- ☐ Crying
- ☐ Desire to participate in activities
- ☐ Overspending
- ☐ Decrease in personal hygiene
- ☐ Exploiting others (e.g. money)
- ☐ Being exploited by others
- ☐ Low/flat mood
- ☐ Fidgeting
- ☐ Scratching self
- ☐ Pulling at hair
- ☐ Throwing objects
- ☐ Sleeping for long periods
- ☐ Missing appointments
- ☐ Refusing to attend appointments
- ☐ Smiling for no apparent reason
- ☐ Laughing at unseen stimuli

- ☐ Increased contact with opposite sex
- ☐ Refusing to take advice
- ☐ Shaking/trembling
- ☐ Repetitive/fidgety behaviours
- ☐ Increased requests to be discharged
- ☐ Playing loud music
- ☐ Watching television loudly
- ☐ Wearing headphones
- ☐ Over-friendly
- ☐ Frottage
- ☐ Lying
- ☐ Hoarding/saving money
- ☐ Hoarding medication
- ☐ Superficial cuts/ burns to self
- ☐ Lack of consideration for others
- ☐ Seeking contact with particular individuals
- ☐ Requesting

- medication (increased dose)
- ☐ Requesting medication (PRN)
- ☐ Urinating and defecating inappropriately
- ☐ Observed difficulty in concentrating
- ☐ Inadvertently entering other clients' rooms
- ☐ Inadvertently entering opposite-sex toilets
- ☐ Standing/hanging around entrances/ exits
- ☐ Buying/collecting objects to use as weapons
- ☐ Taking measures to avoid being observed
- ☐ Other (please specify)
- ....
- ....
- ....

VERBAL EARLY WARNING SIGNS

The following EWS-R may be identified through engaging in a 1:1 with the client

- ☐ Sexually inappropriate speech
- ☐ Erratic speech

- ☐ Over-talkative
- ☐ Increased preoccupation with delusions
- ☐ Increased conviction in delusions
- ☐ Complaints of physical health problems
- ☐ Increased

- complaints about staff
- ☐ Increased complaints about clients
- ☐ Increase in negative comments about self
- ☐ Increase in ideas of reference
- ☐ Asking

inappropriate
personal
information
☐ Repeatedly asking
the same questions
☐ Expressing

unhappiness about
present living
conditions
☐ Inappropriately
disclosing personal
information

☐ Other (please
specify)
....
....
....

References

Addington, D., Addington, J., and Maticka-Tyndale, E. (1993). Assessing depression in schizophrenia: the Calgary Depression Scale. *British Journal of Psychiatry*, *163*, 39–44.

Alanen, Y. O. (1997). *Schizophrenia: It's origins and need-adapted treatment*. London: Karnac.

Amador, X. F., Strauss, D. H., Yale, S. A., Flaum, M. M., Endicott, J. and Gorman, J. M. (1993). Assessment of insight in psychosis. *The American Journal of Psychiatry*, *150*, 873–879.

American Psychiatric Association (2000). *Diagnostic and statistical manual of mental disorders* (4th edition, text revision). Washington, DC: American Psychiatric Association.

American Psychiatric Association (2003). *Practice guidelines for the assessment and treatment of patients with suicidal behaviours*. Washington, DC: American Psychiatric Association.

Andrews, D. and Bonta, J. (1995). *The Level of Service Inventory – Revised (LSI-R)*. Toronto, Canada: Multi-Health Systems.

Andrews, D. and Bonta, J. (2003). *The psychology of criminal conduct* (3rd edition). Cincinnati, OH: Anderson.

Andrews, D. A., Bonta, J. and Hoge, R. D. (1990). Classification for effective rehabilitation: rediscovering psychology. *Criminal Justice and Behavior*, *17*, 19–52.

Andrews, D. A., Bonta, J., and Wormith, J. S. (2006). The recent past and near future of risk and/or need assessment. *Crime and Delinquency*, *52*, 7–27.

Appelbaum, P. S., Robbins, P. C. and Monahan, J. (2000). Violence and delusions: data from the MacArthur Violence Risk Assessment Study. *American Journal of Psychiatry*, *157*, 566–572.

Ayllon, J. M., and Azrin, N. H. (1965). The measurement and reinforcement of behavior of psychotics. *Journal of Experimental Analysis of Behavior*, *8*, 357–383.

Aziz, M. A., Razik, G. N. and Donn, J. E. (2005). Dangerousness and management of delusional misidentification syndrome. *Psychopathology*, *38*, 97–102.

Barrowclough, C. and Hooley, J. M. (2003). Attributions and expressed emotion: a review. *Clinical Psychology Review*, *23*, 849–880.

Barrrowclough, C. and Tarrier, N. (1992). *Families of schizophrenic patients: Cognitive behavioural intervention*. London: Chapman and Hall.

Barrowclough, C., Haddock, G., Lowens, I., Conner, A., Pidliswyi, J. and Tracey, N.

(2001). Staff expressed emotion and causal attributions for client problems on a low security unit: an exploratory study. *Schizophrenia Bulletin, 27*, 517–526.

Bartels, S. J., Drake, R. E., Wallach, M. A. and Freeman, D. H. (1991). Characteristic hostility in schizophrenic outpatients. *Schizophrenia Bulletin, 17*, 163–171.

Beck, A. T., Epstein, N., Brown, G. and Steer, R. A. (1988). An inventory for measuring clinical anxiety: psychometric properties. *Journal of Consulting and Clinical Psychology, 56*, 893–897.

Beech, A. R., and Ward, T. (2004). The integration of aetiology and risk in sex offenders: a theoretical model. *Aggression and Violent Behaviour, 10*, 31–63.

Beer, B. (2006). Managing challenging behaviour. In G. Roberts, S. Davenport, F. Holloway and T. Tattan (eds) *Enabling recovery: The principles and practice of rehabilitation psychiatry* (pp. 211–231). London: Gaskell.

Belfrage, H. and Douglas, D. S. (2002). Treatment effects on forensic psychiatric patients measured with the HCR-20 Violence Risk Assessment Scheme. *International Journal of Forensic Mental Health, 1*, 25–36.

Bell, M. D. and Bryson, G. (2001). Work rehabilitation in schizophrenia: does cognitive impairment limit improvement? *Schizophrenia Bulletin, 27*, 269–279.

Belcher, T. L. (1988). Overall reduction of overworked hallucinatory behavior in a chronic schizophrenic. *Journal of Behavior Therapy and Experimental Psychiatry, 19*, 69–71.

Berry, K., Barrowclough, C. and Wearden, A. (2009). A pilot study investigating the use of psychosocial formulations to modify psychiatric staff perceptions of service users with psychosis. *Behavioural and Cognitive Psychotherapy, 37*, 39–48.

Bieling, P. J. and Kuyken, W. (2003). Is cognitive case formulation science or science fiction? *Clinical Psychology: Science and Practice, 10*, 52–69.

Binder, R. L. and McNeil, D. E. (1988). Effects of diagnosis and context on dangerousness. *American Journal of Psychiatry, 145*, 728–732.

Birchwood, M. and Trower, P. (2006). The future of cognitive-behavioural therapy for psychosis. Not a quasi-neuroleptic. *British Journal of Psychiatry, 18*(8), 107–108.

Birchwood, M. J., Smith, J., MacMillan, F., Hogg, B., Presad, R., Harvey, C. and Bering, S. (1989). Predicting relapse in schizophrenia: the development and implementation of an early signs monitoring system using patients and families as observers. *Psychological Medicine, 19*, 649–656.

Birchwood, M., Mason, R., MacMillan, F. and Healy, J. (1993). Depression, demoralization and control over psychotic illness: a comparison of depressed and nondepressed patients with chronic psychosis. *Psychological Medicine, 23*, 387–395.

Birchwood, M., Spencer, E. and McGovern, D. (2000). Schizophrenia: early warning signs. *Advances in Psychiatric Treatment, 6*, 93–101.

Birchwood, M., Tower, P. and Meaden, A. (2010). Appraisals. In F. Larøi, F. and A. Aleman (eds) *Hallucinations: A practical guide to treatment* (pp. 81–103). Oxford: Oxford University Press.

Blumenthal, S. and Lavender, T. (2000). *Violence and mental disorder: A critical aid to the assessment and management of risk.* London: Jessica Kingsley Publishers.

Boer, D. P., Wilson, R. J., Gauthier, C. M. and Hart, S. D. (1997). Assessing risk for sexual violence: guidelines for clinical practice. In C. D. Webster and M. A. Jackson (eds) *Impulsivity: Theory, assessment, and treatment* (pp. 326–342). New York: Guilford Press.

Boer, D. P., Tough, S. and Haaven, J. (2004). Assessment of risk manageability of intellectually disabled sex offenders. *Journal of Applied Research in Intellectual Disabilities, 17,* 275–83.

Bonta, J., Law, M. and Hanson, K. (1998). The prediction of criminal recidivism among disordered offenders: a meta-analysis. *Psychological Bulletin, 123,* 123–142.

Brekke, J. S., Prindle, C., Bae, S. W. and Long, J. D. (2001). Risks for individuals with schizophrenia who are living in the community. *Psychiatric Services, 52,* 1358–1366.

Brett-Jones, J., Garety, P. and Hemsley, D. (1987). Measuring delusional experiences: a method and its application. *British Journal of Clinical Psychology, 26,* 257–265.

Brewin, C. R., MacCarthy, B., Duda, K. and Vaughn, C. E. (1991). Attributions and expressed emotion in the relatives of patients with schizophrenia. *Journal of Abnormal Psychology, 100,* 546–554.

Brickman, P., Rabinowitz, V. C., Karuza, J., Coates, D., Cohn, E. and Kidder, L. (1982). Models of helping and coping. *American Psychologist, 37,* 368–384.

Broadbent, E., Petrie, K. J., Main, J. and Weinman, J. (2006). The Brief Illness Perception Questionnaire. *Journal of Psychosomatic Research, 60,* 631–637.

Brown, M. Z., Comtois, K. A. and Linehan, M. M. (2002). Reasons for suicide attempts and nonsuicidal self-injury in women with borderline personality disorder. *Journal of Abnormal Psychology, 111,* 198–202.

Brown, S. (1997). Excess mortality of schizophrenia. *British Journal of Psychiatry, 171,* 502–508.

Buchanan, A. (1993). Acting on delusions: a review. *Psychological Medicine, 23,* 123–134.

Buchanan, A., Reed, A., Wessely, S., Garety, P., Taylor, P., Grubin, D. and Dunn, G. (1993). Acting on delusions II: the phenomenological correlates of acting on delusions. *British Journal of Psychiatry, 163,* 77–81.

Burgess, P. W. and Shallice, T. (1997). *The Hayling and Brixton tests.* Bury St. Edmunds: Thames Valley Test Company.

Bush, S. S., Ruff, R. M., Tröster, A. I., Barth, J. T., Koffler, S. P., Pliskin, N. H., Reynolds, C. R. and Silver, C. H. (2005). Symptom validity assessment: practice issues and medical necessity: NAN Policy and Planning Committee. *Archives of Clinical Neuropsychology, 20,* 419–426.

Byrne, S., Trower, P., Birchwood, M. and Meaden, A. (2006). *Cognitive therapy for command hallucinations.* Hove: Brunner-Routledge.

Caldwell, C. B. and Gottesman, I. I. (1990). Schizophrenics kill themselves too: a review of risk factors for suicide. *Schizophrenia Bulletin, 16,* 571–589.

Cappa, S. F., Benke, T., Clarke, S., Rossi, B., Stemmer, B. and van Heugten, C. M. (2005). EFNS guidelines on cognitive rehabilitation: report of an EFNS task force. *European Journal of Neurology, 12,* 665–680.

Care Programme Approach Association (2008). *The CPA and care standards handbook.* Chesterfield: Care Programme Approach Association.

Care Services Improvement Partnership, Royal College of Psychiatrists and Social Care Institute for Excellence (2007). *A common purpose: Recovery in mental health services.* London: Social Care Institute for Excellence.

Chadwick, P. (2006). *Person based cognitive therapy for distressing psychosis.* Chichester: John Wiley & Sons.

Chadwick, P. and Birchwood, M. (1995). The omnipotence of voices II: the Beliefs About Voices Questionnaire. *British Journal of Psychiatry, 166,* 773–776.

Chadwick, P. Birchwood, M. and Trower, P. (1996). *Cognitive therapy for delusions, voices and paranoia*. Chichester: John Wiley & Sons.

Chadwick, P., Trower, P. and Dagnan, D. (1999). Measuring negative person evaluations: the Evaluative Belief Scale. *Cognitive Therapy and Research*, *23*, 549–559.

Chadwick, P., Lees, S. and Birchwood, M. (2000). The revised Beliefs About Voices Questionnaire (BAVQ-R). *British Journal of Psychiatry*, *177*, 229–232.

Chadwick, P., Williams, C. and Mackenzie, J. (2003). Impact of case formulation in cognitive behaviour therapy for psychosis. *Behaviour Research and Therapy*, *1*, 671–680.

Checkley, H. (1941). *The mask of insanity*. St. Louis, MO: Mosby.

Cheung, P., Shweitzer, I., Crowley, K. and Tuckwell, V. (1997). Violence in schizophrenia: role of hallucinations and delusions. *Schizophrenia Research*, *26*, 181–190.

Chou, K., Lu, R. and Mao, W. (2002). Factors relevant to patient assaultive behavior and assault in acute inpatient psychiatirc units in Taiwan. *Archives of Psychiatric Nursing*, *16*, 187–195.

Cicerone, K. D., Dahlberg, C., Malec, J. F., Langenbahn, D. M., Felicettti, T., Kneipp, S., Ellmo, W., Kalmar, K., Giacino, J. and Harley, J. (2005). Evidence-based cognitive rehabilitation: updated review of the literature from 1998 through 2002. *Archives of Physical Medicine and Rehabilitation*, *86*, 1681–1692.

Clifford, P., Leiper, R., Lavender, A. and Pilling, S. (1989). *Assuring quality in mental health services: The quartz system*. London: RDP in Association with Free Association Books.

Cole, J. D. and Kazarian, S. S. (1988). The Level of Expressed Emotion Scale: a new measure of expressed emotion. *Journal of Clinical Psychology*, *44*, 392–397.

Collins, M. and Munroe, P. (2004). Preventing and managing violence and aggression in in-patient settings. In P. Campling, S. Davies and G. Farquharson (eds) *From toxic institutions to therapeutic environments: Residential settings in mental health services* (pp. 131–166). London: Gaskell.

Commander, M. and Rooprai, D. (2008). Survey of long-stay patients on acute psychiatric wards. *The Psychiatrist*, *32*, 380–383.

Conroy, A. M. and Murrie, D. C. (2007). *Forensic assessment of violence risk: A guide for risk assessment and management*. Hoboken, NJ: John Wiley & Sons.

Cormac, I., Martin, D. and Ferriter, M. (2004). Improving the physical health of long-stay psychiatric in-patients. *Advances in Psychiatric Treatment*, *10*, 107–115.

Cowan, C., Meaden, A., Commander, M. and Edwards, T. (in preparation). Inpatient psychiatric rehabilitation services: a survey of residents' clinical and demographic characteristics and service resources in rehabilitation services within three West Midlands areas.

Cowdrill, V. and Dannahy, L. (2009). Running reflective practice groups on an in-patient unit. In I. Clarke and H. Wilson (eds) *Cognitive behaviour therapy for acute inpatient mental health units: Working with clients, staff and the milieu* (pp. 116–128). Hove: Routledge.

Craig, L. A., Browne, K. D. and Beech, A. R. (2008) *Assessing risk in sex offenders: A practioner's guide*. Chichester: John Wiley & Sons.

Craig, T. (2006). What is psychiatric rehabilitation. In G. Roberts, S. Davenport, F. Holloway and T. Tattan (eds) *Enabling recovery: The principles and practice of rehabilitation psychiatry* (pp. 3–18). London: Gaskell.

Cunningham, M. D. and Reidy, T. J. (1998). Antisocial personality disorder and psychopathy: diagnostic dilemmas in classifying patterns of antisocial behavior in sentencing evaluations. *Behavioral Sciences and the Law, 16*, 331–351.

Curtis, J. L. and Silberschatz, G. (1997). Plan formulation method. In T. D. Eells (ed.) *Psychotherapy case formulation* (pp. 116–136). New York: Guilford Press.

D'Zurilla, T. J. and Goldfried, M. R. (1971). Problem solving and behavior modification. *Journal of Abnormal Psychology, 78*, 107–126.

Daffern, M. and Howells, K. (2002). Psychiatric inpatient aggression: a review of structural and functional assessment approaches. *Aggression and Violent Behavior, 5*, 477–497.

Daffern, M., Mayer, M. M. and Martin, T. (2004). Environment contributors to aggression in two forensic psychiatric hospitals. *International Journal of Forensic Mental Health, 3*, 105–114.

Daffern, M., Howells, K. and Ogloff, J. R. P. (2006). What's the point? Towards a methodology for assessing the function of psychiatric inpatient aggression. *Behaviour Research and Therapy, 45*, 101–11.

Daffern, M., Howells, K. and Ogloff, J. R. P. (2007). The interaction between individual characteristics and the function of aggression in forensic psychiatric inpatients. *Psychiatry, Psychology and Law, 14*, 17–25.

Dagnan, D. and Cairns, M. (2005). Staff judgments of responsibility for the challenging behaviour of adults with intellectual disabilities. *Journal of Intellectual Disability Research, 40*, 95–101.

Dagnan, D. and Weston, C. (2006). Physical intervention in aggressive incidents with people with intellectual disabilities: the influence of cognitive and emotional variables. *Journal of Applied Research in Intellectual Disabilities, 19*, 219–222.

Dagnan, D., Trower, P. and Smith, R. (1998). Care staff responses to people with learning disabilities and challenging behaviour: a cognitive-emotional analysis. *British Journal of Clinical Psychology, 37*, 59–68.

Davenport, S. (2002). Acute wards: problems and solutions. *Psychiatric Bulletin, 26*, 385–388.

Davenport, S. (2006). Psychodynamic considerations in rehabilitation. In G. Roberts, S. Davenport, F. Holloway and T. Tattan (eds) *Enabling recovery: The principles and practice of rehabilitation psychiatry* (pp. 187–199). London: Gaskell.

Davies, W. (1993). *The RAID programme for challenging behaviour*. Leicester: Association for Psychological Therapies.

Delis, D. C., Kaplan, E. and Kramer, J. H. (2001). *Delis–Kaplan Executive Function System technical manual*. San Antonio, TX: The Psychological Corporation.

DH (Department of Health) (1990). *The Care Programme Approach for people with a mental illness referred to specialist psychiatric services* (HC(90)23). London: DH.

DH (1999). *A National Service Framework for Mental Health: Modern standards and service models*, London: DH.

DH (2000). *Improving working lives*. London: DH.

DH (2001). The mental health policy implementation guide. London: DH (http://www. dh.gov.uk/dr_consum_dh/groups/dh_digitalassets/@dh/@en/documents/digitalas set/dh_4058960.pdf).

DH (2002). *National Suicide Prevention Strategy for England*. London: The Stationery Office.

DH (2003). *Improving staff morale*. London: DH.

DH (2007). *Best practice in managing risk*. London: DH.

Donahoe, G. and Robertson, I. H. (2003). Can specific deficits in executive functioning explain the negative symptoms of schizophrenia? A review. *Neurocase, 9,* 97–108.

Donnellan, A. M., La Vigna, G. W., Negri-Shoultz, N. and Fassbender, L. L. (1988). *Progress without punishment: Effective approaches for learners with behaviour problems.* New York: Teachers College Press.

Doren, D. M. (2002). *Evaluating sex offenders: A manual for civil commitments and beyond.* London: Sage.

Douglas, K. S. and Skeem, J. L. (2005). Violence risk assessment: getting specific about being dynamic. *Psychology, Public Policy and Law, 11,* 347–383.

Douglas, K. S., Vincent, G. M. and Edens, J. F. (2006). Risk for criminal recidivism: the role of psychopathy. In C. J. Patrick (ed.) *Handbook of psychopathy* (pp. 533–554). New York: Guilford Press.

Douglas, K. S., Guy, L. S., Reeves, K. A. and Weir, J. (2008) HCR-20 Violence Risk Assessment Scheme: Overview and annotated bibliography. Retrieved from http://kdouglas.wordpress.com/hcr-20.

Dowden, C. and Brown, S. L. (2002). The role of substance abuse factors in predicting recidivism: a meta-analysis. *Psychology, Crime and Law,* 8, 243–264.

Drake R. E. (2007). Suicide attempts and completed suicides among schizophrenia patients. In R. Tatarelli, M. Pompili and P. Girardi (eds) *Suicide in schizophrenia* (pp. 77–81). New York: Nova Science Publishers.

Drake, R. E. and Mueser, K. T. (2001). Substance abuse comorbidity. In J. Lieberman and R. M. Murray (eds) *Comprehensive care of schizophrenia.* London: Martin Dunitz.

Dryden, W. (1998). *Brief rational emotive behaviour therapy.* Chichester: John Wiley & Sons.

Duncan, A. (2005). The impact of cognitive and psychiatric impairment of psychotic disorders on the Test of Memory Malingering (TOMM). *Assessment, 12,* 123–129.

Elliot, P. A., Barlow, F., Hooper, A. and Kingerlee, P. E. (1979). Maintaining patients improvements in a token economy. *Behavioural Research and Therapy, 17,* 355–367.

Emerson, E. (2001). *Challenging behaviour: Analysis and intervention in people with learning difficulties* (2nd edition). Cambridge: Cambridge University Press.

Estroff, S. E., Zimmer, C., Lachicotte, W. S. and Benoit, J. (1994). The influence of social networks and social support on violence by persons with serious mental illness. *Hospital and Community Psychiatry, 45,* 669–679.

Evans, J. J. (2006). Memory rehabilitation – should we be aiming for restoration or compensation? *Journal of Neurology, 253,* 520–521.

Evans, J. J., Emslie, H. and Wilson, B. A. (1998). External cueing systems in the rehabilitation of executive impairments of action. *Journal of the International Neuropsychological Society, 4,* 399–408.

Fadden, G. (2006). Family interventions. In G. Roberts, S. Davenport, F. Holloway and T. Tattan (eds) *Enabling recovery: The principles and practice of rehabilitation psychiatry* (pp. 158–169). London: Gaskell.

Fadden, G., Birchwood, M., Jackson, C. and Barton, K. (2004). Psychological therapies: implementation in early intervention services. In P. McGorry, and L. Gleeson, (eds) *Psychological interventions in early psychosis: A treatment handbook* (pp. 261–280). Chichester: John Wiley & Sons.

Farebrow, N. L., Shneidman, E. S. and Leonard, C. V. (1961). Suicide among schizophrenic mental hospital patients. In N. L. Farebrow and E. S. Shneidman (eds) *The cry for help* (pp. 78–97). New York, Toronto and London: McGraw-Hill.

Farquharson, G. (2004). Leadership and management in therapeutic institutions. In P. Campling, S. Davies and G. Farquharson (eds) *From toxic institutions to therapeutic environments: Residential settings in mental health services* (pp. 108–118). London: Gaskell.

Ferrel, R. B. and McAllister, T. W. (2008). Intellectual disability and other neuropsychiatric populations. In K. T. Meuser and D. V. Jeste (eds) *Clinical handbook of schizophrenia* (pp. 437–447). New York: Guilford Press.

Festinger, L. (1957). *A theory of cognitive dissonance.* Stanford, CA: Stanford University Press.

Foxx, R. M., McMorrow, M. J., Davis, L. A. and Bittle, R. G. (1988). Replacing a chronic schizophrenic man's delusional speech with stimulus appropriate responses. *Journal of Behavior Therapy and Experimental Psychiatry, 19,* 43–50.

Freeman, D., Garety, P. A. and Kuipers, E. (2001). Persecutory delusions: developing the understanding of belief maintenance and emotional distress. *Psychological Medicine, 31,* 1293–1306.

Freeman, D., Garety, P. A., Kuipers, E., Fowler, D., Bebbington, P. E. and Dunn, G. (2007). Acting on persecutory delusions: the importance of safety seeking. *Behaviour Research and Therapy, 45,* 89–99.

Freese, R., Hiscoke, U. and Hodgins, S. (2002). The treatment of mentally ill patients with a history of criminality or violence: What works and what doesn't work? Paper presentation at 11th Congress of the Association of European Psychiatrists, Stockholm, Sweden, September.

Gallop, R., Lancee, W. and Shugar, G. (1993). Residents' and nurses' perceptions of difficult to treat short stay patients. *Hospital and Community Psychiatry, 44,* 352–357.

Gillespie, M. and Meaden, A. (2009) Engagement. In C. Cuppit, (ed.) *Reaching out: The psychology of assertive outreach* (pp. 15–42). London: Brunner-Routledge.

Glisky, E. L. (2005). Can memory impairment be effectively treated? In P. W. Halligan and D. T. Wade (eds) *Effectiveness of rehabilitation for cognitive deficits.* New York: Oxford University Press.

Goffman, E. (1961). *Asylums.* New York: Doubleday.

Goldiamond, L. (1974). Toward a constructional approach to social problem: ethical and constitutional issues raised by applied behavioural analysis. *Behaviourism, 2,* 1–84.

Graham, H. L., Copello, A., Birchwood, M. J., Mueser, K., Orford, J., McGovern, D. Atkinson, E., Maslin, J., Preece, M., Tobin, D. and Georgiou, G. (2004). *Cognitive-behavioural integrated treatment (C-BIT): A treatment manual for substance misuse in people with severe mental health problems.* Chichester: Wiley.

Gray, A. and Mulligan, A. (2009). Staff stress and burnout. In C. Cuppit, (ed.) *Reaching out: The psychology of assertive outreach* (pp. 119–141). London: Brunner-Routledge.

Green, C., Garety, P. A., Freeman, D., Fowler, D., Bebbington, P., Dunn, G. and Kuuipers, E. (2006). Content and affect in persecutory delusions. *British Journal of Clinical Psychology, 45,* 561–577.

Green, M. F. (1996). What are the functional consequences of neurocognitive deficits in schizophrenia? *American Journal of Psychiatry, 153,* 321–330.

Greenhalgh, T., Robert, G., Macfarlane, F., Bate, P., Kyriakidou, O. and Peacock, R. (2004). Diffusion of innovations in service organisations: systematic review and recommendations. *Milbank Quarterly, 82*, 581–629.

Grisso, T., Davis, J., Vesselinov, R., Appelbaum, P. S. and Monahan, J. (2000). Violent thoughts and violent behavior following hospitalization for mental disorder. *Journal of Consulting and Clinical Psychology, 68*, 388–398.

Hacker, D., Birchwood, M., Tudway, J., Meaden, A. and Amphlett, C. (2008). Acting on voices: omnipotence, sources of threat and safety-seeking behaviours. *British Journal of Clinical Psychology, 47*, 201–213.

Hacker, D., Meaden, A. and Fountain, R. (in preparation). Exploring staff attributions about challenging behaviour in schizophrenia: the effect of behavioural topography and staff attributions on staff emotional response and helping intention.

Haddock, G. and Shaw, J. J. (2008). Understanding and working with violence, aggression and psychosis. In K. T. Meuser and D. V. Jeste (eds) *Clinical handbook of schizophrenia* (pp. 398–411). New York: Guilford Press.

Haddock, G., McCarron, J., Tarrier, N. and Faragher, E. B. (1999). Scales to measure dimensions of hallucinations and delusions: the psychotic symptom rating scales (PSYRATS). *Psychological Medicine, 29*, 879–889.

Haddock, G., Lowens, I., Brosnan, N., Barrowclough, C. and Novaco, R. W. (2004). Cognitive-behaviour therapy for inpatients with psychosis and anger problems within a low secure environment. *Behavioural and Cognitive Psychotherapy, 32*, 77–98.

Haddock, G., Barrowclough, C., Shaw, J. J., Dunn, G., Novaco, R. W. and Tarrier, N. (2009). Cognitive-behavioural therapy v. social activity therapy for people with psychosis and a history of violence: randomised controlled trial. *British Journal of Psychiatry, 194*, 152–157.

Hall, M., Meaden, A., Smith, J. and Jones, C. (2001). Brief report: the development and psychometric properties of an observer-rated measure of engagement with mental health services. *Journal of Mental Health, 10*, 457–465.

Hansen, L., Jones, R. M. and Kingdon, D. (2004) No association between akathisia or parkinsonism and suicidality in treatment-resistant schizophrenia. *Journal of Psychopharmacology, 18*, 384–387.

Hanson, R. K. (1997). *The development of a brief actuarial risk scale for sexual offence recidivism.* User Report 1997–04. Ottawa: Department of the Solicitor General of Canada.

Hanson, R. K. and Bussière, M. T. (1996). Predictors of sexual offender recidivism: A meta-analysis. *Journal of Consulting and Clinical Psychology, 66*, 348–362.

Hanson, R. K. and Thornton, D. M. (1999). *Static 99: Improving actuarial risk assessments for sex offenders.* Ottawa, Canada: Public Works and Government Services.

Hare, R. D. (2003). *The Hare Psychopathy Checklist – revised* (2nd edition). Toronto and Ontario, Canada: Multi-Health Systems.

Harris, E. C. and Barraclough, B. (1998). Excess mortality of mental disorder. *British Journal of Psychiatry, 173*, 11–53.

Harris, G. T., Rice, M. E. and Quinsey, V. L. (1993) Violent recidivism of mentally disordered offenders: the development of a statistical prediction instrument. *Criminal Justice and Behaviour, 20*, 315–335.

Harrison, T. (2006). Rolling the stone uphill: leadership, management and longer-term mental healthcare. In G. Roberts, S. Davenport, F. Holloway and T. Tattan (eds) *Enabling recovery: The principles and practice of rehabilitation psychiatry* (pp. 299–309). London: Gaskell.

Hartley, P. and Kennard, D. (2009) *Staff support groups in the helping professions: Principles, practice and pitfalls*. London: Routledge.

Harvey, P. D. and Sharma, T. (2002). *Understanding and treating cognition in schizophrenia: A clinician's handbook*. London: Taylor Francis.

Hastings, R. P. and Brown, T. (2002). Behavioural knowledge, causal beliefs and self-efficacy as predictors of special educators' emotional reactions to challenging behaviours. *Journal of Intellectual Disability Research, 46*, 144–150.

Hastings, R. P. and Remington, B. (1994). Staff behaviour and its implications for people with learning disabilities and challenging behaviours. *British Journal of Clinical Psychology, 33*, 423–438.

Hastings, R. P., Remington, B. and Hopper, G. M. (1995). Experienced and inexperienced health care workers' beliefs about challenging behaviours. *Journal of Intellectual Disability Research, 39*, 474–483.

Hawkins, P. and Sholet, R. (2000). *Supervision in the helping profession* (2nd edition). Milton Keynes: Open University Press.

Hawton, K., Fagg, J., Simkin, S., Bale, E. and Bond, A. (1997). Trends in deliberate self-harm in Oxford, 1985–1995: implications for clinical services and the prevention of suicide. *British Journal of Psychiatry, 171*, 556–560.

Hawton, K., Sutton, L., Haw, C., Sinclair, J. and Deeks, J. (2005). Schizophrenia and suicide: systematic review of risk factors. *British Journal of Psychiatry, 187*, 9–20.

Haynes, S. N. and Williams, A. E. (2003). Case formulation and design of behavioral treatment programs. *European Journal of Psychological Assessment, 19*, 164–174.

Healy, D., Harris, M., Tranter, R., Gutting, P., Austin, R., Jones-Edwards, G. and Roberts, A. P. (2006). Lifetime suicide rates in treated schizophrenia: 1875–1924 and 1994–1998 cohorts compared. *British Journal of Psychiatry, 188*, 223–228.

Henry, J. D. and Crawford, J. R. (2005). A meta-analytic review of verbal fluency deficits in schizophrenia relative to other neurocognitive deficits. *Cognitive Neuropsychiatry, 10*, 1–33.

Hiday, V. A., Swartz, M. S., Swanson, J. W., Borum, R. and Wagner, H. R. (1999). Criminal victimization of persons with severe mental illness. *Psychiatric Services, 50*, 62–68.

Hildebrandt, H., Bussmann-Mork, B. and Schwendemann, G. (2006). Group therapy for memory impaired patients: a partial remediation is possible. *Journal of Neurology, 253*, 512–519.

Hinshelwood, R. D. (2004). *Suffering insanity: Psychoanalytic essays on psychosis*. Hove: Brunner-Routledge.

Hodgins, S., Hiscoke, U. L. and Freese, R. (2003). The antecedents of aggressive behaviour among men with schizophrenia: a prospective investigation of patients in community treatment. *Behavioural Science and the Law, 21*, 523–546.

Hogg, L. and Hall, J. (1992). Management of long term impairments and challenging behaviour. In M. Birchwood and N. Tarrier (eds) *Innovations in the psychological management of schizophrenia: Assessment, treatment and services* (pp. 171–203). Chichester: Wiley.

Holloway, F. (2005). *The forgotten need for rehabilitation in contemporary mental health services: A position statement from the Executive Committee of the Faculty of Rehabilitation and Social Psychiatry, Royal College of Psychiatrists.* London: Royal College of Psychiatrists (http://www.rcpsych.ac.uk/pdf/frankholloway_oct05.pdf).

Holloway, F. (2006). Pulling it all together: the Care Programme Approach at its best. In G. Roberts, S. Davenport, F. Holloway and T. Tattan (eds) *Enabling recovery: The principles and practice of rehabilitation psychiatry* (pp. 231–242). London: Gaskell.

Holmes, J. (2004). What can psychotherapy contribute to improving the culture on acute wards. In P. Campling, S. Davies and G. Farquharson (eds) *From toxic institutions to therapeutic environments: Residential settings in mental health services* (pp. 208–215). London: Gaskell.

Inskip, H. M., Harris, E. C. and Barraclough B. (1998). Lifetime risk of suicide for affective disorder, alcoholism and schizophrenia. *British Journal of Psychiatry*, *172*, 35–37.

Jansen, W., Noorthoorn, E., van Linge, R. and Lendemeijer, B. (2007). The influence of staffing levels on the use of seclusion. *International Journal of Law and Psychiatry*, *30*, 118–126.

Jimenez, J. M., Todman, M., Perez, M., Godoy, J. F. and Landon-Jimenez, D. V. (1996). The behavioral treatment of auditory hallucinatory responding of a schizophrenic patient. *Journal of Behavior Therapy and Experimental Psychiatry*, *27*, 299–310.

Johnstone, L. and Dallos, R. (2006). *Formulation in psychology and psychotherapy*. London: Routledge.

Jones, C., Cormac, I., Silveira da Mota Neto, J. I. and Campbell, C. (2002). Cognitive behaviour therapy for schizophrenia (Cochrane Review). *The Cochrane Database of Systematic Reviews* (1).

Jones, C., Hacker, D. A., Cormac, I., Meaden, A. and Irving, C. (2010). Cochrane systematic review of CBT for schizophrenia: cognitive therapy vs other psychological therapies. *The Cochrane Database of Systematic Reviews* (1).

Jones, C. A. and Meaden, A. (in press). Psychological therapy and psychosocial interventions in the treatment and the management of schizophrenia. In P. Sturmey and M. Hersen (eds) *Handbook of evidence-based practice in clinical psychology. Volume II. Adults.* Chichester: John Wiley & Sons.

Jones, L. (2004). Offence paralleling behaviour (OFB) as a framework for assessment and intervention with offenders. In A. Needs and G. Towl (eds) Applying psychology to forensic practice (pp. 34–64). Oxford: Blackwell Publishing.

Junginger, J., Parks-Levy, J. and McGuire, L. (1998). Delusions and symptom-consistent violence. *Psychiatric Services*, *49*, 218–264.

Kahneman, D. and Tversky, A. (1979). Prospect theory: an analysis of decision under risk. *Econometrica*, *47*, 263–291.

Kay, S., Wolkenfeld, F. and Murrill, L. (1988). Profiles of aggression among psychiatric inpatients: nature and prevalence. *Journal of Nervous Mental Disease*, *176*, 539–546.

Kay, S. R. (1991). *Positive and negative syndromes in schizophrenia: Assessment and research*. New York: Brunner/Mazel.

Kessels, R. P. C. and de Haan, E. H. F. (2003). Implicit learning in memory rehabilitation: a meta-analysis on errorless learning and VCs methods. *Journal of Clinical and Experimental Neuropsychology*, *25*, 805–814.

Kho, K., Sensky, T., Mortimer, A. and Corcos, C. (1998). Prospective study into factors associated with aggressive incidents in psychiatric acute admission wards. *British Journal of Psychiatry*, *172*, 38–43.

Kinderman, P. and Lobban, F. (2000). Evolving formulations: sharing complex information with clients. *Behavioural and Cognitive Psychotherapy*, *28*, 307–310.

Kingdom, D. G. and Turkington, D. (2005). *Cognitive therapy of schizophrenia: Guides to individualised treatment*. New York: Guilford Press.

Kiresuk, T. J., Smith, A. and Cardillo, J. E. (1994). *Goal attainment scaling: Applications, theory and measurement*. Mahwah, NJ: Lawrence Erlbaum Associates, Inc.

Kisely, S. and Campbell, L. E. (2007). Does compulsory or supervised community treatment reduce 'revolving door' care? Legislation is inconsistent with recent evidence. *British Journal of Psychiatry*, *191*, 373–374.

Klassen, O. and O'Connor, W. A. (1988). Crime, inpatient admissions, and violence among male mental patients. *International Journal of Law and Psychiatry*, *11*, 305–312.

Krawiecka, M., Goldberg, D. and Vaughan, M. (1977). A standardized psychiatric assessment scale for rating chronic psychotic patients. *Acta Psychiatrica Scandinavica*, *55*, 299–308.

Kropp, P. R., Hart, S. D., Webster, C. D. and Eaves, D. (1999). *Manual for the spousal assault risk assessment guide* (3rd edition). Toronto, Canada: Multi-Health Systems.

Kuipers, L., Leff, J. P. and Lam, D. (2002). *Family work for schizophrenia: A practical guide* (2nd edition). London: Gaskell.

Kuyken, W., Fothergill, C. D., Musa, M. and Chadwick, P. (2005). The reliability and quality of cognitive case formulation. *Behaviour Research and Therapy*, *43*, 1187–1201.

Kuyken, W., Padesky, C.A. and Dudley, R. (2009). *Collaborative case conceptualization: Working effectively with clients in cognitive behaviour therapy*. New York: Guilford Press.

Landis, J. and Koch, G. G. (1977). The measurement of observer agreement for categorical data. *Biometrics*, *33*, 159–174.

Larkin, W. and Morrison, A. P. (2006). *Trauma and psychosis: New directions for theory and therapy*. London: Routledge.

Laws, K. R. (1999). A meta-analytic review of Wisconsin card sort studies in schizophrenia: General intellect deficit in disguise? *Cognitive Neuropsychiatry*, *4*, 1–35.

Leff, J. and Vaughan, C. (1985). *Expressed emotion in families: Its significance for mental illness*. New York: Guilford Press.

Leff, J., Thornicroft, G., Coxhead, N. and Crawford, C. (1994). The TAPS project: a five-year follow-up of long-stay psychiatric patients discharged to the community. *British Journal of Psychiatry*, *165*, 13–17.

Leggett, J. and Silvester, J. (2003). Care staff attributions for violent incidents involving male and female patients: a field study, *British Journal of Clinical Psychology*, *42*, 393–406.

Lelliott, P., Audini, B., Knapp, M. and Chisholm, D. (1996). The mental health residential care study: classification of facilities and description of residents. *British Journal of Psychiatry*, *169*, 139–147.

Levine, B., Robertson, I. A., Clare, L., Carter, G., Hong, J., Wilson, B. A., Duncan, J. and Stuss, D. T. (2000). Rehabilitation of executive functioning: an experimental–clinical validation of goal management training. *Journal of the International Neuropsychological Society*, *6*, 299–312.

Liberman, R. P., Teigen, J., Patterson, R. and Baker, V. (1973). Reducing delusional speech in chronic, paranoid schizophrenics. *Journal of Applied Behavior Analysis*, *6*, 57–64.

Link, B. G. and Stueve, A. (1994). Psychotic symptoms and the violent/illegal behavior of mental patients compared to community controls. In J. Monahan and H. J. Steadman (eds) *Violence and mental disorder: Developments in risk assessment* (pp. 137–159). Chicago, IL: University of Chicago Press.

Link, B. G., Monahan, J., Stueve, A. and Cullen, F. T. (1999). Real in their consequences: a sociological approach to understanding the association between psychotic symptoms and violence. *American Sociological Review*, *64*, 316–322.

Link, B. G., Andrews, H. and Cullen, F. T. (1992). The violent and illegal behavior of mental patients reconsidered. *American Sociological Review*, *57*, 275–292.

Lloyd, C. (1995). *Forensic psychiatry for health professionals*. London: Chapman and Hall.

Lobban, F., Barrowclough, C. and Jones, S. (2005). Assessing cognitive representation of mental health problems II: the illness perception questionnaire for schizophrenia: relatives' version. *British Journal of Clinical Psychology*, *44*, 163–179.

Lynch, D., Laws, K. R. and McKenna, P. J. (2010). Cognitive behavioural therapy for major psychiatric disorder: does it really work? A meta-analytical review of well controlled trials. *Psychological Medicine*, *4*, 9–24.

McCarrick, A. K., Manderscheid, R. W., Bertolucci, D. E., Goldman, H. and Tessler, R. C. (1986). Chronic medical problems in the chronic mentally ill. *Hospital and Community Psychiatry*, *37*, 289–291.

McKenna, P. J. (2007). *Schizophrenia and realted syndromes* (2nd edition). London: Routledge.

Magaña, A. B., Goldstein, M. J., Karno, M., Miklowitz, D. J., Jenkins, J. and Falloon, I. R. H. (1986). A brief method for assessing expressed emotion in relatives of psychiatric patients. *Psychiatry Research*, *17*, 203–212.

Maley, R. F., Feldman, G. L. and Ruskin, R. S. (1973). Evaluation of patient improvement in a token economy treatment program. *Journal of Abnormal Psychology*, *82*, 141–144.

Manly, T., Hawkins, K., Evans, J., Woldt, K. and Robertson, I. H. (2002). Rehabilitation of executive function: facilitation of effective goal management on complex tasks using periodic auditory alerts. *Neuropsychologia*, *40*, 271–281.

Margison, F. (2005). Integrating approaches to psychotherapy in psychosis. *Australian and New Zealand Journal of Psychiatry*, *39*, 972–981.

Markham, D. and Trower, P. (2003). The effects of the psychiatric label 'borderline personality disorder' on nursing staff's perceptions and causal attributions for challenging behaviours. *British Journal of Clinical Psychology*, *42*, 243–256.

Marshall, M., Lockwood, A., Green, G., Zajac-Roles, G., Roberts, C. and Harrison, G. (2004). Systematic assessments of need and care planning in severe mental illness. *British Journal of Psychiatry*, *185*, 163–168.

Martin, R. L., Cloninger, C. R., Guze, S. B. and Clayton, P. J. (1985). Mortality in a follow-up of 500 psychiatric outpatients: I. Total mortality. *Archives of General Psychiatry*, *42*, 47–54.

Maslach, C. (1978). The client role in staff burnout. *Journal of Social Issues, 34,* 111–124.

Maslach, C. (1982). *Burnout: The cost of caring.* Upper Saddle River, NJ: Prentice Hall.

Mawson, A., Cohen, K. and Berry, K. (2010). Reviewing evidence for the cognitive model of auditory hallucinations: The relationship between cognitive voice appraisals and distress during psychosis. *Clinical Psychology Review, 30,* 248–258.

Meaden, A. and Farmer, A. (2006). A comprehensive approach to assessment in rehabilitation settings. In G. Roberts, S. Davenport, F. Holloway and T. Tattan (eds) *Enabling recovery: The principles and practice of rehabilitation psychiatry* (pp. 64–70). London: Gaskell.

Meaden, A. and Van Marle, S. (2008). When the going gets tougher: the importance of long-term supportive psychotherapy in psychosis. *Advances in Psychiatric Treatment, 14,* 42–49.

Meaden, A., Birchwood, M. and Trower, P. (2010). Cognitive therapy for command hallucinations. In F. Larøi and A. Aleman (eds) *Hallucinations: A practical guide to treatment* (pp. 104–121). Oxford: Oxford University Press.

Meaden, A., Hacker, D. A. and Spencer, M. (in preparation a). The early warning signs of risk checklist: a new tool for identifying and monitoring acute dynamic risk factors.

Meaden, A., Vaughan, R., Rudman, N. and Bowyer, S. (in preparation b). Staff beliefs and care responses to problematic behaviour in psychosis.

Meichenbaum, D. (1977). *Cognitive behaviour modification: An integrative approach.* New York: Plenum.

Meltzer, H. Y., Conley, R. R., De Leo, D., Green, A. I., Kane, J. M., Knesevich, M. A., Lieberman, J. A., Linenmayer, J. P. and Potkin, S. G. (2003). Intervention strategies for suicidality. *Journal of Clinical Psychiatry, 6,* 1–16.

Mental Capacity Act 2005. Chapter 9. Retrieved 27 December 2007 from the Office of Public Sector Information website: http://www.legislation.gov.uk/ukpga/2005/9/contents.

Mental Health Act 2007. Retrieved 14 November 2008 from the Department of Health website: http://www.legislation.gov.uk/ukpga/2007/12/contents.

Menzies, R. J. and Webster, C. D. (1995). Construction and validation of risk assessments in a six-year follow-up of forensic patients: a tridimensional analysis. *Journal of Consulting and Clinical Psychology, 63,* 766–778.

Millon, T. (1994). *Millon Clinical Multiaxial Inventory III.* Coral Gables, FL: Dicandrien.

Mitto, E. C., Evans, J. J., Souza De Lucia, M. C. and Scaff, M. (2008). Rehabiliation of executive dysfunction: a controlled trial of an attention and problem solving treatment group. *Neuropsychological Rehabilitation, 19,* 517–540.

Monahan, J. (1992). Mental disorder and violent behavior: perceptions and evidence. *American Psychologist, 47,* 511–521.

Monahan, J., Steadman, H. J., Silver, E., Appelbaum, P. S., Robbins, P. C., Mulvey, E. P., Roth, L., Grisso, T. and Banks, S. (2001). *Rethinking risk assessment: The MacArthur study of mental disorder and violence.* New York: Oxford University Press.

Moore, E., Ball, R. A. and Kuipers, L. (1992). Expressed emotion in staff working with the long-term adult mentally ill. *British Journal of Psychiatry, 161,* 802–808.

Moos, R. H. (1996). *Ward Atmosphere Scale* (3rd edition). Redwood City, CA: Mind Garden.

Morgan, C. and Fearon, P. (2007). Social experience and psychosis: insights from studies of migrant ethic minority groups. *Epidemiologia and Psichiatria Sociale*, *16*, 118–123.

Morgan, S. (1998). The assessment and management of risk. In C. Brooker and J. Repper (eds) *Serious mental health problems in the community: Policy, practice and research* (pp. 265–290). Oxford: Baillière Tindall.

Morrison, A. P., Renton, J. C., Dunn, H., Williams, S. and Bentall, R. P. (2004). *Cognitive therapy for psychosis: A formulation based approach*. London: Routledge.

Morse, G. A., Calsyn, R. J., Klinkenberg, W. D., Trusty, M. L., Gerber, F., Smith, R. B., Tempelhoff, B. and Ahmad, L. (1997). An experimental comparison of three types of case management for homeless mentally ill persons. *Psychiatric Services*, *48*, 497–503.

Mulvey, E. P., Shaw, E. and Lidz, C. W. (1994). Why use multiple sources in research on patient violence in the community? *Criminal Behavior and Mental Health*, *4*, 253–258.

Mumma, G. H. and Smith, J. L. (2001). Cognitive–behavioral–interpersonal scenarios: interformulator reliability and convergent validity. *Journal of Psychopathology and Behavioral Assessment*, *23*, 203–221.

Nagi, C., Ostapiuk, E. B., Craig, L. A., Hacker, D. and Beech, A. R. (2009). Using the revised Problem Identification Checklist to predict inpatient and community violence: a pilot study. *British Journal of Forensic Practice*, *11*, 4–13.

National Institute for Clinical Excellence (2002). *Schizophrenia: Core interventions in the treatment and management of schizophrenia in primary and secondary care: Clinical guideline 1*. London: National Institute for Clinical Excellence.

National Institute for Health and Clinical Excellence (2009). *Schizophrenia: Core interventions in the treatment and management of schizophrenia in adults in primary and secondary care (update): NICE clinical guideline 82*. London: National Institute for Health and Clinical Excellence.

Navarro, T. and Lowe, J. (1995) *The TULIP approach: A working paper*. London: TULIP, Haringey.

Nelson, G. L. and Cone, J. D. (1979). Multiple baseline analysis of a total economy for psychiatric patients. *Journal of Applied Behavioral Analysis*, *12*, 255–271.

Newhill, C. E., Mulvey, E. P. and Lidz, C. W. (1995). Characteristics of violence in the community by female patients seen in a psychiatric emergency service. *Psychiatric Services*, *46*, 785–789.

Ng, B., Kumar, S., Ranclaud, M. and Robinson, E. (2001). Ward crowding and incidents of violence on an acute psychiatric inpatient unit. *Psychiatric Services*, *52*, 521–525.

Nicholls, T. L., Ogloff, J. R. P. and Douglas, K. S. (2004). Assessing risk for violence among male and female civil psychiatric patients: the HCR-20, PCR-SV and VSC. *Behavioural Sciences and the Law*, *22*, 127–158.

Nijmen, H. L. I. and Rector, G. (1999). Crowding and aggression on inpatient psychiatric wards. *Psychiatric Services*, *50*, 830–831.

Novaco, R. W. (1994). Anger as a risk factor for violence among the mentally disordered. In J. Monahan and H. Steadman (eds) *Violence and mental disorder: Developments in risk assessment*. Chicago IL: University of Chicago Press.

Novaco, R. W. (2003). *Novaco Anger Scale and Provocation Inventory*. Los Angeles, CA: Western Psychological Association.

NSW Health Department (2002). *NSW framework for rehabilitation for mental health* Sydney: NSW Health Department.

O'Brien, W. H., Collins, A. and Kaplar, M. (2003). Case formulation. In: R. Fernandez-Ballesteros (ed.) *Encyclopaedia of psychological assessment* (volume 1, p. 164). London: Sage.

Oberlander, L. B. (1990). Work satisfaction among community-based mental health service providers: the association between work environment and work satisfaction. *Community Mental Health Journal, 26,* 517–532.

Otto, R. (2000). Assessing and managing risk in outpatient settings. *Journal of Clinical Psychology, 56,* 1239–1262.

Padesky, C. A. and Greenberger, D. (1995). *Mind over mood: Change how you feel by changing the way you think.* New York: Guilford Press.

Paget, A. T., Meaden, A. and Amphlett, C. (2009). Can engagement predict outcome in assertive outreach? *Journal of Mental Health, 18,* 73–81.

Palmer, B. A., Pankratz, V. S. and Bostwick, J. M. (2005). The lifetime risk of suicide in schizophrenia: a reexamination. *Archives General Psychiatry, 62,* 247–253.

Payne, R. (1999). Stress at work: a conceptual framework. In J. Firth-Cozens and R. Payne (eds) *Stress in health professionals: Psychological and organisational causes and interventions.* London: Wiley.

Penn, D. L., Mueser, K. T., Tarrier, N., Gloege, A., Cather, C., Serrano, D. and Otto, M. W. (2004). Supportive therapy for schizophrenia: possible mechanisms and implications for adjunctive psychosocial treatments. *Schizophrenia Bulletin, 30,* 101–112.

Perkins, R. (2001). What constitutes success? The relative priority of service users' and clinicians' views of mental health services. *British Journal of Clinical Psychology, 179,* 9–10.

Persons, J. B. (1989). *Cognitive therapy in practice: A case formulation approach.* New York: Norton.

Persons, J. B. and Bertagnolli, A. (1999). Inter-rater reliability of cognitive-behavioral case formulations of depression: a replication. *Cognitive Therapy and Research, 23,* 271–283.

Persons, J. B., Mooney, K. A. and Padesky, C. A. (1995). Interrater reliability of cognitive behavioural case formulations. *Cognitive Therapy and Research, 19,* 21–34.

Phelan, N., Stradins, L. and Morrison, S. (2001). Physical health of people with severe mental illness. *British Medical Journal, 322,* 442–444.

Phillips, H. K., Gray, N. S., MacCulloch, S. I., Taylor, J., Moore, S. C., Huckle, P. and MacCulloch, M. J. (2005). Risk assessment in offenders with mental disorders: relative efficacy of personal demographic, criminal history, and clinical variables. *Journal of Interpersonal Violence, 20,* 833–847.

Pompili, M., Amador, X. F., Girardi, P., Harkavy-Friedman, J., Harrow, M., Kaplan, K., Krausz, M., Lester, D., Meltzer, H. Y., Modestin, J., Montross, L. P., Mortensen, P. B., Munk-Jørgensen, P., Nielson, J., Nordentoft, M., Saarinen, P. I., Zisook, S., Wilson, S. T. and Tatarelli, R. (2007). Suicide risk in schizophrenia: learning from the past to change the future. *Annals of General Psychiatry, 6,* 10.

Potkin, S. G., Alphs, L., Hsu, C., Krishnan, K. R., Anand, R., Young, F. K., Meltzer, H. and Green, A. (2003). Predicting suicidal risk in schizophrenic and schizoaffective patients in a prospective two year trial. *Biological. Psychiatry, 54,* 444–452.

Powell, J., Geddes, J. and Hawton, K. (2000). Suicide in psychiatric hospital in-patients: risk factors and their predictive power. *British Journal of Psychiatry*, *176*, 266–272.

Priebe, S., Fakhoury, W., White, I., Watts, J., Bebbington, P., Billings, J., Burns, T., Johnson, S., Muijen, M., Ryrie, I. and White, C. (2004). Characteristics of teams, staff and patients: associations with outcomes of patients in assertive outreach. *British Journal of Psychiatry*, *185*, 306–311.

Prosser, D., Johnson, S., Kuipers, E., Szmukler, G., Bebbington, P. and Thornicroft, G. (1996). Mental health burnout and job satisfaction among hospital and community-based mental health staff. *British Journal of Psychiatry*, *169*, 334–337.

Punter, J. (2007). A commentary on Ashton. *Group Analysis*, *40*, 96–101.

Quinsey, V. L., Harris, G. T., Rice, M. E. and Cormier, C. (1998). *Violent offenders: Appraising and managing risk*. Washington, DC: American Psychological Association.

Quinsey, V. L., Book, A. and Skilling, T. A. (2004). A follow-up of deinstitutionalized men with intellectual disabilities and histories of antisocial behavior. *Journal of Applied Research in Intellectual Abilities*, *17*, 243–254.

Quinsey, V. L., Jones, G. B., Book, A. S. and Barr, A. N. (2006). The dynamic prediction of antisocial behaviour among forensic psychiatric patients: a prospective field study. *Journal of Interpersonal Violence*, *21*, 1539–1565.

Randolph, E. T. (1998). Social networks and schizophrenia. In K. T. Mueser and N. Tarrier (eds) *Handbook of social functioning in schizophrenia* (pp. 238–246). Needham Heights, MA: Allyn Bacon.

Rath, J. F., Simon, D., Langenbahn, D. M., Sherr, L. and Diller, L. (2003). Group treatment of problem solving deficits in outpatients with traumatic brain injury: a randomised outcome study. *Neuropsychological Rehabilitation*, *13*, 461–488.

Read, J., van Os, J., Morrison, A. P. and Ross, C. A. (2005). Childhood trauma, psychosis and schizophrenia: a literature review with theoretical and clinical impli-cations. *Acta Psychiatrica Scandinavica*, *112*, 330–350.

Reininghaus, U. A., Morgan, C., Simpson, J., Dazzan, P., Morgan, K., Doody, G. A., Bhugra, D., Leff, J., Jones, P., Murray, R., Fearon, P. and Craig, T. J. K. (2008). Unemployment, social isolation, achievement-expectation mismatch and psychosis: findings from the AESOP study. *Social Psychiatry and Psychiatric Epidemiology*, *43*, 743–751.

ReThink (2004) *Lost and found: Voices from the forgotten generation*. London: Rethink. Online. Available from http://www.mentalhealthshop.org/document. rm?id=113 (accessed 1 February 2010).

Richie, J. H., Dick, D. and Lingham, R. (1994). *The report of the enquiry into the care and treatment of Christopher Clunis*. London: HMSO.

Robbins, P. C., Monahan, J. and Silver, E. (2003). Mental disorder, violence, and gender. *Law and Human Behavior*, *27*, 561–571.

Robertson, I. H., Tegner, R., Tham, K., Lo, A. and Nimmo-Smith, I. (1995). Sustained attention training for unilateral neglect: theoretical and rehabilitation implications. *Journal of Clinical and Experimental Psychology*, *17*, 416–430.

Ross, D. (1990). Programmatic structures for the preparation of the reflective prac-titioner. In R. I. Cliff, W. R. Houston and M. C. Pugach (eds) *Encouraging reflective practice in education*. New York: Teachers College Press.

Roy, A. (1982). Suicide in chronic schizophrenia. *British Journal of Psychiatry*, *141*, 171–177.

Rudolph, U., Roesch, S. C., Greitemeyer, T. and Weiner, B. (2004). A meta-analytic review of helpgiving and aggression from an attributional perspective: contributions to a general theory of motivation. *Cognition and Emotion*, *18*, 815–848.

Salekin, R. T., Rogers, R. and Sewell, K. W. (1996). A review and meta-analysis of the Psychopathy Checklist – Revised: predictive validity of dangerousness. *Clinical Psychology: Science and Practice*, *3*, 203–215.

Sambrook, S. (2008). Working with crisis: the role of the clinical psychologist in a psychiatric intensive care unit. In I. Clarke and H. Wilson (eds) *Cognitive behaviour therapy for acute inpatient mental health units: Working with clients, staff and the milieu* (pp. 129–143). Hove, Sussex: Routledge.

Sartory, G., Zorn, C., Groetzinger, G. and Windgassen, K. (2005). Computerized cognitive remediation improves verbal learning and processing speed in schizophrenia. *Schizophrenia Research*, *75*, 219–223.

Schaufeli, W. (1999). Burnout. In J. Firth-Cozens and R. Payne (eds) *Stress in health professionals: Psychological and organisational causes and interventions*. London: Wiley.

Seeman, M. V. (2007). Mental health reform not always beneficial. *Psychiatry*, *70*, 252–259.

Shah, A. and Ganesvaran, T. (1999). Suicide among psychiatric in-patients with schizophrenia in an Australian mental hospital. *Medicine, Science and the Law*, *39*, 251–259.

Shang-Li, F. and Wang, M. A. (1994). A behavioural training programme for chronic schizophrenic patients: a three-month randomised controlled trial in Beijing. *British Journal of Psychiatry*, *164*, 32–7.

Sharma, T. and Antonova, L. (2003). Cognitive function in schizophrenia: deficits, functional consequences, and future treatment. *Psychiatric Clinics of North America*, *26*, 25–40.

Sharrock, R., Day, A., Qazi, F. and Brewin, C. R. (1990). Explanations by professional care staff, optimism and helping behaviour: an application of attribution theory. *Psychological Medicine*, *20*, 849–855.

Shepherd, G. (1995). Care and control in the community. In J. Crichton (ed.) *Psychiatric patient violence: Risks and response* (pp. 111–126). London: Duckworth.

Shepherd, M. and Lavender, T. (1999). Putting aggression into context: an investigation into contextual factors influencing the rate of aggressive incidents in a psychiatric hospital. *Journal of Mental Health*, *8*, 159–170.

Sheridan, M., Henrion, R., Robinson, L. and Baxter, V. (1990). Precipitants of violence in a psychiatric inpatient setting. *Hospital Community Psychiatry*, *41*, 776–780.

Sherrer, M. V. and O'Hare, T. O. (2008). Clinical case management. In K. T. Meuser and D. V. Jeste (eds) *Clinical handbook of schizophrenia* (pp. 309–319). New York: Guilford Press.

Silva, J. A., Harry, B. E., Leong, G. B. and Weinstock, R. (1996). Dangerous delusional misidentification and homicide. *Journal of Forensic Science*, *41*, 641–644.

Simeon, D. and Favazza, A. R. (2001). Self-injurious behaviors: phenomenology and assessment: I. In D. Simeon and E. Hollander (eds) *Self-injurious behaviors: Assessment and treatment*. Washington, DC: American Psychiatric Publishing.

Siris, S. G. (2001). Suicide and schizophrenia. *Journal of Psychopharmacology*, *15*, 127–135.

Skeem, J. L., Miller, J. D., Mulvey, E., Tiemann, J. and Monahan, J. (2005). Using a five-factor lens to explore the relation between personality traits and violence in psychiatric patients. *Journal of Consulting and Clinical Psychology*, *73*, 454–465.

Skinner, B. F. (1953). *Science and human behavior*. New York: Macmillan.

Spielberger, C. D. (1996). *State-Trait Anger Expression Inventory: Professional manual*. Odessa, FL: Psychological Assessment Resources.

Spielberger, C. D., Gorsuch, R. L., Lushene, R., Vagg, P. R. and Jacobs, G. A. (1983). *Manual for the State-Trait Anxiety Inventory*. Palo Alto, CA: Consulting Psychology Press.

Stanley, B. and Standen, P. J. (2000). Carers' attributions for challenging behaviour. *British Journal of Clinical Psychology*, *39*, 157–168.

Staznickas, K., McNiel, D. and Binder, R. (1993). Violence towards family caregivers by mentally ill relatives. *Hospital and Community Psychiatry*, *44*, 385–387.

Steadman, H. J., Mulvey, E. P., Monahan, J., Clark Robbins, P., Appelbaum, P. S., Grisso, T., Roth, L. H. and Silver, E. (1998). Violence by people discharged from acute psychiatric inpatient facilities and by others in the same neighborhoods. *Archives of General Psychiatry*, *55*, 393–401.

Stompe, T., Ortwein-Swoboda, G. and Schanda, H. (2004). Schizophrenia, delusional symptoms and violence: the threat to control/override the concept re-examined. *Schizophrenia Bulletin*, *30*, 31–44.

Summers, A. (2006). Psychological formulations in psychiatric care: staff views on their impact. *Psychiatric Bulletin*, *30*, 341–343.

Sun, F., Long, A., Boore, J. and Tsao, L. (2006). Patients and nurses' perceptions of ward environmental factors and support systems in the care of suicidal patients. *Journal of Clinical Nursing*, *15*, 83–91.

Swanson, J. E., Rudman, L. A. and Greewald, A. (2001). Using the implicit association test to investigate attitude–behaviour consistency for stigmatised behaviour. *Cognition and Emotion*, *15*, 207–230.

Swanson, J. W., Holzer, C. E., Ganju, V. K. and Jono, R. T. (1990) Violence and psychiatric disorder in the community: evidence from the Epidemiologic Catchment Area surveys. *Hospital and Community Psychiatry*, *41*, 761–770.

Swanson, J. W., Borum, R., Swartz, M. S. and Monahan, J. (1996). Psychotic symptoms and disorders and the risk of violent behavior in the community. *Criminal Behaviour and Mental Health*, *6*, 309–329.

Swartz, M. S., Swanson, J. W., Hiday, V. A., Borum, R., Wagner, R. and Burns, B. J. (1998). Violence and severe mental illness: the effects of substance abuse and nonadherence to medication. *American Journal of Psychiatry*, *155*, 226–231.

Szasz, T. (1963). *Law, liberty, and psychiatry: An inquiry into the social uses of mental health practices*. New York: The Macmillan Company.

Tarrier, N. (1992). Management and modification of residual positive symptoms. In M. Birchwood and N. Tarrier (eds) *Innovations in the psychological management of schizophrenia* (pp. 147–171). Chichester: Wiley.

Thomas, P. (3003). A study of the effectiveness of professional development groups. *Nursing Times*, *99*, 32–34.

Thornicroft, G. (1994). The NHS and Community Care Act 1990. *Psychiatric Bulletin*, *18*, 13–17.

Tombaugh, T. N. (1996). *Test of memory malingering*. North Tonawonda, NY: Multi-Health Systems.

Trower, P., Birchwood, M., Meaden, A., Byrne, S., Nelson, A. and Ross, K. (2004). Cognitive therapy for command hallucinations: randomised controlled trial. *British Journal of Psychiatry, 184*, 312–320.

Turkington, D. and McKenna, P. (2003). Is cognitive–behavioural therapy a worthwhile treatment for psychosis. *British Journal of Psychiatry, 182*, 477–479.

Tversky, A. and Kahneman, D. (1974). *Judgement under uncertainty: Heuristics and biases. Science, 185*, 1124–1131.

Vanderhoff, H. A. and Lynn, S. J. (2001). The assessment of self-mutilation: issues and considerations. *Journal of Threat Assessment, 1*, 91–109.

Wade, D. T. and de Jong, A. (2000). Recent advances in rehabilitation. *British Medical Journal, 320*, 1385–1388.

Wanless, L. K. and Jahoda, A. (2002). Responses of staff towards people with mild to moderate intellectual disability who behave aggressively: a cognitive emotional analysis. *Journal of Intellectual Disability Research, 46*, 507–516.

Warm, A., Murray, C. and Fox, J. (2003). Why do people selfharm? *Psychology, Health and Medicine, 8*, 71–79.

Watts, D. and Morgan, G. (1994). Malignant alienation: dangers for patients who are hard to like, *British Journal of Psychiatry, 164*, 11–13.

Wearden, A. J., Tarrier, N., Barrowclough, C., Zastowny, T. R. and Rahill, A. A. (2000). A review of expressed emotion research in health care. *Clinical Psychology Review, 20*, 633–666.

Webster, C. D., Douglas, K. S., Eaves, D. and Hart, S. D. (1997). *HCR-20: Assessing the risk for violence (version 2)*. Vancouver: Mental Health, Law, and Policy Institute, Simon Fraser University.

Weiner, B. (1985). An attributional theory of achievement motivation and emotion. *Psychological Review, 92*, 548–573.

Weiner, B. (1988). Attribution theory and attribution therapy: some theoretical observations and suggestions. *British Journal of Clinical Psychology, 27*, 93–104.

Weiner, N. (1995). *Judgements of responsibility: A foundation for a theory of conduct*. New York: Guilford Press.

Westermeyer, H. (2003). On the structure of case formulations. *European Journal of Psychological Assessment, 19*, 210–216.

Whittington, R. (1994). Violence in psychiatric hospitals. In T. Wykes (ed.) *Violence and mental health care professionals*. London: Chapman and Hall.

Wilson, B. A., Baddeley, A., Evans, J. J. and Shiel, A. (1994). Errorless learning in the rehabilitation of memory impaired people. *Neuropsychological Rehabilitation, 4*, 307–326.

Wilson, B. A., Alderman, N., Burgess, P. W., Emslie, H. and Evans, J. J. (1996). *Behavioural assessment of the dysexecutive syndrome*. Bury St Edmunds: Thames Valley Test Company.

Wincze, J. P., Leitenberg, H. and Agras, W. S. (1972). The effects of token reinforcement and feedback on the delusional verbal behavior of chronic paranoid schizophrenics. *Journal of Applied Behavior Analysis, 5*, 247–262.

Wing, J. K. (1963).The rehabilitation of psychiatric patients. *British Journal of Psychiatry, 109*, 462–635.

World Health Organization (1999). *ICIDH-2: International classification of functioning and disability*. Beta-2 draft, full version. Geneva: World Health Organization.

Wykes, T. and Reeder, C. (2005) *Cognitive remediation therapy for schizophrenia*, New York: Brunner-Routledge.

Wykes, T., Steel, C., Everitt, B. and Tarrier, N. (2007). Cognitive behaviour therapy for schizophrenia: effect sizes, clinical models, and methodological rigor. *Schizophrenia Bulletin*, *10*, 1–15.

Young, J. E. (1994). *Young Parenting Inventory*, New York: Cognitive Therapy Centre of New York.

Young, J. E. (1995). *Young Compensation Inventory*. New York: Cognitive Therapy Centre of New York.

Young, J. E. and Brown, G. (1990). *Young Schema Questionnaire*. New York: Cognitive Therapy Centre of New York.

Young, J. E. and Rygh, J. (1994). *Young–Rygh Avoidance Inventory*. New York: Cognitive Therapy Centre of New York.

Zarkowska, E. and Clements, J. (1994). *Problem behaviour and people with severe intellectual disabilities: The STAR approach*. London: Chapman and Hall.

Zubin, J. and Spring, B. (1977). Vulnerability: a new view of schizophrenia. *Journal of Abnormal Psychology*, *86*, 103–126.

Index